FOR BETTER OR WORSE

LIFE, LOVE AND SUPPORTING CHELSEA IN THE 1990s

JASON GIBBINS

Cover design: Mark Worrall
www.gate17books.co.uk

CONTENTS

ACKNOWLEDGEMENTS 1

CHAPTER ONE – 1990/1991 5

CHAPTER TWO – FA Cup Third Round 20

CHAPTER THREE – 1991/1992 26

CHAPTER FOUR – FA Cup Fourth Round 41

CHAPTER FIVE – 1992/1993 47

CHAPTER SIX – FA Cup Fifth Round................................61

CHAPTER SEVEN – 1993/1994 67

CHAPTER EIGHT – FA Cup Fifth Round Replay 85

CHAPTER NINE – 1994/1995...................................92

CHAPTER TEN – FA Cup Sixth Round 108

CHAPTER ELEVEN – 1995/1996 115

CHAPTER TWELVE – FA Cup Semi-Final 131

CHAPTER THIRTEEN – 1996/1997 139

CHAPTER FOURTEEN – FA Cup Final 155

CHAPTER FIFTEEN – 1997/1998 168

CHAPTER SIXTEEN – European Cup Winners' Cup Final ..186

CHAPTER SEVENTEEN – 1998/1999 200

CHAPTER EIGHTEEN – Bolton and beyond.......................219

POSTSCRIPT 225

DEDICATION 228

ACKNOWLEDGEMENTS

The Bounder Friardale website (www.bounder.friardale.co.uk) is an incredible resource and was the starting point for basic information such as match dates, scores and line-ups, although all information was double checked against Chelsea FC programmes or newspaper reports where possible.

I turned to newspaper cuttings, match videos and the Chelsea Independent and Red Card fanzines to refresh memories of matches, while www.sporting-heroes.net was another excellent resource to remind me of the finer details of the careers of certain players.

Additional research materials included 'Chelsea FC: The Official Biography' by Rick Glanvill, 'Chelsea Azzurri' by Brian Scovell, and 'The Bridge' by Colin Benson.

All other information and quoted conversations are based on real events although, due to the passing of time, I acknowledge that recollections of others may vary.

Finally, I offer sincere thanks to Mark Worrall of Gate 17 for his support and guidance, and for agreeing to put this vanity project to print, and Kim Clark for invaluable assistance with the cover.

You can follow me on Twitter: @Jgibbins

#ForBetterOrWorseChelsea

FOR BETTER OR WORSE

We'd just bid farewell to 1996, party poppers had been firmly popped, and 1997 - a year that would see a new Labour Government, and the Princess of Wales killed in a Paris car crash - was in its embryonic stages.

And it was at that point that the question was asked…
    "So then, when are you going to ask me to marry you?"
    Leaning back - pausing only to take a brief sip of a pint and a drag on a Marlboro Light - the response came naturally:
    "I'll marry you sweetheart when Chelsea win the FA Cup."

There were several witnesses…

CHAPTER ONE
1990/1991

As English football entered a new decade, it remained largely in the grip of gloom.

The Hillsborough Disaster which resulted in the eventual death of 97 Liverpool fans in April 1989 continued to cast a heavy shadow over the following season, with not a single club recording an average attendance above 40,000 and the underlying threat of hooliganism and racism continuing to ensure a trip to the game - any game - predominantly remained a past-time only for the addicted or those of limited ambition.

You could count me in the former, as well as the latter.

The 1990 World Cup brought some respite for the 'beautiful game' as England exceeded expectations to reach the semi-finals, but a John Barnes rap and Gazza's plastic breasts were no more than a tentative first step on the road towards English football's rehabilitation.

From a Chelsea perspective the 1989/90 season offered a more-than-creditable fifth-place finish to mark the club's return to the top flight following a year in the second tier, but it was a campaign that lacked star-dust; a functional team with limited stand-out talent that was never in the hunt for honours.

In reality - despite early highlights such as a 4-1 win at Tottenham and a brief-flirtation with top spot in November - it is most clearly remembered by those that witnessed its duration for back-to-back 5-2 Stamford Bridge humiliations by Wimbledon and Liverpool, and early domestic cup exits to lower-league opposition in the form of Scarborough and Bristol City.

But new seasons equal new dawns, and with arguably the best bit of summer transfer business since former Chelsea boss John Neal assembled a promotion-winning team in the single summer of 1983 the Blues had made two stellar pre-season signings worthy of back-page attention.

So - with apologies to the third summer signing, German-born Welshman Darren Barnard - enter stage left Dennis Wise and

Andy Townsend.

Five-foot five-inch Wisey, chief tormentor in Wimbledon's 5-2 win at the Bridge the previous season, had made the short trip up the District Line for a club record £1.6 million, while Townsend made a £1.2m switch from Norwich on the back of a hugely successful World Cup which saw him play all five games and meet the Pope as his Republic of Ireland side reached the quarter-finals.

Not bad for an English lad from Maidstone, Kent.

And the buzz created by the new signings was evident for the season opener against Derby County, which saw a bumper crowd of 26,000 eventually squeeze through the turnstiles despite long queues created by the failure of a new crowd-control system.

And for only the third time in my memory, among them was my mum.

For the record, her only previous games were the 1986 Full Members' Cup win at Wembley and, prior to that, my first ever Chelsea match - a riotous 3-3 draw before a capacity crowd at Luton on New Year's Day 1980.

On that occasion, quite sensibly, her attendance was entirely based on monitoring the safety of her beloved six-year-old son lacking, also quite sensibly, any faith in my dad to fulfil said duty to the required standards.

On this occasion, her attendance was a direct result of a family holiday in Pembrokeshire being cut short on the morning of the game as the pull of a Townsend and Wise double debut proved too great for the male members of her family to ignore.

"Forget that, you're going to Chelsea..." we announced as poor Mum revealed plans to spend the final day of her holiday sauntering around the shops of Tenby.

What she got to see instead was Chelsea get the new season off to a flier, when a fifth-minute far-post header from David Lee was allowed to stand despite being prevented from crossing the line by a blatant Derby hand.

She also saw Dean Saunders pull the visitors level in the opening minutes of the second half, before Peter Nicholas struck from outside the box to put Chelsea back in front in the 72nd minute.

And, finally, she got to enjoy some late, late drama when a Saunders penalty - the last kick of the game - was saved by David Beasant to secure three opening-day points.

The investment in Wise and Townsend was a statement of

intent from Chelsea chairman Ken Bates and manager Bobby Campbell as they set out to secure Chelsea's first major trophy since the European Cup Winners' Cup success of 1971.

The aim was to close the gap on the likes of Tottenham and Arsenal - both top four finishers in the previous season and both, respectively, beaten to the signings of Wise and Townsend - but the post-Derby reality was immediate back-to-back defeats against two other London irritants.

First up was a midweek 2-1 reverse at Crystal Palace - where Dennis Wise was sent off for kicking out at Andy Gray in only his second appearance - followed by a 1-0 loss at Queens Park Rangers in which 20-year-old defender Jason Cundy was given his Chelsea debut.

With David Lee conceding penalties in both games, and Kerry Dixon missing one at QPR, the impact on expectations was immediate, with the Stamford Bridge attendance for the visit of Sunderland more than 6,000 down on the opening day.

Those of us who kept the faith saw Cundy retain his place alongside fellow home-growns Gareth Hall, Graeme Le Saux and David Lee.

Dennis Wise, meanwhile, took responsibility for penalty duties to score his first for the club and Chelsea's third of the day to take the points by the odd goal in five.

The incredible run of penalties continued at Highbury the following week, with David Lee tripping Anders Limpar to concede his third spot-kick of the embryonic campaign before Chelsea were awarded another of their own.

Naturally, Lee Dixon scored for Arsenal while Kevin Wilson - handed responsibility in the absence of the suspended Wise - spectacularly fired over the bar with Chelsea already heading to a 4-1 defeat.

With the season gathering pace I, meanwhile, was settling into the routine of the final year of my A' Levels.

Living in a town that had taken the bold step of scrapping traditional sixth-form facilities in favour of a short-lived 'tertiary college', we were given as much freedom as we desired to do what we desired in the many, many free hours that filled the time between occasional lectures.

In my case this involved sessions in the pub, playing football or making the convenient 10-minute walk to my girlfriend's house for some fumbled biology lessons.

It was the latter past-time, of course, that was most enjoyable -

coming-of-age lunchtimes and afternoons spent falling in love, finally discovering there was more to life than football, and regularly putting far too much faith in the barks of her family dog to warn of returning parents...

In the evenings I'd work at the local bingo hall, arranging shifts around the Chelsea fixture list to ensure I was always free on a Saturday or when midweek games required my presence.

As part-time jobs go, it was perfect - shifts of no more than four hours, and a happy mixture of roles that included working the bar, lingering for tips as you delivered cash prizes to the floor, and taking to the stage to call the numbers that could make or break an octogenarian's Christmas.

Courtesy of a strong lisp, my calling sessions were also likely to bring me out in a cold sweat as certain number combinations popped up on screen... "all the ssixes, ssixty-ssix," I'd say with as much confidence as I could muster, before following up with, "free and four, firty-four".

And, lisp or no lisp, there was also the one number that would test any bingo caller's professionalism to the full...

"Six and nine, 69," I would announce as straight-faced as possible while - in the furthest corner of the room - an adolescent work-mate would discreetly stick their tongue into the side of their mouth in a bid to make me crack.

But my bingo earnings meant I was back at Stamford Bridge to see Kevin Wilson cancel out Mark Ward's (surprise, surprise) penalty opener for Manchester City in a league clash, before heading to fourth-tier Walsall's new Bescot Stadium for a 5-0 romp in the first-leg of a second-round League Cup tie.

With Townsend on target twice, it was a good night out and the start of a cup run that would prove to provide the most excitement - and disappointment - in the months ahead.

Walsall was followed by a return to Stamford Bridge for visit of Division One new boys Sheffield United; a game in which Northern Irishman Kevin Wilson - an ever-present thus far due to the absence of the injured Gordon Durie - continued his good run of form with a first-half double before Vinnie Jones gave the visitors hope on the stroke of half-time.

In a match which Chelsea largely dominated but failed to gain control, it felt inevitable that Sheffield United would grab a late equaliser... and they did, courtesy of Brian Deane in the 90th minute to leave Chelsea in a distinctly-average 13th place after seven games.

I gave Chelsea's next game at Southampton a miss, instead opting to join a couple of college mates to travel to Chesterfield to watch our local team - and my occasional bit on the side - Northampton Town.

The Cobblers make for the perfect affair as they ask nothing of me and I offer little in return.

They know they are never going to be, quite literally, in the same league as my first love and they know that when they do see me it will only ever be on my terms - a selfish desire for a bit of dirty football against the bins before heading home ridden with guilt, vowing never to do it again.

And my shameful two-timing got what it deserved at Chesterfield.

While the Cobblers didn't even bother to brush their hair for a dismal 0-0 Division Four clash at a freezing Saltergate, Bobby Campbell's Chelsea put on their party dress for a six-goal thriller at The Dell.

Durie made his first start of the season but Wilson retained his place and was again among the scorers alongside Steve Clarke and Dennis Wise, who scored the last of the game in a see-saw 3-3 draw from… hello again… the penalty spot.

The remainder of October saw Chelsea wrap up the Walsall cup tie with a 4-1 second-leg win, drift to a less than memorable 0-0 draw against Nottingham Forest and slip to a 2-0 Anfield defeat to title favourites Liverpool - extending Chelsea's winless run on the red side of Stanley Park to 34 years.

A 1-0 home league win against Aston Villa got November off to a winning start, but it was the return to the League Cup action against second-tier Portsmouth that grabbed the headlines.

Following a stale-mate at the Bridge, the south coast replay proved to be a five-goal thriller on a night that saw away fans evacuated from Fratton Park's main stand when creaking wooden floorboards threatened to send them tumbling onto a concrete concourse below.

With those fans safely relocated to the terrace, Chelsea were trailing 2-0 with fewer than 10 minutes to go when David Lee headed home to reduce the deficit.

Two minutes later Wise levelled from the spot after Townsend was upended before - on 90 minutes - Kevin Wilson picked up a Kerry Dixon knock-down to complete a remarkable turnaround in front of a giddy travelling support.

Whisper it quietly, but a cup run was on.

Dennis Wise then maintained his 100% record from the penalty spot to earn a point in a 1-1 draw at home to Norwich, before a late Kevin Wilson effort was ruled out to deny Chelsea another draw in a 2-1 defeat at Wimbledon.

In the week before the trip to Wimbledon's Plough Lane, centre-half and former captain Graham Roberts was finally shipped out of the club via a £200,000 move to West Brom.

The ex-Tottenham and Rangers favourite was a popular and commanding figure in the Blues promotion team of 1988/89, but started to look woefully exposed in the December of the following season as Chelsea shipped 19 goals in five games.

It would be unfair to say Roberts was entirely at fault for the defensive shitshow, but he was certainly shitshow-adjacent…

He hung around long enough to help Chelsea get dumped out of the 1990 FA Cup on a grim day at Bristol City, but made his last appearance before the end of February.

Also nearing the end of his Chelsea career was Welshman Peter Nicholas.

Like Roberts the likeable midfielder had joined ahead of the 1988/89 campaign but, also like Roberts, was now the wrong side of 30 and looking the wrong side of 40 so was finding it increasingly difficult to keep up with the pace and demands of the top flight.

After putting through his own net at Wimbledon and with Chelsea now just three points above the relegation places, he was among the casualties for a televised clash at Manchester United as Bobby Campbell put further trust in the youth to give Graham Stuart and Damien Matthew their first starts of the season following debuts at the end of the previous campaign.

It was an inspired decision from the amiable Scouser, with the duo bringing fresh energy and pace to a show-stopping performance that saw Chelsea win 3-2 courtesy of a Gary Pallister own goal, an Andy Townsend drive across United keeper Les Sealey and yet another Dennis Wise penalty.

The die was cast for Nicholas, who would appear just once more in a Chelsea shirt, and Stuart and Matthew retained their starting spots for a 2-1 League Cup success at Oxford United that secured a quarter-final spot for the first time since 1985.

Forward momentum continued with home league wins against Tottenham and Palace and a Zenith Data Cup dismissal of Swindon to extend the winning run of the developing side to five games in all competitions.

The Spurs game attracted a season high attendance of 33,478 as Kerry Dixon, John Bumstead and Gordon Durie each found the net in a captivating affair that saw Paul Gascoigne and Gary Lineker, who also missed a penalty, respond for the visitors.

There are ample opportunities to laugh at Tottenham as the decade unfolds so I'll spare their blushes here, other than to state - just for the record - that this was the first in a 26-game run in which Tottenham would fail to beat Chelsea in any competition.

It was the first in a 32-game, 16-year run in which they'd fail to beat Chelsea in the league.

And it was the first in a 27-game run, stretching all the way to 2018, in which they'd fail to win a single league game at Stamford Bridge. We had six World Cups, five Prime Ministers, four General Elections and three Popes in that time. Just for the record.

With Chelsea now sitting a much-more comfortable ninth in the league, a blue and white Santa hat was the dubious headwear of choice for a proportion of an away following old enough to know better for the next game at Derby.

Handing out the festive gifts, meanwhile, were both defences.

Kerry Dixon scored just his third league goal of the season to put Chelsea 1-0 ahead in the 11th minute, before it all went a bit Christmas crackers with goals galore and the occasional minor pitch invasion: 1-1; 2-1 Chelsea; 3-1 Chelsea; 3-2 Chelsea; 3-3; 4-3 Derby; 4-4; 5-4 Chelsea; and, finally, 6-4 to the Chels.

At the final count Dixon and Durie both struck twice, Wise and Le Saux completed the madness, and those in Santa hats headed home singing about how much fun it was to see Chelsea win away...

Chelsea extended the winning run to seven on the final weekend ahead of Christmas when Townsend and Wise cancelled out a Kevin Gallacher opener for Coventry City, before the Football League handed them a 400-mile round trip to Elland Road, Leeds, on Boxing Day.

It was ludicrous scheduling, and to add to the challenges for Chelsea fans there were no train services available, the game was set for a noon kick-off, and just 1,300 tickets had been made available.

In a fixture known for its long history of violence between both sets of fans, it was almost as if they didn't want us to go...

Chelsea beamed the game back to Stamford Bridge for those unable or unwilling to travel, but for those that made the trip it was a miserable day out as the winning run came to an end courtesy of a 4-1 thumping in a near monsoon.

But if getting to Leeds proved difficult for travelling fans, next up was a visit to Luton Town - where away supporters had been banned since 1986 as a direct result of an infamous riot by visiting Millwall fans in an FA Cup clash.

By now though, the final season the away-fan ban was in existence, it was common knowledge that beating the system was more of an expectation than a challenge.

The well-prepared applied for a Luton membership card ahead of each season, while the ill-prepared simply rocked up and tried their luck.

On this occasion we did precisely that - turned up a couple of hours early, hung around with a few other like-minded individuals, and waited.

Sure enough, it wasn't long before an entrepreneurial young chap wandered across with a pocket full of tickets and an eye for a profit.

Based on the fact that we found ourselves in the middle of the main stand, our assumption was that our marked-up tickets came direct from a Luton employee claiming his Christmas bonus. And based on the number of Chelsea around us for the 2-0 defeat, our further assumption was that anyone daft enough to have gone to Stamford Bridge for the second beamback of the week would have been very lonely indeed.

I spent the night before the New Year's Day game against Everton enthusiastically partaking in a previously undiscovered tipple - brandy mixed with Babycham, with the emphasis on the brandy.

Still 22 days shy of my 18th birthday, it proved to be a toxic mix and I awoke from my alcohol-induced coma on the morning of the game in a very sorry state.

In reality I should never have left the comfort and safety of my bed, and had it not been for the presence of one man I almost certainly wouldn't have done so. But that man was Pat Nevin - the poetic winger from the much-loved mid-Eighties Chelsea team who floated above the turf; the wee wizard who would beat one man, beat another and then beat them again just for fun.

Sold to Everton in the summer of 1988, Nevin had made his first return to Stamford Bridge at the arse-end of the previous season, rounding Dave Beasant in front of a Shed end that still adored him to score the visitors' only goal of the game in a 2-1 Chelsea win. Nobody in Chelsea blue particularly minded.

The journey down was predictably rough and involved at least one emergency dash from the tube in fear of a reappearance of the poison within my system, but the game was even more painful.

Opting for a seat due to my inability to stand, I simultaneously sweated and shivered through 90 miserable minutes, paying little or no attention to a game that was settled 2-1 in Everton's favour when Nevin turned the ball into the path of Jason Cundy to score an own goal.

It was Chelsea's first home defeat of the season but another immediately followed when, the following Saturday, second-tier Oxford gained revenge for their recent League Cup exit to Chelsea with a deeply depressing 3-1 FA Cup upset at a sparsely-populated Stamford Bridge.

On the back of those seven straight wins that took Chelsea into Christmas, it was now four defeats from four so spirits needed raising... and raised they were with the news that Australian forward Dave Mitchell had been sent out on loan to Newcastle.

Widely considered by those unlucky enough to see him in action as the worst player to ever wear the Chelsea shirt because... well... he was... he naturally scored the winner on his Newcastle debut to ensure the Gallowgate End saw him score one more goal than we ever did.

He would return from his loan the following month to delight us with a final stinker in a 0-0 stinker against Wimbledon before being released on a permanent transfer to Swindon Town. They had our sympathies.

The FA Cup defeat left the only chance of silverware resting on the shoulders of the League Cup, with Tottenham now waiting in the quarter finals once we'd concluded some west London league business against a QPR side with Ray Wilkins among their ranks.

From 1973-79 youth team graduate Wilkins scored 30 goals in just shy of 200 Chelsea appearances, becoming the club's youngest ever captain in the process.

Sold to Manchester United for a club record £825,000 to help ease the club's growing financial crisis, a mutual love remained between player and club before 'Butch' came home from 1998-2000 as a club coach and, again, for a second spell from 2008-2010 before his contract was ended without official explanation.

In March 2018, Wilkins had a cardiac arrest resulting in a fall and was placed into an induced coma. He died the following month at the age of 61.

For his value to Chelsea, I turn to his friend and Blues double-winning manager Carlo Ancelotti, who wrote: "Ray is one of those select few, always present, noble in spirit, a real blue-blood, Chelsea flows in his veins ... without him we wouldn't have won a thing."

As a banner now hanging from Chelsea's East Stand correctly says, they don't make them like Ray anymore.

Back on that 1991 January day when Wilkins returned to the Bridge with QPR, he showed his usual cool presence in the centre of the park but finished on the losing side as Gordon Durie scored both in a 2-0 Chelsea win.

Reunions complete, it was now time to turn all attention to the League Cup and Tottenham.

Briefly going back in time to 1981/82, the highlight of an indifferent Chelsea Division Two campaign was an FA Cup run that featured a famous win over European Champions Liverpool ahead of a visit from Spurs in the quarter-final.

Considered far too young and innocent to be taken to the predicted mayhem that was Stamford Bridge that day, by chance I found myself spending the afternoon in the company of a Tottenham-supporting uncle.

Chelsea led at half-time to fuel Wembley dreams, but in the second-half a Tottenham team filled with flair, style and Garth Crooks took control to win the game 3-2.

Listening for updates on the radio, I retain a vivid memory of the precise moment my distrust of all things Tottenham was born - that being the moment Spurs went 2-1 ahead and my uncle celebrated a little too enthusiastically for my nine-year-old sensitivities.

Seven long weeks had passed since the 1991 League Cup quarter-final balls had been pulled from the bag and as we walked up the steps from Fulham Broadway tension hung heavy in the January evening air - but not simply due to the game, or even due to hooliganism that would inevitably form a backdrop to the evening at some point, somewhere, but due to the very real threat of war; an actual, global war.

Following months of military build-up in response to Iraq's invasion of Kuwait the previous August, all talk was that air strikes were due to start in the following hours and there was very genuine concern as to what it would mean for those involved in the conflict and for the country as a whole.

The Fulham Road and Stamford Bridge was raw ahead of war,

and as kick-off approached the atmosphere tumbling down from the back of the Shed and West Stand was as electric as any felt since our last extended run in the same competition in the mid-'80s.

Our chosen venue for the evening's entertainment was the concrete Benches at the front of the West Stand and, to add to the fun, my Spurs-supporting uncle would be sitting by our sides.

No more than 5ft 5ins in his stocking feet, his early-evening bravado - decreasingly on the wane with each passing tube stop towards SW6 - had evaporated completely by the time he approached the turnstiles.

As we sat him down between us we offered two simple, but obvious, words of advice - 'keep quiet'. Surrounded by pure hostility, he wouldn't need telling twice.

The game passed in a blur; a rampant Chelsea side ripping through a Tottenham team missing the suspended England midfielder Paul Gascoigne.

Stuart, Le Saux, Dixon, Durie; Le Saux again, Stuart again, Le Saux once more - time and time again Chelsea pushed Tottenham back with pace and power in an exhilarating performance.

Crosses from the left, crosses from the right; shots from near, shots from far... the Benches bouncing in excitement. But, unbelievably, the goal never came in the most one-sided 0-0 draw anyone present was ever likely to witness.

By the time we'd got home - my shell-shocked uncle finally regaining some colour to his cheeks - British, American and Allied planes had launched a massive campaign of bombing and missile strikes on Iraqi forces; the breaking news footage immediately confirming they'd had more luck than Chelsea in finding the target.

Ahead of the Spurs replay Chelsea were again wasteful in front of goal in a 1-0 defeat at Sunderland but - by this time - the league was little more than a sideshow.

The 6,000 away-end tickets for the White Hart Lane re-match were snapped up as soon as they went on sale, but with Gascoigne returning from suspension the expectation from the press and the neutrals was that Chelsea had missed their chance.

But this was Chelsea, and this was Tottenham.

Chelsea picked up where they'd left off in the first game at Stamford Bridge, burying Tottenham with an onslaught of attacking play. The only difference this time was that it ended in goals - first Townsend, then Dixon and then Wise from the spot to put Chelsea into their first semi-final in a major competition since 1985, and only their second since a League Cup defeat to Norwich in 1973.

In the run-up to the next home game against Arsenal, who were engaged in a title-fight with Liverpool and were still unbeaten after 23 league games, fan favourite Kerry Dixon was informed by the Crown Prosecution Service that no action would be taken in relation to a false allegation that he'd stolen £10,000.

But while the claim was entirely unfounded, it came on the back of previous publicity over a gambling addiction and was an indication that problems may be mounting in our star-striker's life.

On the pitch, however, he remained a potent force; and so it proved against the Gunners when he tapped home a selfless pull-back from Damien Matthew in the 88th-minute to double Chelsea's lead following Graham Stuart's earlier strike.

Alan Smith pulled one back for Arsenal on the stroke of the final whistle, but - in what would prove to be the only league game they would lose all season - their unbeaten run was over.

Those back-to-back wins against both north London rivals had once again got spirits soaring, so it was perhaps inevitable what would happen next... Chelsea, predictably unpredictable Chelsea, would turn to shit.

A 2-1 defeat at Manchester City was followed by the aforementioned Dave Mitchell 0-0 stinker against Wimbledon which, in turn, was followed by a ZDS Cup penalty shoot-out defeat to Luton ahead of the biggest game of the season.

The League Cup semi-final placed Chelsea against Division Two promotion hopefuls Sheffield Wednesday, prompting fond memories of a three-game quarter-final epic between the two clubs in 1985.

The contrast in atmosphere, however, to any of those classic 1985 games could not have been starker thanks to television scheduling the first-leg at Stamford Bridge for a noon Sunday kick-off.

The League Cup's unique selling point is winter nights under the lights; a dull Sunday in February before anyone has put the roast on simply doesn't cut it.

As a result it was a flat, tepid affair that played into the hands of Sheffield Wednesday and edged Chelsea towards their latest cup exit against lower league opposition.

The visitors opened the scoring with a well-worked free-kick down the left, pushing the ball down the line with the Chelsea defence expecting a cross. The ball was eventually centred for Wednesday warhorse Peter Shirtliff - a survivor from those Chelsea cup encounters of the past - to net from close range.

With 10 to go David Hirst burst into the box to double the lead and put one Wednesday foot in the final.

If any consolation could be found it came in the form of Chelsea not having to wait long to be put out of their misery, with the second leg just three days later.

Those who travelled to Sheffield were rewarded for their loyalty by a team that rolled over in a 3-1 defeat, dumping Chelsea out 5-1 on aggregate, and some heavy-handed policing from the officers of South Yorkshire.

February had yet to turn to March, but the season was now over - the record signings of Townsend and Wise failing to bring the desired reward as Chelsea extended the number of years since they last won a major trophy to 20.

But win or lose, up the Blues... so still I kept going, turning up with unquestioned loyalty as Chelsea stumbled through the spring.

The majority of the campaign had been spent zipping up and down the motorways of England in my mate Scott's faded red 1.1-litre Fiesta, a feat of engineering that largely met the heavy demands placed upon it through little more than the power of prayer.

So throughout March and April it continued to deliver us to Stamford Bridge to sit miserably on the Benches or stand solemnly in the Shed as attendances slumped to as low as 12,000.

Scott and I would watch planes on the Heathrow flight path glide overhead, look at the weed-ridden sections of closed terrace that evidenced a ground in decline, and try to blank out the fading 'Save the Bridge' advertising boards that reminded us of the greatest concern of all - Chelsea's home of 86 years remained under the ownership of property developers, and our beloved club's right to stay there remained under serious threat.

On the pitch only the completion of a league double over Manchester United and the rescuing of a point after going three down at home to Luton were worthy of any real note before - more out of duty than desire - I once more jumped into the passenger seat of Scott's car for the penultimate away game of the season at Nottingham Forest.

On a blustery day we arrived to find Forest fans in high spirits after booking their place in the forthcoming FA Cup final the previous weekend, so it was of no great surprise when their energised team went 1-0 ahead in the eighth-minute.

And even less of a surprise when they scored again...

And again...

And again...

And again...

And again...

And again.

Nottingham Forest 7 (seven), Chelsea 0.

"Always look on the bright side of life, de do, de do, de do, de do," we sarcastically sang for much of the second half, the misery of the game and the previous few weeks being eased by terrace humour.

The ditty continued all the way to the final whistle and remained relevant as the next game approached; a game for which we could do nothing other than look on the bright side as we prepared for the visit of a Liverpool side still hot on the coattails of Arsenal in the title race.

But, once more, cue the predictable unpredictables for the final home game of the season...

With Stamford Bridge attracting its second-highest league attendance of the campaign - the majority just turning up to check it really was all over - Chelsea cast aside the previous week's East Midlands nightmare to race into a two-goal lead through a Kerry Dixon header and Dennis Wise penalty, surprising home and away fans in equal measure.

It couldn't last though and, sure enough, fewer than 15 minutes into the second half Liverpool were level through former Stamford Bridge favourite David Speedie and substitute Ronny Rosenthal.

Now on the front foot, Speedie and Ray Houghton both went close to immediately giving Liverpool the lead but - just three minutes after pulling level - the title-chasers were stunned to find themselves behind again when Dixon headed home again, this time from a Wise corner.

As we joyously mocked the shell-suited Scousers on the away terrace, Speedie again went close when he hit the post but there was no coming back this time and Chelsea had the final word - Gordon Durie finishing off a perfect counter-attack to wrap up the 4-2 win with three minutes left on the clock.

The result as good as handed Arsenal the title - an Arsenal

side which, don't forget, had lost its only league game of the season to Chelsea - and once more confirmed what we all knew; this infuriatingly inconsistent team had the ability to compete with the best, but would all-too-regularly come up short against the rest.

The final official business of the season was concluded the following weekend at Aston Villa; a 2-2 draw that confirmed an 11th-place finish but saved the best entertainment for after the final whistle.

With Villa fans gathering on the pitch in their thousands - part end-of-season exuberance, part protest following a narrow escape from relegation - numerous Chelsea fans also spilled into the penalty area in front of the away end to debag departing players of their kit and… the animals… do the conga.

With a hastily arranged line of stewards and police stretching across the 18-yard box to keep rival fans apart a few Chelsea (legend says as few as four or five, but in reality it was probably as many as six or seven) burst through and ran at the Villa fans, who turned quicker than a googly from the late Shane Warne to stampede up and out of the Holte End terrace.

Watching from behind the goal, the only thing that disrupted the thundering sound of thousands of Villa feet was the Chelsea laughter. It was time for the summer…

CHAPTER TWO
FA CUP THIRD ROUND

Chelsea v West Bromwich Albion
Stamford Bridge
Saturday, January 4, 1997

Chelsea: Grodas, Petrescu, Leboeuf, Clarke, Hughes (Vialli, 78), Wise, Duberry, Di Matteo, Minto (Burley, 70), Newton, Zola.

West Bromwich Albion: Crichton, Holmes, Murphy, Sneekes, Burgess, Raven (Taylor, 65), Groves (Butler, 46), Smith (Agnew, 24), Peschisolido, Hunt, Hamilton.

Referee: Mike Riley (Leeds)
Attendance: 27,446

"Burley, obviously…"
"Bumstead."
"Bonetti."
"Borota."
"Barry Bridges."
"Ooh, double B, nice… err, Bodley."
"Britton."
"Bannon."
"Brink."
"Baldwin."
"Barnard."
"Beas… hang on… who the fuck's Brink?"
"Tommy Brink you muppet, Irish international, late '50s, early '60s, carry on…"
"For fuck's sake; Beasant…"
"Barness."
"……."
"Come on Gibbo, no pause, no hesitation…"
"TOMMY BRINK? TOMMY F-ING BRINK??"

And that was the end of that week's Chelsea player alphabet game as the remainder of the journey descended into claim, counter-claim and Scott defending Tommy Brink's career stats, defensive abilities and very (non) existence.

I'll be honest, I can't say with any certainty the above conversation took place on the trip to the West Brom game, but if not that week then the week before, or the week after, or the month before or the month after, but the point is that it was this sort of nonsense that filled our time travelling to and from games.

As any true football fan will tell you, the least important thing about the football is the actual football; it's about the friendship, the beer, the laughs, the one-liners and the opportunities to visit new places - I mean, why else would I ever visit the likes of Preston, Oldham, Hull and Barnsley if not for the Chels?

I first met Scott in 1983 when we played for the same junior football team at the age of nine, an immediate friendship formed by the statistical-oddity of both being fans of Second Division Chelsea in a town 80 miles from London and a dressing room largely filled by supporters of Liverpool, Manchester United or Aston Villa.

Almost 40 years on, Scott, myself and Aidy - a third member of the same team who at the time followed United but quickly saw sense and switched allegiances to Northampton Town - remain the very best of best mates.

I've just messaged them both to tell them I'm writing about Tommy Brink and Scott replied with one word - 'Cock' - which made me laugh. Despite the three of us now living in three separate time zones, I love them both. Genuinely and deeply so.

The start of 1997 saw Prime Minister (and Chelsea fan) John Major under increasing pressure as his bid to put family values at the heart of his party's politics continued to backfire; married Harlow MP Jerry Hayes the latest to have his private life spread across the tabloids as he denied allegations of a bi-sexual affair.

Mired in allegations of sleaze it was another indication that time appeared to be running out for Major's Tories, with a Labour party under the leadership of Tony Blair ahead in the opinion polls and seemingly on track for a return to power for the first time since 1979.

The apparent demand for change was being reflected across society as a whole, with the Cool Britannia era continuing to gather pace.

On the back of Baddiel, Skinner and Euro '96, the cultural

renaissance was stepping up a gear in 1997 with Oasis, Blur, Pulp, Suede and The Spice Girls featuring in the charts, 'Lads Mags' replacing porn mags, artist Damien Hirst pickling sharks, and Chris Evans falling out of favour with the BBC to focus on the hit TFI Friday Channel 4 show - the must-watch meeting-point for all that were capturing the spirit of the age.

And front and centre of football's own sun-lit renaissance was Chelsea FC, with Gullit, Vialli, Zola and Di Matteo among the coolest of the class of European imports that had sparked fresh energy and life into the English national game.

On the first weekend of the new year a seasonal chill sweeping the country resulted in a number of games being postponed, but Chelsea's fixture survived and West Brom were the visitors for the start of the FA Cup campaign.

It would be Chelsea's 289th game in the famous competition but for all that effort - dating back to a 6-1 defeat of 1st Grenadiers in October 1905 - we had just one success and three additional appearances in the final to look back on.

Despite the recent influx of foreign talent and relative upturn in fortunes there would be no real reason to suspect this year would be any different, but we lived in hope; otherwise, what was the point?

On arrival at Chelsea we park as normal beneath the shadows of the Fulham Gasworks in Gwyn Close, walk across the King's Road and past the picture-perfect mews in Wandon Road.

There we pop out opposite the main entrance to Stamford Bridge, clock the cranes creating a new-look Shed-end, turn right and walk along the Fulham Road.

It is then past the stallholders setting up on the opposite side of the bridge, past the Fox & Pheasant and Black Bull, past the gates to Brompton Cemetery and all the way up to the Stargazey opposite Chelsea & Westminster Hospital, where the usual gang is no doubt waiting to carry on conversation from where we left off last time.

It isn't the most fashionable of Chelsea pubs but it is owned by London-brewery Fullers, serves decent beer at decent prices, and rarely attracts the interest of idiots (present company excluded).

For now it serves us well but, just as in the past we've collectively or individually moved on from pubs such as the Slug, the Jolly Malster, the Beer Engine, and the fabulous Ferret & Firkin in the Balloon up the Creek, there'll be a time when we move on again. There'll be no particular reason, no explanation, just somewhere different one week and a new temporary habit will be formed. But for now it is the Stargazey, where the pinball of conversation bounces around the table.

Last week's league win against top-of-the-table Liverpool is discussed, plans for next week's game at Nottingham Forest outlined.

Our chances in the cup are debated, ahead of concluding that someone will turn us over at some point.

But then Scott tells everyone about my promise to propose should Chelsea win the cup.

They laugh, take the piss, and conclude that perhaps it will be our year after-all.

But then I remind them it is now 27 years since Chelsea won their single FA Cup, so the odds are firmly stacked in my favour…

"Nothing to worry about, whose round is it?"

More laughter, more piss-take.

As always we push departure to as late as possible, knowing to the second how long it will take to walk back down the Fulham Road and queue for the turnstiles for our respective spots in the all-seater ground undergoing continued redevelopment.

As we sup up and start walking, someone comments that another good day out is about to be ruined by the football. It has become something of a catchphrase, largely because it is true - over recent years far too many Saturday afternoons in warm pubs, in good company, with good beer, have been spoiled by 90 minutes of a cold dish of disappointment on the pitch.

Today's opponents, despite having a proud history and five FA Cups to Chelsea's one, are struggling along in the second-tier of English football.

To the majority of top-flight clubs it would be seen as the perfect cup draw, but Chelsea are Chelsea and we have serious history in this department.

As recently as October we lost to lower-league opposition in the form of Bolton Wanderers in the League Cup.

Last season, in the same competition, it was Stoke City. The year before that… Millwall in the FA Cup.

And I could go on… year in, year out, Chelsea are too often the wounded Goliaths to the cocky Davids.

It is a part of the club's DNA of which manager Ruud Gullit is aware… "No more stupid results," he said ahead of today's game.

On this occasion, those under his charge have listened - by the time keeper Frode Grodas is forced to make his first save after more than 80 minutes, Chelsea are two up and the contest is over.

Club captain Dennis Wise, recalled to the team following a short spell on the sidelines in favour of Scottish midfielder Craig Burley, scored the opening goal shortly before half-time - guiding the ball between the post and the outstretched arm of Paul Crichton after Mark Hughes had flicked on a Gianfranco Zola cross.

Burley then came from the bench with the game still in the balance but settled matters within five minutes of his arrival, sliding home with one touch after a Roberto Di Matteo pass split the defence.

Further firepower is on the bench in the name of Gianluca Vialli and he is introduced with just over 10 to play, arriving in time to scuff a late left-foot shot from the edge of the box that trundles back off the far post... where his Italian countryman Gianfranco Zola is on hand to side-foot home.

It isn't a game that will live long in the memory, but it is a comfortable, controlled win that puts Chelsea into the next round without any suspense or drama.

And for that rare treat, we can only be grateful.

FA Cup Third Round results

Chesterfield 2 Bristol City 0; Liverpool 1 Burnley 0; Watford 2 Oxford United 0; Reading 3 Southampton 1; Gillingham 0 Derby County 2; Leicester City 2 Southend United 0; Notts County 0 Aston Villa 0 (Replay: Aston Villa 3 Notts County 0); Nottingham Forest 3 Ipswich Town 0; Blackburn Rovers 1 Port Vale 0; Sheffield Wednesday 7 Grimsby Town 1; Wolverhampton Wanderers 1 Portsmouth 2; Crewe Alexandra 1 Wimbledon 1 (Replay: Wimbledon 2 Crewe Alexandra 0); Middlesbrough 6 Chester City 0; Luton Town 1 Bolton Wanderers 1 (Replay: Bolton Wanderers 6 Luton Town 2); Everton 3 Swindon Town 0; Wrexham 1 West Ham United 1 (Replay: West Ham United 0 Wrexham 1); Hednesford Town 1 York City 0; Wycombe Wanderers 0 Bradford City 2; Queens Park Rangers 1 Huddersfield Town 1 (Replay: Huddersfield Town 1 Queens Park Rangers 2); Barnsley 2 Oldham Athletic 0; Brentford 0 Manchester City 1; Coventry City 1 Woking 1 (Replay: Woking 1 Coventry City 2); Manchester United 2 Tottenham Hotspur 0; Norwich City 1 Sheffield United 0; Plymouth Argyle 0 Peterborough United 1;

Carlisle United 1 Tranmere Rovers 0; Crystal Palace 2 Leeds United 2 (Replay: Leeds United 1 Crystal Palace 0); Chelsea 3 West Bromwich Albion 0; Charlton Athletic 1 Newcastle United 1 (Replay: Newcastle United 2 Charlton Athletic 1); Arsenal 1 Sunderland 1 (Replay: Sunderland 0 Arsenal 2); Stoke City 0 Stockport County 2; Birmingham City 2 Stevenage Borough 0.

CHAPTER THREE
1991/1992

So, let's cut straight to the chase.

When the fixtures for the new season were announced, all eyes were on one game - Tottenham.

And the Gods were on our side, sending us to White Hart Lane on just the second weekend of the campaign.

While always a highly-anticipated fixture, excitement was at its peak as we walked along the Tottenham High Road to give a 'warm' welcome to Spurs' £2.2m new summer signing... former Blue Gordon Durie.

The tall, pacey, Scottish international was a popular figure at Chelsea, returning an impressive 51 goals in 123 appearances over the previous five years, so most fans were sympathetic when his wife's home-sickness was reported as a reason he wanted to leave Stamford Bridge to return 'north'.

Glasgow Rangers was the expected destination, so it came as something of a surprise when it was announced in mid-August that he was linking up with the likes of Saint Gary of Lineker at the previous season's FA Cup winners.

Durie's lawyers would ask me to acknowledge that he did indeed go north; even if it was just under an hour on the District and Victoria lines if he was happy to walk the final slog from Seven Sisters.

In an introduction to the Tottenham fans in the programme, Durie said: "There have been reports that I was looking to go back up to Scotland and, while that was half right, I couldn't be more delighted at how this has turned out. I'm happy to be here and looking forward to the future with Spurs.

"It's a coincidence that we're playing Chelsea today but it will be nice to see the boys again. My decision had nothing to do with them or the supporters because I have always got on with both."

As he would soon discover, he should have put more emphasis on 'have'.

The away terrace was packed to capacity well in advance of

kick-off and the vitriol grew with every passing minute…

As the teams were announced:

"Number six, Gary Mabbutt" - *"Boooo"* - "Number seven, Paul Stewart" - *"Boooo"* - "Number eight, welcome to White Hart Lane, Gordon Durie" - *"BOOOOOOOOOOOOOOOO; GORDON DURIE IS A WANKER IS A WANKER, GORDON DURIE IS A WANKER IS A WANKER, GORDON DURIE IS A WANKER IS A WANKER…"*

As the teams came out to warm-up:

"BOOOOOOOOOOOOOOOO; JUDAS, JUDAS, JUDAS; GORDON DURIE IS A WANKER IS A WANKER, GORDON DURIE IS A WANKER IS A WANKER, GORDON DURIE IS A WANKER IS A WANKER; JUDAS, JUDAS, JUDAS…"

And repeat.

By the time Kerry Dixon had headed Chelsea's first through the legs of Erik Thorstvedt with less than three minutes on the clock, Durie was already proving to be 30 years ahead of his time - imposing a strict Covid-like social-distancing policy with regard to the away terrace.

It was a similar story if he was in danger of touching the ball; Chelsea fans quickly learning it was best to keep their lips permanently rounded in preparation if they were to have the time to squeeze in a quick 'booo' or 'wanker' before he moved it on or gave it away with a single touch.

Dixon's opener was followed by an exquisite 22nd-minute lob from Kevin Wilson when Chelsea broke up-field after Durie (chortle) was dispossessed on the edge of the box.

Townsend calmly passed it past Thorstvedt to make it three straight from the restart and, although Lineker reduced the deficit before the hour was out, the script for the day had been written:

"JUDAS, WHAT'S THE SCORE? JUDAS, JUDAS WHAT'S THE SCORE? JUDAS, WHAT'S THE SCORE?…"

Durie was a shell of a figure by the time the day was over and, to our disappointment but to his undoubted relief, was missing due to injury for the January return fixture when Tottenham handed over the remainder of their six-point gift to Chelsea.

His Tottenham career, meanwhile, never fully kicked into gear after that home-debut humiliation and in 1993, after 58 appearances that yielded just 11 goals, he finally got his move to the proper north - all 400 miles to Glasgow Rangers.

The Tottenham game gave Chelsea their first win of the season on the back of an opening weekend draw against Wimbledon and a midweek 3-0 humbling at newly-promoted Oldham following a busy summer of ins and outs.

In addition to Durie, also making their way through the Stamford Bridge exit door was England left-back Tony Dorigo courtesy of a £1.3m switch to Leeds, and Scottish winger Kevin McAllister - the Poundshop Pat Nevin returning to former club Falkirk after six years on the Fulham Road.

Of most note though to those Chelsea fans of a sentimental nature was the departure of John Bumstead. An ever-popular but often under-rated midfielder, Bumstead left for Charlton Athletic on a free transfer after 13 years of loyal Chelsea service that saw him make in excess of 400 appearances.

Boosting the ranks, meanwhile, was classy centre-half Paul Elliott from Celtic for £1.4m, Scotland left-back Tommy Boyd, who joined from Motherwell as a direct replacement for Dorigo, and Joe Allon, a former star of a Newcastle FA Youth Cup winning team who had caught the eye with 35 goals for Hartlepool the previous season.

There was also a new - or returning - face in the manager's office as Ian Porterfield replaced Bobby Campbell, who had announced he was calling it a day at the end of the previous season to move upstairs to support chairman Ken Bates in an advisory role.

Porterfield was Campbell's assistant as Chelsea won Division Two in 1988/89 before his departure to manage Reading in the October of 1989 coincided with a dip in form that saw Chelsea fall away from the early-season Division One frontrunners.

Despite being sacked by Reading, his return to Chelsea was - while not exactly setting pulses racing - a popular choice among the playing staff and accepted without complaint by the majority of fans who recognised his former contributions.

On the opening day of the new season Elliott and Boyd both made their debuts as starters, with Elliott making an instant impression to head home a Kerry Dixon flick after John Fashanu had put Wimbledon ahead.

The star of the show though was Joe Allon, who came on as a late substitute with Chelsea again a goal behind.

With fewer than five minutes left to play, Graeme Le Saux crossed from the left and a grateful Allon sent it flying past Hans Segers with a deflection off his shin.

The scrappy nature of the goal was irrelevant for Allon, who leapt the advertising hoardings and ran to take the acclaim of the

Shed terrace in the style of a man who'd just scored a 40-yard worldie to win the World Cup.

A new cult hero was born.

His legend grew on the Wednesday following the 3-1 win over Spurs when he again made his mark from the bench against a Notts County team managed by Neil Warnock, who had reportedly turned down the Chelsea job ahead of the appointment of Porterfield.

With Chelsea trailing 2-0, Elliott was once more on target to reduce the deficit before Allon levelled.

Quickest to react to a rebound from his own shot, Allon hooked a volley into the net for his second in two home appearances... back over the hoardings, back in front of the Shed, and back on the back pages.

A Zenith Data Systems Cup strike aside, it was his last goal for Chelsea. But it was fun while it lasted.

But if one cult hero wasn't enough, we had another on the books by the time the Chelsea were next back in action.

Step forward Vincent Peter Jones. Vinnie, to his mates.

A key figure in a Wimbledon FA Cup-winning side, a Leeds promotion side and a Sheffield United team that over-achieved ahead of his switch to Chelsea, Vinnie used his strengths - and limitations - to make greater contributions than many were willing to give him credit for.

So with Chelsea already showing signs of the frustrating inconsistency that dogged the previous campaign, they needed someone willing to grab them by the bollocks... and, as Paul Gascoigne will famously testify, Vinnie certainly had form in that department.

Reaction to his signing was mixed, but pre-match clenched fists and a debut assist in a 4-1 romp against Luton did no harm in winning over the numerous doubters.

He then made a quick return to Sheffield United as a Dennis Wise winner moved Chelsea up to second in the early table, but it was Kevin Hitchcock - enjoying a run in goal in the absence of the injured Dave Beasant - who secured all three points with a man-of-the-match display between the sticks.

After a draw at West Ham and lacklustre home defeat to the returning Tony Dorigo's Leeds, Jones scored his first goal in a Chelsea shirt in a 2-0 defeat of Aston Villa to move his new club back up to third.

Meanwhile, Chelsea's fortunes were being played out against

the backdrop of forthcoming change in my own life.

With Oxford and Cambridge both scandalously failing to offer me a university place following my A-Level return of Double D and an E, I was forced to look elsewhere for higher education opportunities if I was to avoid being forced prematurely into the world of work.

Kindly coming to my rescue was the West Surrey College of Art & Design in Farnham, Surrey, which had unwisely deemed me worthy of a place on a journalism course.

Farnham was a small, safe town in which to leave home to study but - as importantly - was fewer than 50 miles from Stamford Bridge.

My match-going companion Scott, though, was heading up to the north-west to further his education, so the September 21 QPR derby at Loftus Road would potentially be the last we were to jointly do until we were reunited for Christmas.

It was almost emotional.

Walking down the South Africa Road at about 2pm for a game that - implausible though it may seem in the modern game - wasn't all ticket, we soon realised we'd perhaps under-estimated quite how many Chelsea would be turning up to see if we could move up to second in the table.

As was always the case at QPR it was obvious Chelsea would be there in their thousands, but this was a White City invasion.

Knowing we'd be wasting our time heading to the Chelsea terrace or seats, we grabbed the first tickets we could lay our hands on in the Ellerslie Road Stand and went in.

We weren't alone, with the attendance of 19,579 containing a minimum of 12,000 Chelsea spread across the ground.

A few home fans around us were brave enough to go up in their own seats when QPR went 2-0 up - former Chelsea player Clive Wilson tucking home the first - but they were restrained in their enthusiasm.

The true weight of numbers became clear in the 70th minute when Townsend put Chelsea back in the game. Moving on to a half-cleared corner 25 yards out, Townsend nonchalantly hit it on the half-volley to send it straight back from where it had come - the ball arrowing into the top corner.

And if that wasn't spectacular enough, in the dying seconds Dutch centre-half Ken Monkou flicked on a long Jones throw for Wise to equalise with an overhead kick from no more than a yard out.

Somewhere in the depths of Google there's a wonderful picture of the moment the ball hits the net, Wise wheeling away in celebration with a tsunami of Chelsea arms aloft in the QPR seats behind.

The Loftus Road game was followed by a 1-1 draw at home to Second Division Tranmere Rovers in the first-leg of a League Cup tie, setting up a tricky trip for the return game at Prenton Park, before Pat Nevin made his latest return to Stamford Bridge as Everton took a share of the points to push Chelsea back down to fifth.

I had a new friend in tow for the following weekend's pilgrimage to Highbury; Dave being an early university acquaintance from Northern Ireland who was tagging along for his first taste of English football.

The queue for the Clock End away terrace stretched up Highbury Hill and not all made it in before the gates were locked, ensuring a strong Chelsea presence in the Arsenal North Bank.

But with my new mate by my side, I was safely wedged in the packed away end in time to see Graeme Le Saux and Kevin Wilson stun the defending champions in the first 20 minutes.

Dave was loving every minute but, based firmly in the neutral camp, didn't have the good grace to stop smiling as Arsenal stormed back to win the game through a Lee Dixon penalty awarded for a dubious handball, and further goals from Ian Wright and Kevin Campbell.

The penalty decision so incensed Andy Townsend he was on the phone to Danny Baker later in the evening to complain on the BBC 606 football fans' phone-in show - this being in the days when a footballer's every word wasn't approved by a club press officer, Danny Baker wasn't persona non grata within the walls of the Beeb, and football phone-ins weren't the radio equivalent of sticking an ice-pick in your ears.

Chelsea fans' nervousness ahead of the Tranmere League Cup return leg proved to be warranted as the hosts secured a 3-1 extra-time win on the night, with former Liverpool forward John Aldridge stuttering in his run-up to score a controversial penalty.

A Damien Matthew sending off added to the misery as Chelsea extended their impressive record of losing to lower league opposition in one - and sometimes both - of the main cup competitions to six years.

Stretching back to 1986/87, the full list of shame now featured Cardiff, Reading, Barnsley, Scunthorpe, Scarborough, Bristol City,

Oxford, Sheffield Wednesday and Tranmere. But as we'll find out, there'd be one more name to add to the list before the season was out.

Jones was again on target in a 2-2 home draw against Liverpool, but the following week's 0-0 draw at Crystal Palace moved Chelsea to five league games without a win as all early-season optimism again started to fade.

A 1-0 win at Coventry briefly stopped the rot, but defeats to Norwich and Southampton put Chelsea back on the downward slide - the 3-0 home thumping by Norwich of particular note for two strikes from outside the box by their highly-rated forward Robert Fleck.

As November moved into December reinforcement was needed, and it came in the form of much-travelled striker Clive Allen.

Allen spent the first half of his career switching from London club to London club - QPR, Arsenal (well, sort of, he sensibly didn't stay long enough to actually play), Crystal Palace, QPR again and Tottenham - before finally discovering the world didn't end at the North Circular ahead of moves to Bordeaux and then Manchester City.

With things starting to go stale at City, he coughed up for a new Travelcard and returned to the capital just in time to go straight into the Chelsea starting line-up for a testing trip to fourth-placed Sheffield Wednesday.

There was to be no dream debut though as David Hirst put the hosts in control with a second-half brace before Chelsea keeper Kevin Hitchcock was sent off for a contretemps with Nigel Worthington.

Vinnie Jones needed little encouragement to take the gloves for the final 20 minutes and got to the brink of the final whistle without conceding, only for Wednesday to grab a third in the 90th minute.

Clive Allen scored his first Chelsea goal in the next league game, a televised 3-1 home defeat to Manchester United that sent the visitors above Leeds to the top of the table, and again showed the ability that made him such a popular signing throughout his career with a further two in a 4-2 defeat of Oldham.

So, here's a thing that is probably true for most football fans...

In the periods of life when you are only an occasional visitor to games you remember every match in vivid detail; but in those periods that you go regularly it's the games that you don't attend that stand out, presumably due to some inbuilt guilt for not being there.

Which makes Chelsea's 2-0 defeat at Notts County on Boxing Day 1991 something of a personal curiosity because, despite everything pointing to my presence, I have absolutely no recollection of being there or - for that matter - no recollection of not being there.

I've watched the goals, read match reports and even studied the away terrace to see if it sparks a recollection. But nothing. It's a blank.

The real mystery, however, lies in the fact that I remain in possession of three match programmes from the game. Why would I have three programmes if I didn't go? Or, equally, why would I have three programmes if I did go?

But I digress...

The following Saturday Chelsea made another festive return to Luton with the away fan ban now lifted. Just like the previous year, however, it ended in a 2-0 defeat with Boyd sent off after the damage had already been done.

Clive Allen then continued his strong start as a Chelsea striker to score in a 1-1 New Year's Day home draw against his former club Manchester City before attention turned to the FA Cup and another trip to lower league opposition.

Waiting in the wings to potentially humiliate Chelsea on this occasion was Division Three Hull City.

What could possibly go wrong?

Well, on this occasion, nothing. Jones and Wise scored in a relatively comfortable 2-0 win that meant everyone had to go for a lie down, while the big upset of the day came from The Racecourse Ground in Wrexham where former Chelsea cult hero Mickey Thomas scored a stunning free-kick to help give his struggling Division Four side a 2-1 win over Arsenal.

Clive Allen maintained his fine run of scoring form in league wins against Tottenham and Wimbledon, before grabbing the only goal of the game in an FA Cup Fourth-Round defeat of Everton which required Kevin Hitchcock to save a late Tony Cottee penalty to secure progress.

The cup clash - in the pre-Premier League days, only the fourth game to ever be televised live from Stamford Bridge - put Chelsea into the fifth round for only the third time since the 1977/78 season.

The draw paired them with an enticing home clash against

Sheffield United, but before attention could switch back to the Road to Wembley there was league duty to be completed at Liverpool and at home to Crystal Palace and Southampton.

Chelsea had not won at Liverpool since a cup success in 1966 and had to go back to 1935 for their last league victory, so hopes were not exactly high among the travelling support.

On a memorable day, however, Dennis Wise and Vinnie Jones called on some of their former Wimbledon Crazy Gang spirit to stick a poster saying 'Bothered' over the 'This is Anfield' sign in the players' tunnel and then both found the net in a 2-1 win. The margin of victory would have been even greater if not for Wise having a penalty saved by Bruce Grobbelaar, but the win would still go down as one of the most impressive, and unexpected, in the first half of the decade.

Of less historic note from the game at Anfield is that it was Tommy Boyd's last in a Chelsea shirt, with the Scot returning north of the border just five months after making the journey south.

Boyd was shipped out to Celtic in a period of business that saw centre-forward Tony Cascarino heading in the opposite direction to provide increased competition for Kerry Dixon.

With Andy Townsend still pulling strings in midfield, Cascarino doubled Chelsea's contingent of Kent-born Republic of Ireland internationals to two and made an instant impact with the goal that gave his new side a point against Palace.

The following 1-1 home draw against Southampton was notable only for the attendance.

A figure of just 7,148 registered the club's lowest ever post-war crowd for a top-flight game, with even the Zenith Data Systems Cup clash between the same sides just two weeks earlier attracting more as Chelsea exited the sideshow competition at the regional semi-final stage.

While the league no-show could be partly explained by the game being held midweek, poor weather and inconsistent league form, it was also a result of all attention being on the forthcoming weekend FA Cup Fifth Round clash.

In direct contrast to the Southampton game Stamford Bridge was packed for the visit of Sheffield United with a season-high of 34,447 clicking through the turnstiles, although not all arrived in time to see Vinnie Jones booked after just three seconds for 'putting down a marker' on former teammate Dane Whitehouse.

Choosing a spot directly in the middle of a packed Shed, Scott and I had already been carried by various surges up and down the steps of the terrace long before Graham Stuart picked up a 24th-minute Andy Townsend pass on the right touchline.

Taking a couple of touches to bring it under control, Stuart swerved past two Sheffield United markers to drive into the box, and side-foot home past a diving Phil Kite.

Cue a Shed surge to end all surges...

Despite still having more than an hour to play Chelsea retained control for the remainder of the game, with only a Brian Deane header against the crossbar coming close to spoiling the party.

You could forget the league now; Chelsea weren't pushing for honours and, barring a complete collapse, were unlikely to face the threat of going down, so all focus was on the cup and a quarter-final home draw against Sunderland - struggling Division Two Sunderland - on a Monday night in the second week of March.

Chelsea last faced the Wearsiders in knock-out competition in the 1985 League Cup last four, going out after two legs and a night of violence at Stamford Bridge.

On that occasion, me and my dad found ourselves locked out on the Fulham Road as the game kicked off before finally being allowed access to a section of the North End terrace next to the Sunderland support.

Standing directly alongside the away fans only added to the fun on a night that saw pitch invasions, smoke bombs, seats used as missiles and Sunderland score while officers from the Metropolitan Police were enjoying a canter through the Shed-end penalty area.

On this occasion, however, we were on the West Stand Benches safely surrounded by our own as Chelsea boss Ian Porterfield - famously the scorer of the goal that gave Sunderland a 1973 FA Cup Final win over Leeds - brought Kevin Wilson into midfield for the suspended Vinnie Jones and recalled Kerry Dixon in place of recent starter Cascarino.

On a poor pitch that made any good football a struggle, Chelsea took the lead in the 36th-minute when Clive Allen pounced in the six-yard box to send the Bridge into raptures.

We were now just a clean sheet from a first FA Cup semi-final appearance since 1970, in which we already knew we'd face a tie against Norwich City.

The overriding memory of the second half is simply one of tension as Chelsea failed to kill off the game and Sunderland looked increasingly likely to take one of the growing number of chances coming their way.

And so it was, with less than 10 minutes left to play, that Chelsea missed opportunities to clear upfield, Paul Bracewell hooked a ball into the box and 31-year-old John Bryne - a consistent pain in the arse who loved a goal or two against Chelsea in seasons gone by - headed back across a flat-footed Kevin Hitchcock for the ball to loop agonisingly in at the far post.

The packed Sunderland away terrace, quite understandably, went loopy.

Minutes later, game over, I bid farewell to my dad and brother and headed back to my Farnham student digs hoping a housemate with benefits might be willing to lighten my dark mood.

The replay in the north-east was scheduled for the following Wednesday, but before then Chelsea had to squeeze in two league games - a trip to Norwich, and a visit of Coventry.

Both ended 1-0 - one in victory, one in defeat - with the legendary Kerry Dixon scoring a cracking strike that would prove to be the last of his 193 in a Chelsea shirt in the trip to Carrow Road, before Townsend and Allen were both sent off in the Coventry loss.

The struggles of student finance meant I couldn't afford the 600-mile round-trip to Roker Park for the cup replay, but may I take this opportunity to offer my condolences to the thousands of loyal Chelsea fans that did travel and still bear the mental scars to this day.

For what it's worth I was locked in my bedroom in Surrey, with Jonathan Pearce and Capital Gold radio for company; hoping for the best, expecting the worst.

The intense Roker Park atmosphere was coming across loud and clear on the radio and it was no surprise when Peter Davenport gave the hosts the lead in the 20th-minute.

In a reverse of the Stamford Bridge tie though it was Chelsea that pushed and pushed in the second-half, chasing the goal that would take the tie to extra-time.

With just under five minutes remaining Dave Beasant pumped a long free-kick into the Sunderland area. The attempted clearance was knocked down to Vinnie Jones who lifted it back into the area, where a grateful Dennis Wise tucked it under the body of Tony Norman.

"YEEEEESSSSSSSSSSSSS......"

I set off on a lap of honour, bursting through the door of my ground-floor bedroom and up the stairs to dive on top of my

Middlesbrough-supporting housemate who - in an ideal world - wanted both Boro's north-east rivals Sunderland and his gobby mate's Chelsea to lose.

With a quick "eff off" from him, I ran back downstairs and into my room to hear the Chelsea fans in full voice as Pearce described Sunderland preparing to take a corner from their right.

"WE SHALL NOT, WE SHALL NOT BE MOVED …." sang the Chelsea fans.

"It's Brian Atkinson with an out-swinging corner," is what, using my imagination to the full, Pearce probably said.

"…WE SHALL NOT, WE SHALL NOT BE MOVED…" continued the away support.

"Gordon Armstrong beats Andy Townsend in the air…" Pearce would have noted.

"UNTIL WE WIN THE FA……."

Shit. Arse. Fuck. Bollocks.

The stunned mid-song silencing of the Chelsea fans told me all I needed to know.

The sound of Pearce squealing like a stuck pig simply confirmed it.

It was now 21 years since Chelsea had last won a major trophy.

And it hurt, it really, really bloody hurt, because a clear, winnable route to a Wembley FA Cup Final had been snatched from our grasp by the latest in a long line of Chelsea embarrassments against lower-league opposition.

The resulting dark mood was long and deep, and I was one of just 11,000 stupid enough to show up for the wake at the following Saturday's league clash against Sheffield United. We lost, of course, with Jason Cundy the Chelsea scorer in a 2-1 defeat.

It felt as though things couldn't get much worse but, in the following days, Chelsea proved once more that they are always happy to kick you in the bollocks while simultaneously smacking you in the mouth.

One of our own, Cundy was a rising star who came through the youth ranks to establish himself as a popular centre-half.

With the right guidance and support he had clear potential to be a club stalwart for years to come, so it was something of an annoyance that, in the days following the Sheffield United defeat, Chelsea announced they were sending him - against his wishes - on loan to bitter rivals Tottenham Hotspur.

We were, to put it mildly, a bit pissed off.

To add to our fury, in the same week Kevin Wilson was sold to Notts County and Clive Allen - after fewer than four months at Stamford Bridge - was told he'd be adding another stamp to his London collectors' card with a move along the District Line to West Ham.

'Willo' had been a loyal and consistent servant who scored some valuable goals across six seasons at the club, but a move to pastures new was probably overdue. No real complaints.

Natural finisher Allen, however, while not necessarily a long-term solution, had scored nine goals in just 22 appearances in this short time at the club so his premature departure added to the sense of gloom surrounding the loss of Cundy.

So with the dark clouds gathering, I was joined by Aidy on a trip north to stay at Scott's university digs for a visit to Manchester City.

It was a waste of time and money, and the drab 0-0 is remembered only for two reasons.

First, while the away support was among the smallest in all my years following Chelsea, it was vitriolic in its concerns over the direction of the playing squad as it consistently told the management team that it wanted Cundy back. They didn't listen, and his move to Spurs was made permanent in the summer.

Second, Scott, Aidy and I spent the night of the match in the Deansgate area of Manchester looking for a decent club in which to drink away our memories of the game.

Failing miserably we called it an early night, grumbling about the lack of a decent nightlife in the city... only discovering sometime later that we'd managed to walk right past the doors of the famous Hacienda club at the peak of its powers.

If there was a metaphor for my life as a Chelsea fan in the post-Sunderland spring of 1992, there it was - so tantalisingly near, yet so agonisingly far.

West Ham's Clive Allen then made an immediate return to Stamford Bridge to score a predictable peach in front of the Shed, albeit in a 2-1 defeat for the East End barrow boys, before we all headed north to Yorkshire to see Rod Wallace, Lee Chapman and Eric Cantona put Chelsea to the sword and Leeds one step closer to the league title. It never rains, but it pours.

With a defeat of QPR followed by defeat at Aston Villa, I was looking forward to putting a miserable end to the season behind me as I jumped on the train from Farnham for the final home league game of the season against Arsenal.

Spotting my Chelsea shirt, a woman sitting opposite took the immediate opportunity to engage me in conversation about the season and, after a few niceties, asked for my view on the Sunderland games.

I gave the politest response possible, but it was an itch she clearly wanted to keep scratching.

"Did you go?"; "Did you think it was your year?"; "What did you think when Byrne scored at the Bridge?"; "What did you think when Armstrong scored the Roker winner?" etc, etc, etc.

Eventually I took the bait: "Go on then, I assume you are a Sunderland fan?"

"Well, not a fan as such," she said, "but my husband's the manager..."

Sitting in front of me was Carole Crosby, wife of Sunderland boss Malcolm who, by this stage, had guided his side to the FA Cup Final against Liverpool.

She then proceeded to spend the rest of the journey ripping it out of me, recounting every fine detail of the cup run, outlining the celebrations on the night they beat Chelsea and telling me - in exhausting, excessive detail - about the magic of John Byrne's 'lucky boot'.

Like I gave a shit.

So fast forward to 2020 and, because it still occasionally keeps me awake at night, I told the story about Malcolm Crosby's wife on Twitter.

So imagine my surprise when, the following day, I received a reply with the simple message: "Hi Jason, Mrs C here. Fancy a train journey!!"

It was the first Tweet she'd sent of any description in 15 months, adding one final twist of the knife to a 28-year wound. I'm sure she found it funnier than I did.

With the Arsenal game that followed my encounter with 'Mrs C' finishing 1-1, the season concluded with a 2-1 defeat at Everton.

The trip to Goodison saw a debut for youth-team graduate Eddie Newton, but was also to be the final appearances for 1990 Player of the Year Ken Monkou - the classy Dutchman having impressed across more than 100 appearances - and, most notably, Kerry Dixon.

The star signing of a number who turned out to be star signings in the summer of 1983, Dixon served Chelsea with distinction for nine seasons, scoring 193 goals to become - at the time of his departure - the club's second-highest scorer of all-time, just nine shy of Bobby Tambling's record.

The scorer of 34 goals in his debut season, 36 in his second and 25 in Chelsea's return to the top-flight in 1989/90, the 6ft blond had the looks to match his talent.

For me, aged just 10 when he first arrived at the Bridge, he was the ultimate boyhood hero; a Roy Race-type figure who built his legend on being a big figure in big games - Leeds, Grimsby, Highbury, Hillsborough to name just a few.

Off the field, however, he has written and spoken openly about his personal life being increasingly on the edge as the Chelsea years passed by - failed business ventures and a gambling addiction being his primary downfalls.

Dixon has said this in no way impacted on his form on the pitch, but when it was announced in the summer that he'd be moving on to Southampton the news wasn't perhaps met with the sense of loss it fully deserved.

In reality, while the return of just six goals in his final season could be partly waved away by an improved all-round contribution, Dixon's long-term place at the very top of Chelsea folklore may have been better served had he departed a season earlier.

So rather than leaving to cheers from the Shed, Dixon eventually exited through the side door and we'd have to wait until he faced us in the colours of his boyhood club Luton Town to say an emotional, and proper, farewell.

But that would come in due course because, in the meantime, we had a new centre-forward to learn to love.

So, hello Robert Fleck...

CHAPTER FOUR
FA CUP FOURTH ROUND

Chelsea v Liverpool
Stamford Bridge
Sunday, January 26, 1997

Chelsea: Hitchcock, Petrescu, Leboeuf, Clarke, Vialli, Wise, Di Matteo, Minto (Hughes, 46), Sinclair, Newton, Zola.

Liverpool: James, Kvarme, McAteer, Wright, McManaman, Collymore, Fowler, Barnes, Redknapp, Bjornebye (Berger, 74), Matteo.

Referee: Steve Dunn (Bristol)
Attendance: 27,950

"Let it through, Roy Evans has just had a heart-attack."

Ken, always good for a one-liner, brought guffaws of laughter from those around him on the Fulham Road as an ambulance on blues and twos tried to edge its way through the ecstatic post-match crowds.

A London boy who moved to Northamptonshire in the 1960s for work, Ken was the very definition of 'proper Chels' and had a stand-up routine of stories from the '50s through to the '90s to keep us entertained.

Back in the days before motorways were built, and still living in London, he was one of the original Chelsea away supporters; one of a ground-breaking, ground-hopping group that would jump on a Fulham Road coach after Friday-night last orders to arrive - A-roads all the way - in the likes of Manchester, Liverpool, Blackpool or Burnley in time for the following day's game.

A wonderful story-teller, you could taste the 'doorstep' cheese sandwich he was forced to eat after walking home a girl in early-60s' Bolton - this sharp-suited London boy something of a novelty to her northern parents…

And you could picture yourself standing in a 'black and white' Shed as Ken told tales of Greaves, Bentley, Osgood, Cooke and more…

And years later, without thought, you'd find yourself pointing at a pub on the way to the Bridge to say 'someone was shot in that pub once', knowing no more than that because Ken knew no more than that, but would still remind us of the fact every time we passed the pub when he joined us on trips to the game.

And in my home town Ken was a football legend, combining his love of Chelsea with launching both a Sunday football league for adults and a junior side that still runs to this day; an institution that has supported thousands of children across the best part of nearly 50 years.

It was when signing for his junior side that I first met him in 1982 - my pin-striped Le Coq Sportif Chelsea shirt bringing a look of sympathy to his face - and in later years I would became good friends, and football companions, with his equally-Chelsea-mad sons Gary and Paul.

Gaz and Paul were both alongside their dad when we bumped into them on this particular Sunday, all of us buzzing with child-like excitement at what we had just witnessed as Ken cracked his gag at the expense of Liverpool boss Evans.

The FA Cup Fourth Round day had started with Sunday papers still full of images of Diana, Princess of Wales, walking through landmines on a visit to Angola the previous week, and the latest developments on the increasingly tense battle for power in the corridors of Westminster.

The collapsing Conservative government found itself in a House of Commons minority on January 16 after the death of 56-year-old Meriden MP Iain Mills, only for green-bench parity to be restored four days later with the passing of Labour's Martin Redmond.

The back pages of those same Sunday papers, meanwhile, were focusing on an entirely different 'blue v red' battle for dominance.

Chelsea v Liverpool was the undeniable tie of the round, pitching Ruud Gullit's continental collection of Leboeuf, Vialli, Zola and Di Matteo against Roy Evans' table-topping 'Spice Boys' of James, Redknapp, McManaman and McAteer.

The late Sunday-afternoon kick-off meant for a change of routine, with food a greater priority than beer to soak up the previous night's excesses.

In a greasy-spoon where the North End Road meets the Fulham Road, chat was keen, anticipation high as - mugs of tea bubbling, January windows steaming - we talked of the threat of Robbie Fowler, the pace of Stan Collymore, and of Clarke v Barnes and of Zola v Wright.

We talked of Liverpool's league defeat at the Bridge just weeks previously, and of their comfortable win at Anfield earlier in the campaign.

We talked of Chelsea's recent return to form, and signs of a Liverpool dip.

And then, wiping the last of the crumbs from our mouths and pulling down hats, we walked out the café into the afternoon air, turned right, lit a Marlboro Light and joined the walk of all walks - the few hundred yards from Fulham Broadway station to Stamford Bridge that drip with the sights, the smells, the sounds, the taste and the touch of Chelsea.

There is no better walk to awaken the senses... even if the game doesn't always go to plan.

To our left, filling both sides of the East Stand lower tier, Liverpool's away support is spending the half-time break singing of Wembley; to our right, Chelsea fans in the West Stand are silent.

Liverpool had laughed in the face of our pre-match predictions of a close game, taking the lead in the 10th-minute when Robbie Fowler touched home a cross from Stig Inge Bjornebye.

They doubled the advantage after 20 minutes, this time Collymore racing through the middle to slide home after Eddie Newton mis-controlled a short ball from Zola.

They could be, should be, leading by three, four, or even five with Fowler and McManaman, twice, going close to adding to the tally in a dominant first-half display.

Chelsea's only chance of note fell to Vialli but the Italian - restored to the starting line-up after a lengthy spell on the bench - lifted over from 12 yards with the game already looking beyond reach.

For the first time since his summer arrival there were groans of frustration aimed in his direction; a significant minority calling for him to be hooked in favour of Hughes.

And now, at half-time, black humour is to the fore as 1971 European Cup Winners' Cup final scorer John Dempsey is paraded in front of the despondent Matthew Harding Lower.

"*Bring him on, bring him on, bring him on*" we're chanting, no doubt doing nothing to boost the confidence of Vialli and others who have walked down the tunnel out-thought, out-fought and on their way to being out of the cup.

"There's one thing I suppose…" says Scott, disrupting my dark thoughts. "It doesn't look like you're getting married any time soon."

"Every cloud…" I reply, without a hint of humour.

Those calling for change to the starting 11 get their wish as the teams return for the second half but, to the surprise of most, it isn't Vialli making way for Hughes but the left-sided Scott Minto.

Releasing an attacking trio of Hughes, Vialli and Zola, Ruud Gullit is putting all his chips on black to beat a team of reds that hasn't lost from a two-goal advantage for 33 years.

And the effect is immediate.

A fast, pressing, passionate start to the half disrupts the previously-comfortable Liverpool defence and is rewarded within five minutes when Hughes - steam from his nostrils - controls on his chest on the edge of the box, spins to his left and fires low with his right foot beyond the out-stretched hand of David James.

Smelling blood, Hughes limits his celebration and heads straight back to the centre circle to restart.

The pressing continues, and eight minutes later Leboeuf plays long to the edge of the area.

Petrescu hustles and harries the rattled Liverpool defence and Hughes toes the loose ball back to Zola.

From just outside the 'D' Zola takes one touch to control, takes aim, and fires a left-footed arrow beyond the full reach of a diving James.

The net bulges. It's in. We're back from the dead. 2-2. Fucking hell.

"*Zola, la la la la Zola, la la la la Zola …*"

Chelsea are now flying, Liverpool floundering, the Bridge a cauldron of noise - jumping, rocking, bouncing, thumping in excitement.

"*COME ON CHELSEA, COME ON CHELSEA, COME ON CHELSEA…*"

No pause for breath, everyone as one, moving from one inspiring song to the next.

"*CHELSEA (CLAP, CLAP, CLAP), CHELSEA (CLAP, CLAP, CLAP), CHELSEA (CLAP, CLAP, CLAP)…*"

And now - momentum still building - Zola switches the ball from left to the centre, from left to Dan Petrescu.

Petrescu takes a touch... Petrescu turns... Petrescu pauses...
Vialli holds his line... Vialli times his run...

Petrescu threads a pass... and Vialli's one-on-one.

Heads up... necks strained... we're stretching to our toes...

And with an outstretched Vialli touch... we're tumbling down the rows.

It's Chelsea 3 Liverpool 2. It's bedlam.

The long, deep, guttural roar of celebration - the type for which there is no word - blends seamlessly into tribute for the goal-scorer.

"VIALLI, VIALLI, VIALLI, VIALLI, VIALLI, VIALLI, VIALLI, VIALLI..."

The game is back under way as we dust ourselves down, check ourselves, compose ourselves and realise there is still nearly half an hour to play.

"For fuck's sake Chelsea hold on, just fucking hold on..."

But Chelsea remain breathless, relentless, and the play remains down the far end, the end we are attacking.

James, flapping, is forced to make a further save from Di Matteo. And then another from Vialli.

"We should have finished them off... they'll make us pay."

But then, beneath a dark January sky, daylight...

A Zola free-kick from the right, a perfect Vialli header... Chelsea 4 Liverpool 2.

Another explosion of noise, but this time with a subtle hint of laughter mixed with the roar.

It's a laughter that signifies the joy, delight and disbelief at what we're watching.

It's a laughter that means we know the game is won, that we know the day is done... a 26-minute four-goal blitz that is game changing, season-changing, possibly even history-changing.

To our left Liverpool fans are now silent, beaten, battered. On the pitch, their centre-half Mark Wright is shell-shocked, dazed, confused; the haunted look of a man walking from the wreck of a car crash.

Their misery, their trauma, is the ripest cherry on the sweetest icing on the most delicious cake.

Two-nil down, 4-2 up.

Poor-old Scousers fucked it up.

This is why we do this.

This is why we love this.

This is why we're Chelsea.

FA Cup Fourth Round results

Leicester City 2 Norwich City 1; Blackburn Rovers 1 Coventry City 2; Bolton Wanderers 2 Chesterfield 3; Hednesford Town 2 Middlesbrough 3; Derby County 3 Aston Villa 1; Everton 2 Bradford City 3; Newcastle United 1 Nottingham Forest 2; Manchester City 3 Watford 1; Queens Park Rangers 3 Barnsley 2; Portsmouth 3 Reading 0; Manchester United 1 Wimbledon 1 (Replay: Wimbledon 1 Manchester United 0); Carlisle United 0 Sheffield Wednesday 2; Chelsea 4 Liverpool 2; Arsenal 0 Leeds United 1; Peterborough United 2 Wrexham 4; Birmingham City 3 Stockport County 1.

CHAPTER FIVE
1992/1993

"You'd have to pay me to watch that crap...."

The assessment of Chelsea's less than magnificent end to the previous campaign came from Des, an uncle by marriage who was responsible for injecting the first dose of the Blue drug into Gibbins veins when he took my teenage dad to Stamford Bridge in the 1950s.

A south Londoner by birth who had witnessed first-hand the skills of Bentley, Tambling and Greaves, Des was now more than happy to be told about the ills of Beasant, Townsend and Jones from afar. And quite frankly, who could blame him.

But his comment got me thinking...

With a number of undeniably more attractive options now fighting for the attention of my ever-decreasing student funds, the chances of visiting Stamford Bridge and beyond with continued, unquestioned loyalty were looking, well, slim...

So what if Chelsea were to, you know, "pay me to watch that crap...??"

And that is how on the first day of the 1992/93 season - the first day of the all-singing, all-dancing, all-new Premier League - I was handed possession of an illuminous orange stewards' bib, pointed towards a gangway at the top of the main entrance to the Shed terrace and told to get on with it.

Quite what 'it' was wasn't clear, but in return I'd be given a used £10 note straight from the turnstile takings, a matchday programme and - as danger money - a free burger or hotdog of doubtful origin from either of the high-class catering sheds in the Shed.

Not only did I now have the means for watching another season of crap, I was contractually obliged.

The new season represented historic change for top-flight football, with its soul sold to the masters of satellite television for £300 million.

The dawn of the new 'razzle, dazzle, every game's a big game, *bigger than the last game'* Premier League era saw the launch of Monday night football, three substitutes on the bench and the 'bastards in the black' turning out in green, purple and yellow.

New additions to the Chelsea squad, meanwhile, included the experienced full-back Mal Donaghy from Manchester United, vertically-challenged striker John Spencer from Glasgow Rangers and - balancing out the glamour of the Premier League's new Sky Striker cheerleaders - Mick Harford from Luton.

But the big money was reserved for Norwich striker Robert Fleck; the £2.1m fee for a man with a recent history of scoring spectacular goals against Chelsea setting a new club record.

The Fleck signing, in particular, had to work for manager Ian Porterfield, who was finding himself increasingly short of friends following the previous season's spring failings.

Porterfield threw Donaghy, Harford and Fleck straight into the starting line-up for the opening-day clash against Oldham Athletic and, although Fleck was the liveliest of the three, it was Harford that looked like he'd given his new boss a winning start with an impressive 25-yard debut strike with only six minutes remaining.

We hadn't, however, accounted for goalkeeper Dave Beasant.

The Wimbledon FA Cup winner was an inspired signing in the 1988/89 runaway promotion season, adding stability at a point in the campaign when the first signs of a wobble were threatening to appear.

But during the previous campaign the first cracks in his form had started to show, and so it was that he gifted a point to visitors when he miskicked a clearance straight to the feet of a gleeful Nick Henry who returned it into an unguarded net from the edge of the centre-circle.

Across Stamford Bridge Chelsea fans were silenced, but none more so than a woman under the watchful eye of my Shed stewarding who promptly fainted. Dave Beasant, we would continue to learn, had the knack of doing that to people.

Defeat at Norwich - a game in which Fleck was prevented from playing as part of his transfer agreement - was followed by a 3-3 thriller at Sheffield Wednesday.

Otherwise engaged on an afternoon's work placement at the BBC Saturday afternoon sports show Grandstand, I was delighted to discover that I could take advantage of being able to watch a livestream of the game being fed into the back of the studio.

That, therefore, is why somewhere in the BBC archives is footage of me going loopy behind the head of presenter Bob

Wilson as Graham Stuart picks up the ball deep in his own half, completes a solo-run, slides between late attempted-tackles and finally slips the ball beneath Chris Woods to score one of Chelsea's best goals of the '90s.

It took Chelsea five games to register their first win of the campaign, a 1-0 home win against QPR, but when the Blues travelled to Aston Villa for a midweek game at the start of September 'star striker' Fleck had yet to find the net and pressure was starting to show.

But fear not. On a comfortable night in the Midlands Eddie Newton and Dennis Wise completed the scoring in a 3-1 win, but it was Fleck that grabbed the headlines after bundling home in the six-yard box for Chelsea's first goal of the game.

"We all live in a Robbie Fleck world, a Robbie Fleck world, a Robbie Fleck world..." we sang from the away end in support of a new goal-getter that was either going to push us up among the title challengers or... spoiler alert... score just one more league goal all season.

For now though, things were ticking along relatively nicely and the pressures on Porterfield were starting to ease as his blend of home-grown and experienced players began to gel.

Sitting firmly in the experienced camp was Paul Elliott, the previous season's player of the year.

A near ever-present since his signing, he was a graceful, intelligent footballer who also chipped in with the odd goal along the way.

On the back of two wins, and with Elliott managing the backline, confidence was high ahead of a trip to Liverpool that Chelsea could repeat the previous season's long-awaited away success at Anfield.

But little over ten minutes in, Elliott's career was over.

Going in for a tackle on the halfway line, Elliott had started to go to ground when Liverpool's Dean Saunders planted his right foot on to the defender's right knee.

The seriousness was immediate, with Andy Townsend - who would go on to become a future teammate of Saunders at Aston Villa - starting to signal to the bench for support before Elliott had even hit the floor.

In respect of balance, at first viewing the incident was at high speed and that may have offered some mitigation for referee John Key's decision to not only leave Saunders unpunished for the incident but to award the free kick in the Liverpool player's favour.

But was the Saunders challenge damaging? Clearly; it ended a player's career.

Was it reckless? Well, there were plenty who thought so... but the legal system said not.

Elliott took Saunders to the High Court to seek damages but lost the case, with Mr Justice Drake ruling that 'Dean Saunders was not guilty of dangerous or reckless play' and that 'Elliott failed to prove Saunders was in breach of the duty of care he owed to Elliott in all the circumstances of this case'.

Elliott has since gone on record as saying he no longer holds any malice, but it's not a view shared by any Chelsea supporter who witnessed the incident and, to this day, Saunders remains a hate figure on the Fulham Road.

After Elliott had been stretchered off Saunders added insult to injury when - to the backdrop of taunts of *"Vinnie's going to get you"* from the Chelsea end - he proceeded to open the scoring with a header before running to celebrate in front of the Chelsea fans and high-fiving home supporters in the main stand.

The final injustice, after Mick Harford levelled the scores, was another howler from Beasant - the keeper allowing a cross across the box to squirm through his body to hand Jamie Redknapp a late winner.

The Elliott incident diverted attention away from Beasant's error, but there was to be no hiding place when Norwich visited Stamford Bridge seven days later.

Post-Anfield Chelsea made further changes to the squad with Vinnie Jones heading back to former club Wimbledon after 12 months on the Fulham Road and Nigel Spackman - a popular figure in the Chelsea mid-1980s' team - returning for a second spell at Stamford Bridge.

Another new arrival was full-back Anthony Barness from Charlton and, along with Spackman, he went straight into the starting line-up for the visit of the Canaries.

They couldn't have got off to a better start as Mick Harford and Andy Townsend put Chelsea in control before 30 minutes were on the clock, but they - along with the 16,800 present - had no idea of the horrors that lay ahead.

A minute into the second-half Mark Robins stretched a foot to meet a cross in to the box. Lacking power or precision, Beasant could only help scoop the ineffectual effort into the net.

Half an hour later Beasant went absent without leave to the left of his six-yard box to gift Robins an empty net in which to poke home the equaliser.

But the best was yet to come when, just five minutes later, David Phillips sent a weak shot goal-bound.

Beasant went down to gather the trundling ball, only to complete a spectacular hat-trick of dropped bollocks by allowing it to bobble through his grasp.

The howls of derision from the Chelsea support were followed by boos on the final whistle, and further humiliation came when manager Ian Porterfield promptly announced to media that the former England stopper would never play for the club again.

While that proved not strictly true, it would be the last time he'd play for Porterfield.

With Kevin Hitchcock restored between the posts Chelsea went on a run of three clean sheets with a win at Manchester City, a second visit in three years to Walsall in the League Cup and a drab, goalless, affair at home to Nottingham Forest before falling to a 2-1 defeat in a feisty fixture at Arsenal that saw four Chelsea players go in the book.

With League Cup progression effectively secure following the 3-0 first-leg win at Walsall, little over 7,500 were present to see formalities completed in the second-leg.

The afternoon following the 1-0 win - Fleck scoring the winning penalty - I was lacing my football boots for West Surrey College of Art and Design's journalism team ahead of a left-back appearance against students from one of the art courses.

"Did you go to Chelsea last night?" asked a course colleague/team-mate.

"Yeah, it wasn't too bad all things considered..." replied I, "... at least I saw Fleck score again."

"You what...?" said a voice from the opposing team who hadn't been asked, "...it was fucking shit."

The dissenting voice belonged to Stewie, and just like that I had a new Chelsea mate who would become a regular match-day companion across the '90s and whom I still try to catch-up with once or twice a season when I fancy buying someone an overpriced craft gin or cider.

Regardless of the rights or wrongs of Porterfield's decision to go public over the 'sacking' of Dave Beasant, there was no denying that the change of number one had a positive effect on results as October and November saw Chelsea complete league wins against Ipswich, Coventry, Crystal Palace, Everton and defending-champions Leeds.

A League Cup third-round home defeat of Newcastle was followed up by creditable fourth-round 2-2 draw at Everton that ensured both teams would try again in SW6 and, as Chelsea prepared to go to Tottenham in the first week of December, only a 2-1 defeat at home to Sheffield United had slowed progress in the previous nine games.

On the back of his debut at the tail end of the previous season Eddie Newton had now graduated to become a regular starter, but it was the trip to White Hart Lane that firmly put him on the map when - in the absence of the injured Robert Fleck - the Hammersmith-born midfielder became stand-in striker to twice burst in to the box to score in the final quarter of the game.

A debutant by the name of Sol Campbell gave Spurs late hope, but the 2-1 win moved Chelsea up to an unlikely joint-second in the table behind Norwich.

What we didn't know as we left White Hart Lane was that it would be the last time we'd celebrate a Chelsea away win for more than 12 months.

The Tottenham win was followed by a 0-0 draw at Middlesbrough and a 1-0 League Cup replay dismissal of Everton to put Chelsea into a cup quarter-final for the third successive season.

And if things were starting to go well on the pitch, there was even better news off it.

Ahead of the final league game before Christmas, a 1-1 draw at home to Manchester United in which Eric Cantona scored his first goal for the visitors, it was announced that Chelsea had won their nine-year legal battle to secure the ownership of Stamford Bridge.

It was a cause for celebration far greater than any goal that had put us among the season's league front-runners.

The battle to Save the Bridge was long and complex but, in summary, dated back to the moment Ken Bates took ownership of Chelsea Football Club in 1982 for £1 plus responsibility for club debts.

But while Bates may have got the club for a quid, he did not get the freehold to the ground - that remaining under the ownership of holding company SB Property, of which club directors David Mears and Viscount Chelsea remained major shareholders.

Within their rights to sell said shares to whomever they pleased, whenever they pleased, they did just that in 1983 when property developers Marler Estates took a 70% share in SB Property.

The handing of power to Marler - and subsequently Cabra Estates - meant Chelsea's continued existence on the site they had played at since formation in 1905 was on the whim of a company which now owned a prime piece of development land within a Dave Beasant miskick of London's West end.

Marler gave the club notice to quit once their lease expired in 1989 and it was only through Bates' skills in the boardroom and the courts that, through a series of filibustering legal proceedings, Chelsea remained at Stamford Bridge three years after the deadline had passed.

The delays proved crucial - just long enough for the UK economy to fall into recession and the property market to collapse, resulting in Cabra going into liquidation in November 1992.

The Royal Bank of Scotland stepped in to assume control of the freehold and arranged a deal with Chelsea to renew the lease for another 20 years with an option to buy the site outright.

While Chelsea were now secure for the foreseeable future and a rebuild of the crumbling stadium was ready to begin, Bates' next masterstroke would be to create Chelsea Pitch Owners - an independent company that would buy the freehold before selling shares to fans under a structure that would mean no single person could unduly influence the company.

In 1997 CPO completed the purchase of the Stamford Bridge freehold and pitch, and granted the club a 199-year lease to play there at a peppercorn rent.

When Bates eventually handed over the Chelsea reins to Russian oligarch Roman Abramovich in 2003 the club was once again on the brink of financial collapse but - unlike in 1982 - was a much more attractive option for purchase with a fully-redeveloped ground, associated hotels and restaurants, and a team punching at the top-end of the English game.

As for the fans, they could welcome the new owner safe in the knowledge CPO held the power should there ever be - as indeed proved to be the case - any future moves to sell Stamford Bridge and relocate.

But back to the start of 1993, and with Chelsea still in both cups and just six points off top spot following festive period draws against Southampton and Wimbledon there was plenty of reason for optimism - the only warning sign that all was not right within the camp coming when Graeme Le Saux angered fans by throwing his shirt to the ground after being substituted against the Saints.

The FA Cup paired Chelsea with the long trip to

Middlesbrough's Ayresome Park on the opening Sunday of the new year, to be followed in the midweek by a trip across London to Selhurst Park for a League Cup quarter final against Crystal Palace.

Scott and I set off for Middlesbrough on the afternoon of Saturday, January 2 looking forward to a night out in Redcar, where my Boro-supporting university housemate had promised to proudly show us streets littered with the frozen vomit stains from the New Year celebrations.

Beneath the shadows of the nearby Teesside steelworks, we found ourselves traipsing from empty seaside bar to empty seaside bar seeking some warmth, any warmth, as the temperature plummeted from arctic to dark side of Uranus.

The Maldives it was not, but the loss of frozen limbs would be a small price to pay for a Chelsea cup win.... or they might have been, had the game not been postponed.

We had our fears at 2am when we failed to complete the low-tech referee's test of a car key penetrating the frozen surface, but confirmation came early on the Sunday morning to at least offer the consolation of an early departure from Redcar.

We spent the next three days defrosting at our parental homes in the Midlands before heading down to the Selhurst Park as attention turned to the League Cup.

Redcar Sunday, Croydon Wednesday; you only live once.

On the back of the long car trip to Middlesbrough, Scott and I let the train take the strain for this one and stepped from Thornton Heath station to discover rain bouncing above our ankles.

Taking shelter in the first pub we could find, the doors burst open about an hour before kick-off and a Chelsea fan delivered the news we'd feared... "Game's off lads."

Oh, FFS. Four days, two games, more than 12 hours of travel, and not a single ball kicked.

It turned out, however, to be nothing more than wishful thinking from our sodden town crier, with others reporting the game was not yet officially off but a pitch inspection was due.

Getting another round in to await confirmation, referee Gerald Ashby generously passed the pitch playable just half an hour ahead of kick-off.

I don't know what he'd been drinking, but I wanted some...

It was a filthy, filthy night with large puddles in various areas of the pitch - most crucially in the goalmouths - and for those of us pinned into the corner of the open Holmesdale Road terrace it was also going to be a long one.

The misery started less than five minutes in when Frank Sinclair knocked a ball back to keeper Kevin Hitchcock that stuck in a puddle on the edge of the area, allowing Chris Coleman to slide in and poke the ball towards the net with just enough pace for it to travel through the mud on the goal-line.

Townsend levelled for Chelsea with a fine individual left-foot strike before George Ndah put the hosts back in front with another effort that again had just enough power to roll through the surface water.

Grant Watts made it 3-1 shortly after the restart and, despite a spirited second-half effort and a vocal Chelsea support, the closest the Blues came to getting back into the game was when a goal-bound Steve Clarke shot came to an abrupt halt in the same goal-line mud that had been so kind to Palace earlier in the match.

The pre-Christmas optimism had now been replaced with a run of four games without a win in any competition, and that was extended to five with a 4-2 home league defeat to Manchester City ahead of the rearranged Middlesbrough FA Cup game.

Now back at university in Surrey, repeating the trip to Teesside on a Wednesday night was out of the question so - as with the previous season's soul-destroying FA Cup defeat to Sunderland - it was once more over to radio commentary to deliver bad news from the north-east… a 2-1 defeat, despite taking a 68th-minute lead, meaning it was now 22 years since Chelsea had last won a major trophy.

With January not yet two weeks old, all New Year positivity had now gone.

Porterfield finally lost patience with Fleck, dropping his big-money man to the bench for a 3-0 defeat at bottom-of-the-table Nottingham Forest, before - with Kevin Hitchcock injured - handing the gloves to new tracksuit-trouser-wearing Russian signing Dmitri Kharine for a 1-1 midweek draw at QPR.

Three days later Kharine, signed from CSKA Moscow for a reported £400,000, was beaten by Sheffield Wednesday's Paul Warhurst just three minutes into his home debut before being withdrawn at half-time due to injury.

Replaced by 36-year-old Gerry Peyton for his first - and last - 45 minutes as a Chelsea player, Kharine was watching from the stands as John Harkes doubled the visitors lead late on to prompt boos on the final whistle.

Porterfield was now on borrowed time, and following a dismal

3-1 defeat at struggling Oldham - who prior to the visit of Chelsea hadn't scored for eight hours - the winless run stretched to 11 after a dull 0-0 draw at home to Liverpool.

By the time title-contenders Aston Villa travelled to Stamford Bridge on Valentine's weekend, Chelsea had dropped to 11th in the table and nine points off the relegation spots.

The Villa team at least gave Chelsea fans something other than the desperate run of form to focus on as wearing their number nine shirt was Dean Saunders, who had moved from Liverpool to the West Midlands days after ending Paul Elliot's career.

His presence ensured he was booed and barracked every time he touched the ball and contributed to one of the more committed Chelsea performances of recent weeks.

The best of the home side's chances came via midfielder David Hopkin, a 20-year-old signing from Morton playing only his second senior game, but his efforts proved fruitless as Villa left with an underserved 1-0 win.

And that proved to be that for Porterfield, with the Scot becoming the first Premier League manager to be sacked when he was relieved of his duties the following Monday.

Porterfield was a decent man, but one who - particularly after losing the support of his popular and experienced number two Don Howe due to heart problems in December - proved to be incapable of motivating a drifting team back to form.

"When we lost Don Howe, our hopes for that season went with him," Dennis Wise would later, accurately, say.

With the future of the ground secure and planning permission already granted for redevelopment, Ken Bates quite simply couldn't afford the risk of a second relegation in six seasons.

What Bates decided Chelsea needed was someone big on personality, big on motivation, and immediately popular with Chelsea fans.

What Bates decided Chelsea needed was club legend David Webb.

The scorer of the winning goal in Chelsea's 1970 FA Cup win, Webb had no big-club experience as manager but had guided Southend United from the Fourth Division to the Second before clashing with the chairman and walking out 12 months prior to his appointment at Stamford Bridge.

Appointed on a short-term contract, Webb gave an early warning of the style of football we could expect to see under his leadership when he played Mick Harford alongside Tony

Cascarino for his opening game at Blackburn Rovers.

While 6ft 3in Harford had been one of the few relative surprises of the season, chipping in with valuable goals, pairing him with 6ft 2in Cascarino hardly hinted at plans for fast-paced attacking football with the ball played to feet.

The pairing, not surprisingly, failed to click and Harford would only play a further two games for his new boss following the 2-0 defeat at Ewood Park that saw Chelsea reduced to 10 men following the sending off of Frank Sinclair.

There was one significant change for Webb's home debut as manager with Dave Beasant restored between the sticks for a Monday night visit of Arsenal.

Following his Norwich humiliation, Beasant had taken the opportunity to restore some confidence via loan spells at Grimsby and Wolves and he rewarded Webb's faith by keeping a clean sheet as John Spencer set up Graham Stuart to score the only goal of the game and secure Chelsea's first win in 14 attempts.

Spencer's summer signing slipped under the radar compared to the more established Fleck and Harford, but he was one of the few positives during the winless run as he showed enthusiasm and an eye for goal when coming off the bench.

Against Arsenal he was given his chance by Webb as a late replacement for Harford, and nine days later he came off the bench again - and had an impact again - as Chelsea won again.

On this occasion Everton keeper Neville Southall failed to hold a Spencer shot that was prodded home by Stuart, before the wee Scot struck himself with 10 minutes left to play for a 2-1 win.

Three games in and Webb had effectively done the job he was appointed to do - steady the ship and move Chelsea back into the safety of mid-table.

But while the results may have improved, the quality of football and confidence in the future direction of travel remained a cause for concern.

The Everton win was followed by progressively dull 1-1 draws against Crystal Palace, Tottenham and Leeds; Leeds being a particularly grim midweek affair that saw Cascarino sent off for elbowing David Wetherall and - in the shadow of ongoing mainland terrorist attacks - an away terrace that spent most of the night confirming it would not be surrendering to the IRA.

The despondency grew ahead of the next home game against Middlesbrough, with Chelsea shipping out the exciting midfielder-come-defender Graeme Le Saux to Blackburn Rovers in return for forward Steve Livingstone, some loose change and national embarrassment.

While Le Saux had alienated some of the Chelsea support with his Boxing Day petulance, it was clear to even the most casual observer that he was an England international in the making - as was to prove to be the case within 12 months of his departure.

Livingstone, on the other hand, had failed to establish himself at Blackburn after previously failing to establish himself at Coventry.

Still, someone at Chelsea felt it was a good deal, someone at Blackburn managed to keep a straight face, and a future international star was therefore swapped for an appearance-shy, goal-shy journeyman.

While Chelsea went on to dismiss relegation-bound 'Boro with four second-half goals, it remained a largely tepid affair in front of 13,000 fans already starting to question if Webb was the long-term answer to the mediocrity.

Following a draw at Ipswich, Webb gave substitute Neil Shipperley his debut in a 1-0 defeat at Southampton before starting the young striker for the visit of Wimbledon.

Shipperley deservedly scored the last of the Chelsea goals in a 4-2 win but, despite going on to score a further eight over the next couple of years, a 2019 act of public indecency would ultimately see him toss away any chance of being best remembered for his moderate goal-scoring exploits.

With the season drifting to a thankful conclusion, just 700 away tickets were available for a trip to Manchester United due to Old Trafford's Stretford End being redeveloped.

Those who missed out were the lucky ones, because those of us who were there were forced to endure a gutless 3-0 defeat as United closed in on their first title in 26 years, Beasant returned to his old ways with errors in his final Chelsea appearance and - if we hadn't suffered enough - Steve Livingstone made his one and only Blues appearance as an ineffective second-half substitute.

The end of the season could not now come quick enough, but it was more than a release from the weekly misery that I was looking forward to after a 2-1 defeat in the final home game of the season against Coventry City.

I'd heard the rumours throughout the season, but it wasn't until I was told to bring my boots to the game that I knew them to be true - at the conclusion of the match I was to play at Stamford Bridge.

The Stewards' Challenge was a simple format - The Shed v North Stand and West v East, each playing 40-minute games with the winners meeting in a final.

Once the ground had been cleared I found myself pulling on the Chelsea kit while sitting in the away dressing room - trying not to think too much about the fact that just moments earlier the naked, hairy arse of Coventry's Micky Quinn may have been sitting in the exact spot I was now occupying.

Drawing inspiration from great Chelsea full-backs of the past such as Dennis Rofe, Doug Rougvie and John Millar, I played the full 40 minutes before losing in a penalty shoot-out following a 0-0 draw.

Any disappointment at missing out on the chance to play another game, however, was quickly eased upon the discovery that the Chelsea team were still in the tiny players' bar tucked away off the tunnel... and they were on the booze.

I can't reveal too many secrets from the inner sanctum - primarily because I was too pissed to remember - but, with Paul Elliott present, I do recall his teammates being more than happy to share their views on Dean Saunders with very little prompting.

High on alcohol and adrenaline, by the time I decamped to The Cock pub on the North End Road for an end-of-season session with Stewie and others it was threatening to get messy.

I'm not sure what I was thinking as Saturday ticked into Sunday but, in summary, despite being offered a bed for the night by a very kind female companion I had a sudden change of heart as our night bus passed Clapham Junction, mumbled my apologies and dived into the train station....

There was no doubt it was my loss, not hers, and the idiocy of my decision was confirmed when I quickly realised my last train back to Surrey had left a good hour previously.

Reviewing my options I jumped on the last train of the night heading in the other direction to Waterloo, where an officer from the Met suggested I had two options as I drunkenly explained my predicament - arrest, or shut up and bed down for the night in the station.

I wisely took the second option.

After what little sleep I could get I went for a dawn stroll across Waterloo Bridge and found an immediate inner peace as I watched the sun slowly rise to warm the Thames on a beautiful spring morning.

Looking down the river, content with my own happy thoughts, I didn't even notice the battered yellow Ford Cortina pull to a slow stop behind me - the only car on the bridge at this early hour.

"Excuse me mate, excuse me..." said a passenger stepping from the car, finally pulling me from my reflective ponderings, "we're looking for a young boy, can you help?"

"Err, sorry," I naively said, looking around and shrugging my shoulders, "I'm not from around here, but I haven't seen anyone."

My inquisitor looked a little confused, started to return to the car, but then stopped, turned, and spoke again.

"No," he clarified, "I said (he really emphasised 'said') we're looking for a young boy. Do you (he also really emphasised 'you') know where we can find one...?"

The penny finally dropped... the young boy they wanted was me.

I offered them a few choice words, turned, ran, and remained in Waterloo until the first train of the day arrived, but it was a sobering experience - one single night on the streets and there I was being offered cash for sex.

There remained just one outstanding item of 'Any Other Business' before the season concluded - a pitiful 4-2 defeat at Sheffield United only partially rescued by large sections of the 7,000 travelling Chelsea supporters dressing in various interpretations of Yorkshire attire.

The braces, flat caps and occasional stuffed whippet on show provided some much-needed humour to ease us through a dismal conclusion to a mostly dismal campaign that offered little cause for current or future optimism.

As we left Bramall Lane we knew that something had to change, and it had to change soon...

CHAPTER SIX
FA CUP FIFTH ROUND

Leicester City v Chelsea
Filbert Street
Sunday, February 16, 1997

Leicester City: Keller, Grayson, Watts, Prior, Walsh, Campbell (Lawrence, 80), Parker, Taylor, Claridge, Robins (Wilson, 65), Marshall.

Chelsea: Hitchcock, Petrescu, Leboeuf, Clarke, Hughes, Wise, Di Matteo (Gullit, 87), Minto, Sinclair, Newton, Zola (Vialli, 68).

Referee: Mike Reed (Birmingham)
Attendance: 19,125

The meet was arranged for a pub in Watford; not the one with a Junction, the one with a Gap - the picturesque Watford village in Northants that gives its name to its adjacent M1 service station which signifies the point where the south blends into the early fringes of the north. Or the Midlands, as it would more accurately be described.

And as we walked across the rear car park of The Stag - just a gentle 10-minute drive from home - we knew they'd already arrived, as drifting through the doors, generating curious glances from the pre-lunch village walkers, was a familiar chant.

"We all follow the Chelllllsea, over land and sea - AND LEICESTER - we all follow the Chelsea, on to vic-tory, all together now..."

The Stag was an ideal stop-off for Gary's Coaches; his loyal Chelsea clientele easing themselves from their seats in the polluted service station car park, walking up the hidden staff entrance at its rear and - as if popping through the door to another world - stepping into a rural idyll on the other side.

Now behind them were litter-strewn fast-food outlets, slot

machines flashing temptations, and hyper-active kids pestering parents in the shops; in front... neat country verges, sheep in fields, and Bob from the parish council having another quick half before going home to carve the roast - his usual Sunday solitude disturbed by 'The Chels'.

As we step through the doors the familiar faces are plentiful and Stewie is easy to find, sitting at a table with coach-organiser Gary and others; his next cider already waiting as his first one is drained.

A warm hug from Stewie for me and Scott, a handshake for my dad, a slap on the back for my brother Andrew, and then it's 'alright mates' and 'how you doings' all round as Dad does what Dad does and hands me a 20 to go to the bar - 'you go get them, I'll pay for them'.

"Thanks for sorting," Stewie says on my return as I hand him his ticket for the game, "drink up and I'll get you another."

The tickets had been sourced a week-or-so earlier when Scott and I made a clandestine trip to Leicester to secure the five required for the latest huge game in the growing list of huge games.

We may - or may not - have managed to pick up one or two for the Chelsea end, but we would have struggled for three and definitely been over-reaching for four or five with demand as high as it was as another cup run entered the later stages.

So the Leicester end it was.

Buying the tickets had been ridiculously easy, especially considering the recent violent relationship between the two clubs' sets of fans. We simply arrived at the Filbert Street ticket office, queued, waited, smiled, handed over the cash and walked away - no evidence required of being a Leicester fan, no membership cards or booking history needed; just a degree of confidence, some knowledge of local lingo and a straight face.

"Have you still got five together anywhere? Don't really mind where."

"Only in the top of the Double Decker, that OK?"

"Perfect. Let's hope we win eh?"

As we walked away, we remarked that the lack of scrutiny from the Leicester staff was asking for trouble. Quite literally, as it would turn out.

But back in The Stag the atmosphere and pre-match tension continues to build, and then Gary gives the signal, half-finished pints are left on the bar, and all is quiet again; the landlord counting the bonus takings from a well-behaved lunchtime crowd as the coaches refill and we head back out to our car for the onward 25 miles to *'And Leicester'*.

On Dad's insistence we avoid the risk of delays on the M1 for such a short trip - 'nowhere to go if you get stuck on that' - and head up the A5.

Past the new Daventry International Rail Freight Terminal being developed near Crick, past Rugby, a right turn, and across the Leicestershire border.

Through Lutterworth, anticipation rising, and into the suburbs of Leicester.

Blaby, Glen Parva, and then past Grace Road, home to Leicestershire's cricketers, and down to Welford Road, home to its rugby union players.

We park up near the hospital, and are then straight into the city's football territory - tight, Victorian, terraced streets filtering fans down to the ground; it's a Lowry painting but in Leicestershire, not Lancashire.

The homes are all two-up two downs, with front doors that lead straight onto the footpath on one side and straight into small living rooms on the other.

Filthy net curtains in every window hint at a sorry standard of living; properties that once housed workers from the city's declining textile industry now offered as multi-occupancy flea-pits by quick-buck landlords.

And then we are on to Burnmoor Street, where the hot-dog stalls, police vans, programme sellers and replica-shirts blow the secret that a tiny single-tier football stand is hidden behind its own terraced houses; their backyards kissing its corrugated-iron rear.

Chelsea fans are queueing on the corner, ready to take one of the limited number of seats that spread halfway along the stand, but we carry on past to make our way to the two-tier South Stand behind which the terraced homes give way to an electric sub-station and an expanse of land leading down to the River Soar.

I've sat in the top-tier of this stand a couple of times previously and have never had any issue with the home fans, but today is likely to be different as this is no run-of-the-mill league affair; it's a win-at-all-cost tie for both sides - Leicester chasing their first quarter-final appearance in 15 years, Chelsea their first FA Cup success in 27.

Today we need to judge the mood, keep our cover, but Dad hasn't read the memo and is applauding the Chelsea players as they come out to warm up; soliciting a raising of the eyebrows from me and a few early comments from some of the home support.

It's not an unusual experience for me, as growing up Dad regularly took me in the home seats when we watched Chelsea away.

From Villa to United, Wednesday to Forest, and Watford to West Brom, Birmingham and beyond he was of an age that believed rival football fans should be able to sit side-by-side and - with some degree of common sense - of the view that home seats were often a safer option than 1980s' Chelsea away terraces for his pre-teen son.

I'm no longer a pre-teen though and can sense the danger around, eyeing numerous individuals and groups that are unlikely to take kindly to any Chelsea liberties.

But soon the game is under way and the focus is on the pitch.

A Leicester side hampered by injury and suspension hold their own in the early exchanges but, 16 minutes in, Chelsea take the lead when Di Matteo cuts in from the left and fires right-footed across Kasey Keller in front of the stand in which we are sat.

We celebrate the goal, not excessively, but we celebrate, as do plenty of other Chelsea dotted across the top tier.

Shouts of abuse come from the home fans but attention is quickly diverted to the lower tier to our left corner, where something more serious is clearly taking place. We can't see it from our seats above, but we can hear the roars, see a few spilling on to the edge of the pitch and see the police moving in to pull fighting factions apart.

The match is briefly halted but Dad doesn't heed the warning, continuing to roar Chelsea on when play is back under way, continuing to draw attention our way.

Stewie is rightly concerned.

"Jase," he whispers from the corner of his mouth, "for fuck's sake, shut your dad up..."

I do as I'm told, pointing out to Dad that if any slappings are to be dished out then he - much closer to 60 than 50 - might be considered too old, while Andrew - only 13 - would be considered too young.

But me, Scott and Stewie... in our prime at 24? We're Goldilocks' porridge - just right.

Dad takes the hint just in time, because on 35 minutes Chelsea score again - Petrescu releasing Hughes to drive across goal.

Despite exploding inside we're more restrained this time, others again taking the heat, but it adds further fuel to an increasingly nasty atmosphere and we could do without Chelsea taking the piss.

And then the half-time whistle goes, and Dad immediately gets to work on a magic trick that I've seen many times before.

He stands, turns, looks for the closest Leicester fan that he assesses to be of similar age and attitude and says, quite pointedly, that 'these youngsters' dare not open their mouths as he digs into his memory banks for the names of Leicester players past.

"I used to come here when Gordon Banks and David Nish were playing. You've had some bloody good players and sides over the years. Do you remember..." and on he goes, carrying on talking until his chosen victim has little choice but to engage.

On the pitch Alan Birchenall - a former player who represented both clubs - is leading the half-time entertainment so they talk about him. And by the end of break they are new best mates, bringing others in to the conversation and helping defuse some of the volatility in our immediate area.

Old boys united; it's a powerful force.

The teams come back out, Leicester now attacking our end, Dad now doing his best Brian Clough impression and telling anyone still listening that the game is far from over... 'it only takes a second to score', 'get the next goal and you'll probably win this' etc, etc.

Confirming the peace work is done, he's starting to wind me up now...

And just seven minutes in Dad has his 'what did I say?' moment as Steve Walsh outjumps Kevin Hitchcock to head home a Garry Parker free-kick.

We sit back in our seats, everyone around celebrating. Nothing to be done, don't respond, don't react. Take the punishment.

It's a different game now. Leicester continue to push, but Chelsea stay firm and it looks like we are going to hang on.

With fewer than five to play scorer Di Matteo is withdrawn, with Gullit coming on to offer fresh legs and see his side over the line.

But the player-manager's first act is to miss a tackle that leads to Steve Clarke fouling Steve Claridge within striking distance.

It's Parker again with the free-kick, swinging it into the six-yard box from the right.

Hitchcock comes out to meet it but Eddie Newton gets there

first, poking it into his own net.

It's 2-2, and we can't deny the Leicester fans their smugness as they get right in our faces... 'take that you Cockney bastards'.

With the home support distracted, Chelsea nearly win it when Hughes heads over at the death.

We instinctively rise to our feet, let out an involuntary 'ooh' and run hands through our hair, but I immediately find myself thinking I'm glad he didn't score.

The tension is now too high, the risk too great; there is only one way it would end.

On the final whistle we immediately edge out, leaving Leicester fans to celebrate the comeback.

I'm happy to take the draw, happy to head home safe and happy to still be in the cup.

It's back to the Bridge, where we'll attempt to finish the job in 10 days' time...

FA Cup Fifth Round results

Chesterfield 1 Nottingham Forest 0; Leicester City 2 Chelsea 2; Derby County 3 Coventry City 2; Manchester City 0 Middlesbrough 1; Bradford City 0 Sheffield Wednesday 1; Wimbledon 2 Queens Park Rangers 1; Leeds United 2 Portsmouth 3; Birmingham City 1 Wrexham 3.

CHAPTER SEVEN
1993/1994

I had some terrible news in the summer of 1993. I got a job.

After spending two years studying for a not-particularly-challenging Journalism HND in Farnham, the plan had always been to stay a further year to extend the qualification to degree level.

It was a plan I was all in favour of because I still had plenty of unfinished campus business to see to. And, I suppose, it would have been nice to graduate with a degree too.

But, to my intense disappointment, the job as a reporter on my local daily newspaper was too good an opportunity to turn down so I packed my Farnham bags with a heavy heart, pausing only to think about what might have been as I bid farewell to one or two particular focuses of personal attention.

Before my notebook and pen was let loose on the good people of Northampton, however, I was told that I'd be sent on a 20-week internal training course with other new company recruits from across the UK. Think Police Academy, but with Chinos and paisley ties.

Now we were talking. Shipped over to live in digs in Peterborough I had the best part of five months to continue to live the student lifestyle, but with new friends and real money in my pocket - the princely sum of £6,400 per year.

Over those carefree months we worked hard and played harder, with life whizzing by in a blur of shorthand exams, media law refreshers, and alcohol, alcohol and more alcohol.

On one memorable occasion we were taken to Westminster for a day walking the corridors of power. At the end of official proceedings, our course leaders sent us off for a night in the clubs and bars of the West End with a clear warning that they expected to see us all back in the Peterborough office at 9am the next morning.

Like RAF Squadron Leaders they counted us out and - the next day - they counted us back in. It is my sad duty to report that not everyone returned safely.

The Peterborough course started on Monday, August 2 and I began the new phase of my life greatly buoyed by the events of the preceding weekend.

Across the two days of July 31 and August 1, Chelsea joined Ajax, Lazio and Spurs for the four-team pre-season Makita Tournament held at Tottenham's White Hart Lane.

Now under the player-manager guidance of former Spurs superstar Glenn Hoddle, Chelsea beat Ajax on penalties on the Saturday to set up a Sunday final against Tottenham - winners of their own semi-final against Lazio.

What followed was a glorious 4-0 romp, with Chelsea fans celebrating Tony Cascarino's finest hour - the much-maligned centre-forward hitting a hat-trick to steal the headlines from Hoddle and exciting new summer signing Gavin Peacock, the scorer of the third of the four goals on the day.

A meaningless pre-season tournament it may have been, but for success-starved Chelsea fans a trophy was a trophy and Hoddle's possession-based passing game teased an exciting future following the dour, tepid performances of Porterfield's final days and Webb's brief reign.

With the Makita Trophy safely added to the list of Chelsea 'honours', I left a White Hart Lane lacking any of its usual post-match Tottenham menace, raced home, chucked my bags in the car and headed up to Peterborough.

By 9pm I was having a first pint with a new flatmate who was to become a great friend for life and had convinced myself Chelsea were about to rule the world. It was a 10/10 day.

For 'about to rule the world', read in the relegation zone at Christmas...

Hoddle's appointment as player-manager had, in hindsight, perhaps been on the cards for a while.

One of the most gifted players of his generation, he had spent time at Chelsea's Harlington training ground in 1991 to retain and maintain fitness between his departure from Monaco and appointment as player-manager at Swindon Town.

Now on the Chelsea radar, it may have been that Ken Bates would have tried to bring Hoddle in as an immediate replacement for Porterfield the previous February had he not been on the cusp of leading Swindon to an eye-catching promotion to the top flight.

When the much-teased appointment was announced in June, therefore, Webb's short-term contract suddenly made perfect sense - he was unlikely to have ever been anything more than a caretaker waiting to hand over the keys to a new headmaster.

Ken Bates' programme notes for the opening Premier League game against a highly-rated Blackburn Rovers confirmed as much, with the grey-bearded leader writing: "I have always wanted Chelsea to play intelligent, exciting football with style; sadly that has been increasingly lacking in recent years and supporters have rightly voted with their feet.

"In appointing Glenn Hoddle as manager I believe we have taken the first steps to getting Chelsea back to our traditional ways."

Among Hoddle's first acts was to bring in Andy Dow from Dundee to fill a left-back spot that had proved troublesome since the departure of Tony Dorigo two years previously, and sign-off the departures of Andy Townsend to Aston Villa and the occasionally exciting, often frustrating, Graham Stuart to Everton.

While consistently one of the better performers over the past three years, Townsend's commitment to the shirt noticeably waned following the January cup exits of the previous season and he ensured he would be the object of the Stamford Bridge boo boys in future years by citing a desire to 'win trophies' as the reason for wanting away.

Stuart, meanwhile, left after failing to agree a new contract following protracted negotiations that went public when Chelsea managing director Colin Hutchinson used his programme notes to name a 'young player' seeking £4,000 per week. While not directly naming Stuart, he was the only name in the frame... which may have helped him decide his future lay elsewhere.

Adding to the new arrivals was Danish centre-half Jakob Kjeldbjerg and the aforementioned Gavin Peacock - the god-fearing midfield linkman joining from Newcastle for £1.25m.

Hoddle also brought in his own backroom team with former Tottenham manager Peter Shreeves replacing Don Howe as the number two, and ex-Arsenal man Graham Rix taking responsibility for the youth.

Hoddle donned the number 20 shirt for the Blackburn opener as squad numbers became the latest addition to the Premier League era, but it wasn't to prove to be a winning start.

Despite the new boss directing the tempo of the game as part of a back five and Peacock capping his league debut by heading home a Dennis Wise cross, goals from Stuart Ripley and Mike Newell saw Blackburn return to Lancashire with three points that would launch a title challenge.

Chelsea again dropped points from a winning position in a 1-1 draw at Wimbledon, and a 1-0 defeat at Ipswich left them still looking for their first league win when Queens Park Rangers visited the Bridge for a Wednesday-night August clash.

Hoddle switched Peacock from midfield to attack, and was rewarded when the former QPR player scored the first goal and made the second for Cascarino in a 2-0 win.

Progress stalled again though with a 1-1 draw at home to Sheffield Wednesday that saw David Lee come off the bench, open the scoring and then get sent off for two yellows, followed by another 1-1 that saw Cascarino once more on the scoresheet at Tottenham. Chelsea deserved all three points, but Dmitri Kharine was beaten by a late Teddy Sheringham penalty after the scorer collapsed under the slightest of touches.

With just one win in six, Chelsea were in 13th when I stood waiting outside Fulham Broadway to meet Scott ahead of a clash against defending champions Manchester United.

When he popped out of the station I was surprised to see him in the company of Yvette and Celine, two friends from home who fancied a day out with a difference.

Yvette had been a good friend since primary school. Warm, intelligent and sociable, it was always a delight to see her and the day ahead immediately took on added appeal with her unexpected presence.

Celine, meanwhile, was part of a wider friendship group but I knew her less well. Later in the year we'd have an unexpected festive snog followed by a single date held out of mutual politeness, but it was still Scott that would receive most of my attention as we squeezed into a packed Stamford Bridge to see Chelsea attempt to end United's six-month unbeaten run.

United went close to breaking the deadlock in the 16th minute when an audacious 35-yard turn and shot from Eric Cantona bounced and hit the bar with Dmitri Kharine stranded, but - just a minute later - it was Peacock that got the only goal of the game.

Eddie Newton released Steve Clarke, who played to the feet of Hoddle, who lofted a flighted ball into the danger zone. A half-cleared Steve Bruce header was chested down by Clarke, whose shot was parried by Peter Schmeichel in to the path of the on-rushing Peacock to lift it home from within the six-yard box... limbs, as the youth of today like to say.

Peacock was again on target in a 1-1 draw at Coventry, taking his tally to four from eight games, before another 1-1 draw got the League Cup campaign under way in the first leg of a second-round tie at West Brom.

Eighteen-year-old Neil Shipperley had given another glimpse of his potential as a second-half substitute against Manchester United and got his first league goal of the season at home to Liverpool with a helping hand from Bruce Grobbelaar.

Shipperley spun and turned a Wise cross goal-bound, which Grobbelaar juggled one, two, three, four times... before referee Keith Hackett generously judged the ball had crossed the line.

It was a good job he did, as it would prove to be Chelsea's last league win until late December - a run of 12 games in which they scored just four goals.

The only win of any kind during the period, a laboured 2-1 second-leg defeat of West Brom in the League Cup, was sandwiched by a defeat at West Ham in which Dennis Wise saw red for a two-footed tackle and a third home defeat in three seasons to an impressive Norwich City.

Andy Townsend was roundly abused in a 1-0 defeat at Aston Villa, Chelsea exited the League Cup by the same scoreline at Manchester City's Maine Road, and even new £1.5m signing Mark Stein failed to reverse fortunes in another 1-0 defeat at home to Oldham Athletic at the end of October.

One of three professional footballers in his family, Stein failed to live up to early expectations at Luton Town and donned the colours of Queens Park Rangers and Oxford United before finally shooting to attention at third-tier Stoke City in 1992/93, scoring 33 goals in 57 matches.

Following his debut against Oldham, Stein retained his place for a 4-1 stuffing at Leeds United and a 2-0 defeat at home to Arsenal that took the league losing run to six on the bounce - a level of ineptitude that was just one shy of a club record set in 1952.

But, despite the slide towards the relegation zone, the opinion of Hoddle from the terraces remained largely supportive.

Implementing ideas developed during his spell at Monaco under the guidance of future Arsenal manager Arsene Wenger, Hoddle had increased standards off the pitch with a fresh focus on players' fitness, diet and professionalism.

And even against the backdrop of defeats, players such as Wise, Frank Sinclair and Steve Clarke were among those visibly developing under the new regime.

And, aside from all that, we all knew that if Hoddle left the only parties now stupid enough to be interested in the Chelsea job would be journeymen, madmen, or Neil Warnock.

Thanks to some ridiculous Sky TV scheduling Chelsea were back in league action just two days after the Arsenal defeat when they welcomed Manchester City to a sparsely-populated Stamford Bridge.

And although the losing run came to an end, the struggle for goals continued courtesy of a 0-0 draw that was followed by further blanks in defeats at Sheffield United and Blackburn Rovers as Chelsea finally dropped into the bottom three.

Following the postponement of a midweek visit of Wimbledon, the huge financial risk of relegation was there for all to see when Ipswich Town visited Stamford Bridge in December.

At the north end of the ground - where Manchester City fans had stood for the previous home fixture - there now stood bulldozers preparing to demolish the windswept terrace that had watched over the good, the bad and the ugly for all of the near 90 years of Chelsea's existence.

When Ken Bates did his sums for the long-awaited Stamford Bridge redevelopment it was on the basis of top-flight football, so the prospect of relegation at the same time as committing to the re-building of three sides of the ground didn't bear thinking about.

On the pitch there was at least some good news as - after more than 390 minutes without a goal - Chelsea opened the scoring against Ipswich via a diving Gavin Peacock header. Naturally the good cheer didn't last, with a Chris Kiwomya equaliser extending the winless run to 10.

The weather resulted in a second postponement of the month when a visit to QPR was chalked off, so we had to wait for a crucial clash at Southampton two days after Christmas for 10 to become 11.

The Saints were suffering an equally poor campaign and were themselves on a run of five straight defeats that had seen them score just once, but they made light work of Chelsea as the away support started to air its frustrations.

Despite Stein finally getting on the scoresheet at the eighth time of asking, the defeat was the low-point of the league season - a jubilant home crowd celebrating two second-half goals that secured a 3-1 win.

As Scott and I joined other despondent fans walking away from The Dell we knew one thing - defeat in the next two games, at home to Newcastle and away to bottom-of-the-table Swindon, would leave Chelsea at the foot of the top-flight table for the first time since 1979.

Hoddle, meanwhile, was also lacking answers. "We have to turn things around as quickly as possible," he told the press. "A win will do it for us, but right now we're wondering where that win will come from."

But, as is so often said when something more original struggles to come to mind, it's a funny old game.

The Christmas fixture list ensured Chelsea would welcome Newcastle to Stamford Bridge just 24 hours after the defeat at Southampton and - literally overnight - things took an upward turn.

Making three changes from the side that surrendered at The Dell, Hoddle was rewarded with a performance that displayed commitment and character as Stein got his second in two days in a tense 1-0 win.

The goal came in the 11th minute when a long Wise ball released Stein to cut inside, setting up an agonising afternoon that saw the home side regularly pinned back but holding on to move out of the relegation zone.

Across the years there are various games, various moments, that you can look back on as crucial in the future direction of the club, and - while certainly not the most obvious in Chelsea's history - the victory against Newcastle on December 28, 1993 was still one such occasion.

Let's just say Newcastle's Andy Cole, not Stein, had scored the only goal of the game that day...

Would Hoddle have remained if 12 games without a win had become 13, 14, or 15?

If Hoddle had gone, who would have come in?

If Hoddle had gone, would Chelsea have stayed up?

If Hoddle had gone...?

You get the idea.

But, regardless of 'ifs', 'buts', and 'maybes', it was Stein that scored that day and the first step on the road to recovery had been taken.

Buoyed by the defeat of Newcastle, Chelsea fans travelled in their thousands for a New Year's Day clash at Swindon Town to see if their side could now remove another monkey from their collective backs by winning away from home.

Incredibly, since the Eddie Newton-inspired 2-1 win at Tottenham that briefly put Chelsea joint second in December 1992 the Blues had not enjoyed a single win on the road - going 26 games in all competitions and the entirety of 1993 without success.

The Wiltshire club's ramshackle County Ground struggled to cope with the numbers, resulting in brief periods of tension and crushing as the away support attempted to squeeze through inadequate turnstiles that led to the corner of terrace.

Those that got in saw Neil Shipperley give the visitors the lead in the 19th minute before Stein doubled the advantage moments before half-time - Chelsea spoiling us by scoring more than once in a league game for the first time since August.

By the time Wise put the result beyond doubt in the 90th minute Chelsea fans were already happily celebrating the breaking of the away hoodoo, with even a Swindon consolation immediately from the restart failing to lower the mood.

With Chelsea now up 17th, two days later they made it three wins on the bounce with a topsy-turvy 4-2 defeat of struggling Everton.

Craig Burley and man-of-the-moment Stein, with a penalty, put Chelsea two to the good only for Everton to level before Shipperley and Stein, again, restored the advantage.

Chelsea were handed a trip to third-tier Barnet as the FA Cup got under way in January but, due their Underhill ground being deemed unfit to host such an auspicious event, the powers that be switched the tie to Stamford Bridge to set up the prospect of an away tie at home.

But aside from the matchday programme being produced by the north London 'hosts', there was very little noticeable difference to any other Chelsea home game as Barnet - who had won just two league games all season and featured Glenn Hoddle's brother Carl in their starting 11 - narrowly missed out on a major upset by going closest to scoring in a 0-0 draw.

Mark Stein then scored his sixth in as many games as Chelsea drew 1-1 at Norwich, before Barnet were brushed aside in their return to Stamford Bridge for the cup replay - Stein again among the scorers in a 4-0 win as Chelsea made, errr, home advantage count...

"OI, TOWNSEND... YOU WANKER..."

Three days after the Barnet replay win, the booming solo voice came from the back of the West Stand to welcome former Chelsea midfielder Andy Townsend back to Stamford Bridge for the first time since his summer departure to Aston Villa.

If he'd have waited a minute or two he'd probably have got a round of applause, but he chose to express his opinion seconds into a minute's silence for Matt Busby - Manchester United's European Cup-winning manager and Munich air disaster survivor who had passed away two days previously.

The silence descended into inevitable farce as hundreds of others turned to the Townsend abuser to return the compliment, thousands more told them to also shut up, and the remainder did their best to try to stay silent or stifle giggles.

Based on the fact that the despised Dean Saunders was also in the Villa starting line-up, the only real surprise was that the Townsend heckler missed an open goal by not taking the opportunity for a 2-for-1 attack.

The Welshman, however, was on the receiving end of the expected abuse as soon as the game kicked off and the vitriol aimed in his direction only grew in volume when he opened the scoring before the interval.

Stein rescued a point in the second half - becoming the first player to score in six successive Premier League games - but the headlines the following day would be focused on the breaking of the Busby silence.

Bates and Hoddle also confirmed it wasn't an issue the club was taking lightly by raising it in the following week's programme, calling on fans turning up to watch the FA Cup Fourth Round tie against Sheffield Wednesday to name and shame the original offender.

If Chelsea were to extend their cup run to the fifth round the expectation was that it would have to be done at the first time of asking against a Wednesday side missing five players through injury, including the key talents of Chris Waddle, Andy Sinton and Mark Bright.

Despite themselves missing Hoddle, Eddie Newton and Dennis Wise to injury, all appeared to be going to plan for the hosts when Steve Clarke ghosted past numerous Wednesday challenges before placing the ball into the path of Peacock to slide home after 14 minutes.

It was Wednesday, though, that ended the day as favourites to progress thanks to a Graham Hyde equaliser on the hour that meant the sides would have to meet again the following week.

Chelsea travelled for the Hillsborough replay on the back of a 4-2 defeat at Everton that saw Stein net both to continue his remarkable scoring run, but after getting stuck in traffic I was still jogging towards the Leppings Lane turnstiles as the game got under way.

"Six men went to mow, went to mow a meadow..." came the sound as I approached the entrance with my dad and brother; the noise from what was clearly a huge away support leaking from the confines of the stadium

Pulling my ticket from my pocket, the momentum grew... *"Seven men, six men, five men, four men, three men, two men, one man..."*

They'd got to eight as I slipped through the turnstile, nine as I increased my pace up the stairs and - timing my arrival to perfection - ten at the precise moment I caught my first sight of the pitch.

"TEN MEN WENT TO MOW, WENT TO MOW A MEADOW," bellowed the away end, *"Ten men, nine men, eight men, seven men, six men, five men, four men, three men, two men, one man and his dog Spot went to mow a meadow... CHELSEA (clap, clap, clap), CHELSEA (clap, clap, clap), CHELSEA (clap, clap, clap), CHELSEA..."*

We were in position for no more than two or three minutes before we were celebrating... a clever Gavin Peacock overhead kick presenting John Spencer with the simplest of finishes from six yards in front of a stunned Hillsborough Kop.

Mark Bright levelled for Wednesday before the break to set up a humdinger of a second half; a quality Wednesday team pushing for the winner but being denied by a Chelsea side showing the same determination and passion as the away support to take the game to extra-time.

It took just six minutes of the extra period for Chelsea to regain the lead when Stein headed across the box for Peacock to drive back across Wednesday keeper Kevin Pressman before, in the second half of extra-time, Peacock turned provider to cross for Craig Burley to wrap up proceedings.

With the goal sparking an emergency evacuation of the home support - a giant white owl magically appearing in the seats of the Wednesday Kop - the final memory of the night was the first singing of a song that was to become the anthem of the season.

"Forever and ever, we'll follow our team, for we are the Chelsea and we are supreme...

"We'll never be mastered by no (by no, by no, by no) northern bastard; we'll keep the blue flag flying high...

"Flying high up in the sky, we'll keep the blue flag flying high;

from Stamford Bridge to Wembley, we'll keep the blue flag flying high."

News reached us as we left the ground that the much-fancied Arsenal and Newcastle had both lost to lower league opposition in replays of their own, while Chelsea's expected fifth-round opponents Leeds had been dumped out by Oxford.

The cup draw, we noted, was opening up.

Scott had now left the north and was living in the glorious surroundings of Slough when - two days on from Sheffield - I travelled down to celebrate his 21st birthday the night before Chelsea were due to return to league action at Oldham.

Following a raucous night that featured 'top-shelf' pints for the birthday boy and 2am three-legged races for the other assembled drunks, I should never have considered driving to Oldham... but drive to Oldham I stupidly did.

Guided north largely by rumble strips on the inside lanes of various motorways, I somehow completed the 200-mile journey without major incident to see Chelsea lose 2-1 - Scott looking as bad as I felt on a bitterly cold day that extinguished all post-Hillsborough glow.

With a capacity below 11,000, demand was always going to significantly outstrip supply for Chelsea's FA Cup Fifth-Round trip to Oxford United's Manor Ground so - rather than risking missing out in the inevitable scramble - I put my journalism contacts to good use by sourcing a couple of home tickets from Oxford coach and former Northampton Town midfielder Richard Hill.

To no-one's surprise Chelsea flooded the ground in their thousands, and long before kick-off those without tickets were eyeing up trees and the roof of a neighbouring bowls club as potential vantage points to see the game.

Based on league placings alone Chelsea were favourites to progress, but no-one among the travelling support was taking anything for granted for numerous reasons.

Disturbing our sleep in the days ahead of the game were thoughts of Chelsea's continued and consistent cup failure against lower league opposition, memories of Oxford personally dumping us out of the cup just three years previously, and, perhaps most worrying of all, the fact that our 1992 Sunderland nemesis Malcom Crosby was now on the coaching staff at Oxford while his 'lucky-boot-wearing' striker John Byrne was in their starting 11.

Our fears were not eased by a flying start from Oxford - Joey Beauchamp enjoying the freedom of the Home Counties to poke the ball beneath Dmitri Kharine within five minutes before the Russian keeper was again called in to action to prevent Alex Dyer from doubling the lead.

Midway through the half, however, Chelsea took an element of control. First John Spencer juggled, turned and shot from the edge of the box to level in front of the away end and those in the trees, and then Craig Burley fired home from 20 yards to give the visitors the advantage.

Both goals highlighted the number of Chelsea supporters across all four sides of the ground, and the start of the second-half was briefly delayed by skirmishes beneath the low-covered London Road end that housed those Oxford fans most offended by the taking of their turf.

A nervy second-half saw Chelsea hold on to the lead until, with fewer than 10 to play, Gavin Peacock handled in the area to give Oxford a lifeline from the spot.

Mike Ford took responsibility to take the game to a replay but fired his shot against the bar to spark jubilation in the away end and further minor skirmishes elsewhere around the ground.

There was, though, still time for one final let-off when a late cross was swung into John Byrne at the far post.

With every Chelsea fan waiting for the net to bulge, to the surprise of all the former Mackem headed wide... maybe, just maybe, we again dared to think, this year might finally be our year...

The Oxford win set up a Stamford Bridge quarter-final clash against Wolves, but ahead of that - and with relegation still a real threat - Chelsea faced a crucial game at home to fellow strugglers Tottenham and a trip to Old Trafford to face high-flying Manchester United.

With the unbeaten run against Tottenham now in its fourth season and already becoming 'a thing', it looked like it would end as Steve Sedgley and Jason Dozzell put Spurs two clear with less than 20 minutes played.

Come the interval, however, Chelsea were a goal to the good - Mal Donaghy grabbing a rare goal at the near post, Stein then swivelling to fire into the roof of the net and, for the third, Spencer controlling on the outside of his foot to unleash a shot past Ian Walker.

The thrills continued in the second-period when Spurs substitute Andy Gray levelled with a penalty after a needless Erland Johnsen handball, but then missed a second opportunity from the spot - Kharine saving after being fortunate to stay on the pitch after bringing down Ronny Rosenthal in a one-on-one.

With the game tied at 3-3 and moving into stoppage-time, I'd left the Benches and was heading up the steps of the Shed to buy tickets for the forthcoming cup quarter-final when I was stopped in my tracks by a roar.

I turned just in time to see the ref award the third penalty of the day after Peacock was upended by Dean Austin, and delayed my exit to see Mark Stein jubilantly smash home Chelsea's fourth to the delight of the home crowd - the ball hit so hard it bounced back out of the penalty area after thundering against the stanchion. *"Steino, Steino, Steino...!"*

The following week was as good, if not better.

Already the only side to beat champions-elect Manchester United courtesy of the 1-0 win in September, Chelsea repeated the act at Old Trafford with Gavin Peacock once more scoring the only goal of the game when he lifted the ball over the advancing Peter Schmeichel.

It again summed up the perennial frustrations of being a Chelsea fan; supporting a team capable of doing the double over United on one hand, while being on the end of a double defeat to Oldham on the other.

It was that unpredictability, combined with the badly-timed loss of the prolific Mark Stein to an ankle injury at Old Trafford, which caused most concern ahead of the visit of Wolves for the last-eight FA Cup game.

Wolves visited the Bridge on the fringes of second-tier play-off places and were the clear underdogs but, as Chelsea fans could so clearly recall, so were Sunderland at the same stage two years previously.

Cup fever was turned up a notch or two by the debut appearance of a massive blue flag that was passed along The Shed and West Stand Benches ahead of the teams appearing.

Organised by Chelsea Independent Supporters Association and measuring an immense 100ft by 50ft, it had the rampant Chelsea lion at its heart sandwiched by the words 'Pride of London' and 'CFC' and was funded by, among others, one Matthew Harding - a Chelsea-fan-done-good who had recently been appointed to the board of directors in exchange for a few million quid to fund the ongoing development of the new North Stand.

With Stein missing there was a further blow 20 minutes into the game when his partner in crime John Spencer was also withdrawn through injury; Hoddle replacing him from the bench for his first game since November.

With anxiety at a high, however, the calming presence of Hoddle was a blessing in disguise; the boss taking up a spot in midfield to take control of a scrappy encounter.

Hoddle went closest in the first period when a deflected shot was well saved by Wolves keeper Mike Stowell, and was on hand again to lay the foundations for the goal that won the game - Hoddle to Wise to Burley; a Burley cross to Peacock and... get in... the number 10 hooking home on the volley in front of the North End building site.

With 30 minutes still to play, all Chelsea had to do was hold on as the *Ghosts of Sunderland Past* filled the thoughts of the capacity home crowd.

Sixty minutes became 70, 70 became 75. Eighty minutes gone... 81, 82, 83, 84.

Eighty-five, 86, 87...

Eighty-eight, 89, 90...

A couple of agonising minutes of injury-time... and, YEEESSSSSSSSS!!!!...

The whistle was the signal for a pitch invasion; Scott, Stewie and I among those decamping from the Benches as the Blue Flag was quickly unfurled once more to be lofted above the heads in celebration of Chelsea reaching their first FA Cup semi-final since 1970.

In the following weeks Chelsea beat Wimbledon, lost at Liverpool, beat West Ham with Hoddle scoring his one and only Chelsea goal, lost to Sheffield Wednesday, beat Southampton and drew at Newcastle, but it was difficult to focus beyond the forthcoming FA Cup Semi-Final v Luton to be held at Wembley on April 9.

With Stein still on the treatment table, the striker getting most attention ahead of the semi-final was one lining up in Luton colours. He went by the name of Kerry Dixon.

Dixon's spell at Southampton following his departure from Chelsea had been disappointing - making just nine league appearances - but he'd found fresh energy and form following the move to his home-town club and was part of a team that pulled off shocks against both Newcastle and West Ham to reach the semi-finals.

The fear as the Wembley game approached was that if Dixon

was going to reach the first major final that had thus far eluded him - but which every Chelsea fan knew his abilities so richly deserved - it would be sod's bloody law that it would be against the club he had served with such distinction and at which he was so loved.

But Dixon wasn't the only threat; winger Scott Oakes - son of Showaddywaddy guitarist Trevor Oakes – had been finding all the right notes in the Hatters' cup run, while a niggly young Welsh striker called John Hartson was also one to be wary of.

As it turned out, Hartson started on the bench and by the time he was introduced Chelsea were already two to the good through a Gavin Peacock brace.

From the off Chelsea were quicker, stronger, more composed and nerves were settled before 15 minutes had been played when Tony Cascarino headed on a free-kick form the Chelsea half that was moved via the head of John Spencer to Peacock, who scored from 10 yards.

Two minutes after half-time Cascarino, Spencer and Peacock again combined to put Chelsea on the brink of the final.

In all honesty, after waiting so many years to reach an FA Cup Final it was all unexpectedly easy; even, dare I say it, a little anticlimactic.

Luton never threatened, Dixon was largely peripheral to the action and, despite being world leaders in finding unique ways of shattering dreams, even Chelsea couldn't find a way of cocking this one up.

The final whistle brought what is a famous reception for Dixon; Chelsea fans finally getting the chance to properly thank him for his years of service by serenading him from the pitch ahead of Peacock, Hoddle or any of the others of the class of '94 that had just given them their first FA Cup Final in 24 years.

For Dixon, it was an emotional moment. Writing in his autobiography Up Front he said: "What will live me forever was the reaction of the fans. Chelsea's 40,000 supporters broke off from their celebrations to chant *'There's only one Kerry Dixon'*. It was a heart-warming moment, a highlight of my career in terms of pure emotion."

It was our pleasure Kerry, our absolute pleasure.

When I said 'anticlimactic' what I obviously meant was a grin from ear to ear and an immediate trip to the Fulham Road where, with Scott, Stewie and various other acquaintances, I drank the night away in celebration of the breaking of my cup final virginity.

No pun intended, but it had been a long time coming.

Awaiting us in the final was one of two giants from the north - Manchester United or, ahem, Oldham Athletic, who would play their own semi-final at Wembley the following day.

I'm happy to admit that I was desperate for United in the final; not because we had already beaten them twice that season, and not even because facing the champions-elect would automatically guarantee us a place in the following season's European Cup Winners' Cup.

I wanted United - and this is intended with the greatest of disrespect to the Latics - because I hadn't spent a lifetime dreaming of seeing Chelsea play in the final of world's greatest domestic cup competition only to face Oldham Athletic.

Manchester United v Chelsea was north v south, red v blue, Manchester v London. If Chelsea were to win the cup I wanted to see Paul Ince slumped to his knees, not Andy Ritchie or Roger Palmer.

I got my wish, but only just, as United needed a last-minute extra-time equaliser in the Wembley clash before winning the replay at Manchester City's Maine Road.

Ahead of the final we had the annoyance of seven league games to complete.

Chelsea drew at QPR and lost at Arsenal before, in the continued absence of Stein and with Cascarino also now on the treatment table, Robert Fleck made his first appearance since October in a 1-1 draw at home to Leeds.

Fleck retained his place against Swindon before - stop the clocks - he scored the fourth and final goal of his Chelsea career in a 2-2 draw at Manchester City.

Now on a roll, Fleck continued to make an unlikely late run for a place in the cup final team in the penultimate home game of the season - a 2-1 defeat to Coventry watched by just 8,900 - but, to the relief of all but the man himself, was back in the stands when Stein made his long-awaited return for the visit of Sheffield United on the final day of the league campaign.

There was a fair bit to focus on for the visit of the Blades... there were FA Cup Final flags that needed waving, the possibility of an emotional goodbye to The Shed to consider and the chance that Sheffield United - despite starting the day five places off the foot of the table - could be relegated.

With regard to The Shed even the club didn't know if this would be its final game as a famous terrace, confirming in the match programme that they were seeking an extension to the summer deadline for all Premier League grounds to be converted to all-seater venues.

It was a great shame because when we returned in August it had indeed gone, and while we were there for its last breath it meant we were robbed of the chance to say how much we loved it.

The Shed was an open, ramshackle, hotchpotch of a terrace; a jumble of concrete, corrugated iron, rust and piss with distant views of the pitch and cover for only the few.

But the piss was our piss, and standing in the Shed was a rite of passage for all Chelsea fans; the majority of whom who would later find more permanent homes in the East, the West or the Benches from where they would watch the next generation launch into a rousing rendition of Knees Up Mother Brown.

I loved it the first time I saw it, and I miss it to this day.

Sheffield United twice led to all but secure their Premier League safety, with Everton and Ipswich both filling the final relegation spot alongside Oldham and Swindon across the course of the afternoon.

But in the 76th-minute Stein made it 2-2 to put the visitors back on the brink and, with final whistles blowing up and down the land, fired home again in stoppage time to send them into the bottom three for the first time.

Just 30 seconds later referee Keith Cooper brought matters to a close and Sheffield United were down.

FA Cup Final day then.

I could spend a few paragraphs building the excitement, writing the usual Wembley clichés, but what's the point? Every Chelsea fan, regardless of age or whether they were there or not, knows what happened.

Chelsea had the better of the first half against a Manchester United team chasing a league and cup double and went closest when Gavin Peacock hit the bar.

But in the second-half Eddie Newton brought down Dennis Irwin for a penalty converted by Eric Cantona, before referee David Elleray booked his permanent place on the list of Chelsea hate figures - scandalously blowing for a second penalty when Frank Sinclair and Andre Kanchelskis went shoulder-to-shoulder outside the box and the Russian tumbled as he continued into the area.

It wasn't a penalty then, it wouldn't be a penalty now, it won't be a penalty for as long as my arse points south... but David Elleray said it was a penalty and David Elleray must be obeyed.

Cantona again converted and it was now 23 years since Chelsea had last won a major trophy - the only consolation being that the final score was only 4-0 as United threatened a rout once Chelsea heads dropped.

Sitting alongside my dad and brother for this special day, we added our voices to a proud Chelsea support right up to and beyond the moment United captain Steve Bruce lifted the cup *("CHELSEA, CHELSEA, CHELSEA, CHELSEA, CHELSEA, CHELSEEEEA, CHELSEA ...")* before exiting Wembley to dodge the numerous scuffles that were breaking out and to be soaked by heavy rain that was one piss-take too far.

It's the hope, as they say, that kills you. As long as David Elleray doesn't get there first.

CHAPTER EIGHT
FA CUP FIFTH ROUND REPLAY

Chelsea v Leicester City
Stamford Bridge
Wednesday, February 26, 1997

Chelsea: Grodas, Petrescu (Johnsen, 106), Leboeuf, Clarke, Hughes, Wise, Di Matteo, Minto (Vialli, 46), Sinclair, Newton, Zola.

Leicester City: Keller, Grayson, Prior, Elliott, Walsh, Izzet, Lennon, Parker, Marshall, Claridge (Taylor, 71), Heskey.

Referee: Mike Reed (Birmingham)
Attendance: 26,053

I've had an interesting relationship with Leicester across the years; it often being a fixture to which something of additional significance attaches itself.

It was at Leicester where I witnessed my first serious outbreak of football violence.

On a Friday night in October 1981 I was aged eight as I sat alongside my dad with smoke bombs obscuring our view from the Burnmoor Street stand, while Chelsea fans on the terrace to our left seemed to be engaged in near constant scuffles with home supporters, each other, the police or all three.

I had already seen a few outbreaks of trouble in the two years I had now been deemed old enough to go to Chelsea, but this level of violence was something new. The trouble had started in the streets outside and continued into the ground, and the huge plumes of smoke drifting into the air captivated me - adding a previously unknown element to the football experience.

When we got home it wasn't Micky Fillery's goal in a 1-1 Second Division draw that I was talking about, but all the surrounding activity; tales that so incensed my mum that she pulled out the Basildon Bond and fired off a stern letter to

Chelsea, expressing outrage that I should have to witness such scenes while seemingly missing the point that I'd been enthralled from start to finish. Still… they sent back a programme signed by the first team by way of an apology, so it was worth the price of a stamp.

It was also Leicester where I went to watch Chelsea attempt to secure promotion from the Second Division on April 15, 1989. On the back of a run of 27 games without defeat, Chelsea travelled to Filbert Street in search of the final three points that would guarantee an inevitable return to the top-flight with five games still to play.

I was with Scott and his dad Tom on that hot spring day, full of hope. Arriving at around noon for a 3pm kick-off we sought seats in the Chelsea end but were told they were sold out, so instead made do with Leicester seats at the top of the Double Decker stand to which I would return in future years. The early arrival meant early entrance, and as soon as the turnstiles opened we clicked through to make our way to our seats.

"These are Leicester only," a steward at the entrance to the block identified on our tickets told us. "If you are Chelsea, go to the block at the end and sit where you want."

With Chelsea fans comfortably outnumbering the home support it was a comment he and his colleagues would repeat time, and time, and time again as 3pm approached, ensuring many hundreds of away supporters would be herded in to a section of seats simply designed for hundreds. Being among the first in we selected the front row, overlooking the small corner section of terrace that would accommodate the majority of the Chelsea support. As time ticked by, all the other seats were filled. And then the number of bums exceeded the number of seats; people standing up, moving up, allowing others to find their bit of space.

But if the situation in the seats was mildly uncomfortable, on the terrace below it looked unbearable. Well in advance of kick-off we could see from our front-row viewing point that one section of the terrace appeared to be full to capacity, with people pushed up against the fences - those bastard, unforgiving fences - with little room to move. We could then see a fortunate few being removed and placed in a second section until - joined by people still coming in from the back - that too was full to capacity.

As kick-off approached it was worthy of our attention, but it wasn't particularly unusual and we trusted that someone - whoever that 'someone' may be - knew what they were doing.

At half-time the first news of the biggest games of the day came through. Everton were leading Norwich 1-0 in an FA Cup semi-final at Villa Park, while the second of the last-four cup games at Hillsborough between Liverpool and Nottingham Forest had been abandoned due to, according to the Leicester announcement, "crowd trouble".

A half-hearted cheer went up from the Chelsea support, entirely oblivious to the nature of the tragic, fatal events unfolding.

The second half saw Leicester claim a 2-0 win with the assistance of some extraordinary refereeing decisions that delayed Chelsea's promotion by a week, but it was already an irrelevance as news started to filter through of the seriousness of the events at Hillsborough.

"People have died," people were saying as the game neared its conclusion.

Walking back to the car the mood was disgracefully ugly as violence - the initial tumour that led to the fences, that led to all football fans being treated as criminals, that led to the authorities to make decisions that led to death - again littered the streets.

I just wanted to get home.

And once in the car reports from Hillsborough chilled us to the bone. People had died. Not one, not two, but more... many, many more... the reported figure continually rising, the gym at Hillsborough being used by a mortuary.

The deaths were reported as 50, 60, 70 and then, as we all know, 95 in the immediate aftermath before rising to 96 when life support was withdrawn from victim Tony Bland in 1996 and, in 2021, 97 when a coroner ruled 55-year-old Andrew Devine was 'unlawfully killed' 32 years after suffering irreversible brain damage at the game.

When I got home on that fateful day I watched the television pictures but I couldn't comprehend the magnitude of the events.

Only later, when I finally recounted the events from my day at Leicester to my dad, did the anger start to take hold. It took hold because as I spoke I came to the realisation that there had always been an inevitability about 'a Hillsborough'; and as I spoke I came to the realisation that Hillsborough - on that very same day - could potentially have been Filbert Street; and as I spoke I came to the realisation that, in my own small way, I was part of the wider problem.

The eight-year-old that was captivated by the smoke bomb had accepted the hooligan element as he turned into a teen and -

honest truth - even encouraged it; not in an active way, but certainly in a cowardly *"you're going home in a Chelsea ambulance"* cheer-leading type of way.

And because he accepted the hooligan problem, he also too willingly accepted what followed - the appalling mistreatment, the criminalisation of innocents, the fences, the overcrowded terraces, and the gross negligence that cost innocent Liverpool fans their lives. He always trusted that someone - whoever that 'someone' may be - knew what they were doing. Turned out he didn't have a fucking clue.

It took me time to start to process that day and I didn't go to another game for what remained of the season but, of course, the following campaign I did go back and over time some things changed, some things didn't.

The violence that clouded the game didn't completely go away (still hasn't) and some of my own questionable decisions in the name of watching 'The Chels' didn't completely go away (still haven't), but thankfully the fences and the worst of the death-trap terraces were soon no more.

And if we fast forward all the way to April 29, 2015, Filbert Street itself had also long since gone... so it was to Leicester's new all-seater stadium a few yards down the road that I travelled to see Chelsea try to claim a win that would put them within just one more victory of a league title.

This one though would be the Leicester game of greatest personal significance, because this one would be the last time I would go to Chelsea with my dad.

In failing health, it was at Dad's own pace that he walked to the ground as the head of three generations; his two sons and two of his six grand-children by his side.

I didn't know it would be the last game he would see but, in truth, I think Dad perhaps did. As a result, he treated us to the full 'glass half-empty' running commentary that was his Chelsea trademark as he bemoaned Didier Drogba's misfiring first-half performance, begrudgingly acknowledged the Ivorian's equaliser two minutes after the interval and then declared - to the amusement of all - that we were the "worst champions" he had ever seen, despite Chelsea going on to win 3-1 in front of an away end in full celebration mode.

My Dad, my hero, passed away precisely one year and one day later on April 30, 2016, aged 75.

In those 12 difficult months he watched from home as Chelsea slumped to a low of 16th in the defence of their title, sacked manager Jose Mourinho for a second time, and lost 2-0 on their next visit to Leicester as the home fans taunted the away end with a chant of *'you're the worst fucking champions we've ever seen'*.

Dad liked that when me and my brother Andrew gave him our report of the game.

"As I've always told you," he said, "I'm not always right... but I'm never wrong."

And so we head back to 1997, and the cup replay at Stamford Bridge.

Despite always being happy to go above and beyond, regularly doing 12-hour shifts or more in the name of news, my request for an early dart to get to the game is denied. Print deadlines loom, I haven't been able to give enough notice, and I'm needed at my desk for a push into the evening to get papers to bed. It's the curse of not choosing a nine-to-five job.

So when the teams are announced they are relayed to me via a radio perched on my desk - volume just loud enough for me to hear, not loud enough to disturb colleagues.

Half-heartedly proof-reading pages, tweaking headlines, I fail to give the words in front of me my full attention; listening instead to the words transported from Stamford Bridge.

Leicester are close to full strength, with the quartet of Muzzy Izzet, Neil Lennon, Matt Elliott and Emile Heskey all returning and all adding experience to the side that recovered from the 2-0 deficit in the first game. This isn't going to be easy; we're playing a different Leicester tonight.

And so it proves in a first half of limited chances, with the visitors proving resilient as Chelsea are limited to two long-range strikes from Roberto Di Matteo.

My reading of the radio reports is that we sound laboured, the previous week's pointless trip to Italy for a friendly with AC Milan perhaps taking its toll on the legs of players already facing a congested fixture list.

At half-time it's 0-0. I could probably head home now, but I nip out for a cigarette, get in a round of teas for the office and then re-read pages I've already read, conscious they didn't receive my full attention the first time around.

I'll find something on a second reading because I always do - a misspelled name, a missing word - and it will be good to do so as it will mean one less call of complaint when the paper is out, one fewer call from someone who never makes mistakes in their own job but is always happy to swear down the phone for ours.

And while I'm cursing our readers the game is back under way, with Vialli introduced from the bench in favour of Scott Minto in an attacking switch to 4-3-3.

Vialli livens up proceedings, forcing two saves from Kasey Keller in as many minutes, but it's Leicester that make me quickly lift my head and look at the radio - a Heskey shot that results in a cheer from the away support in the East Lower.

'Have they scored? Bollocks, have they scored?'

It's a split second of uncertainty, but the Leicester cheers quickly die out and are followed by a much louder *'waayyyyy'* from the Chelsea fans - a mocking cry that confirms in time with the commentary that the shot only found the side netting.

It's as close as either side have come though and the tie is now 180 minutes old, heading to extra-time, two evenly-matched sides that still can't be separated.

So as the players start looking towards the additional 30 minutes, I start looking to the door... and on the final whistle I make the dash; a couple of minutes to get from desk to car for the period of extra time that will accompany my journey home.

At the end of the extra first period it's still level, one mistake likely to prove crucial as we get ever closer to the torture of penalties to decide the tie.

Perhaps with that in mind Gullit makes his second change of the night, replacing Dan Petrescu with long-serving defensive stalwart Erland Johnsen. It seems a bit negative, but not conceding is now more important than scoring.

One thing is for sure... with just one goal to his name in eight years Johnsen certainly hasn't been brought on to nick a goal.

I'm slowing my driving down now, doing 50 in a 60, 40 in a 50, trying to time my arrival home to coincide with the end of the game, preferring to see it out on the radio rather than risk missing a key moment as I walk from car to house to see the final few minutes on television.

But as I pull into my street Eddie Newton makes a short pass to Johnsen inside the attacking half. I can hear the energy of the crowd rising as Johnsen moves forward, heading towards the Leicester goal.

As he lays off the ball to Vialli, who loops it back in his direction, I'm struggling to assess the level of danger or work out how close to goal he is.

But then there's a roar. It's a committed roar from across the ground, but I know it's not a goal because it's stunted in its nature; it's a roar of desperation, not celebration.

'What? What? What is it?'

'Penalty? Free-kick? What is it?'

I strain to tune into the commentary. They're saying Johnsen has fallen in the box, they think referee Mike Reed has given a penalty.

'Has he? Has he? Has he?'

The confirmation comes. He has.

Get. The. Fuck. In.

There's only three minutes to play.

This is the decisive moment; right here, right now...

But there is a delay.

The Leicester players are furious, still surrounding Reed claiming Johnsen went down too easily.

I don't believe it for a second because the Norwegian isn't that type of player, but so what if he did? I don't care.

I'm now outside my home, engine off, sitting, waiting, tapping the steering wheel, staring hard at the radio, waiting for Frank Leboeuf to take the crucial spot kick.

"Carefree wherever you may be, we are the famous CFC" is ringing around the ground, filling the gap between penalty award and penalty kick... making me again wish I was there, not here.

And then the singing fades, a sign that the Frenchman is stepping up to the spot.

I don't need the commentary; the Stamford Bridge reaction tells me he's scored.

No desperation about this roar, it's an extended roar of joy.

I listen to the final couple of minutes and then step through the door.

I don't say hello but I apologise as I change channels, wanting to see the winning goal and the foul that led to it.

I don't have to wait long, and I smile as I see that Johnsen did indeed 'win' the penalty. Not a dive as such, but an out-of-control tumble, the work of a man expecting a touch that didn't come.

I laugh at our good fortune.

"Do you know what?" I say. "You might want to start looking at wedding dresses..."

FA Cup Fifth Round replay

Chelsea 1 Leicester City 0 (aet)

CHAPTER NINE
1994/1995

With the new season on the near horizon, there was a potentially life-changing decision to be made as the final hours of a boys' boozy week in Kos approached: cancel my flight home, quit my job, and hop around neighbouring Greek islands with Guilia - a wealthy Milanese goddess who had stolen my heart just five days previously - or reject her most persuasive of natural charms and head home for Paul Furlong's Premier League debut against Norwich City.

Guilia was a couple of years my senior with deep ocean-blue eyes, a smile beyond compare, and the time and financial means to spend as long as she wished hopping from one island to the next, and back again if she so desired.

Approaching me outside one of the many bars that lined the streets of Kos Town, her first words were to ask why my left arm was in a cast.

The truth was that it was a football injury. I'd dislocated my elbow and fractured some associated bones after being the victim of a criminal tackle the week ahead of the holiday, but I told her I was a dolphin trainer and explained there are good reasons why you shouldn't run by the pool.

She obviously didn't believe me for a second, but she laughed, humoured me for further detail and rarely left my side for the following days as we walked, talked, drank, laughed, laughed some more and slept on the beach.

Her offer to join her to tour other islands for what was left of the summer was a serious one but, while she may have stolen my heart, she hadn't fully robbed me of my senses... Paul Furlong was a record £2.3m signing, and we were long overdue a home win against Norwich.

Stamford Bridge had undergone radical change as I arrived for the first game of the season on August 20; a first letter from Guilia, meanwhile, confirming she had now reached Mykonos.

At the north end of the ground the new stand that was in development the previous season was now nearing completion, although not yet ready for fans.

At the Fulham Road end The Shed had indeed disappeared and, in its place, stood a small bank of temporary green seats similar to those that surround the 18th green at major golf tournaments.

Even the pitch had changed; moved a few yards closer to the north and east sides of the ground and now as flat as a marble floor after previously featuring a crown running the length of the surface.

Joining former Watford centre-forward Furlong on the new arrivals list was David Rocastle, a classy midfielder who had won two titles at Arsenal before starting to lose his way first at Leeds and then Manchester City, and Scott Minto.

Signed from Charlton Athletic, Minto became the latest lucky winner of the annual raffle to play left-back as Chelsea's search for a long-term successor for the long-since departed Tony Dorigo continued.

Among those off to pastures new, meanwhile, were Tony Cascarino who sealed an unlikely move to former European champions Marseille - now in the French second tier courtesy of a match-fixing scandal - and Mal Donaghy, who hung up his boots after 590 professional appearances.

Injury meant Minto had to wait for his first start, but Furlong and Rocastle both featured strongly.

Rocastle added additional strength to the midfield and was a strong contender for the man-of-the-match award.

Furlong, meanwhile, walked away with a debut goal; controlling a Gavin Peacock cross to score from close range and double the margin of victory after Frank Sinclair opened the scoring shortly before the interval.

On this bright day, however, a dark cloud was cast post-match when a group of Chelsea-aligned thugs from a far-right group attacked innocent Blues fans in a pub on the Finborough Road, a residential street just a five-minute walk from the ground.

The attack - deliberately aimed at members of Chelsea Independent Supporters' Association drinking in the family-friendly pub - caused extensive damage and left a number of those targeted requiring hospital treatment.

It was a sinister throwback to days gone by when organised far-right groups would openly operate on the Fulham Road and, with a season of European football ahead, a worrying reminder that such filth still attached itself to the Chelsea support.

And while we're on the subject of thuggery, next up was Leeds away...

The game was all-ticket for the visiting Chelsea fans and due to nothing more than sloppy personal admin we hadn't applied in time, so were set to sit this one out.

That was the case, at least, until the night before the game when Nick, a long-time Leeds mate we'd bumped into in our local, informed us that he had one spare season ticket sitting next to him and another friend, three spare seats in the car and the confidence that tickets for the Leeds end would be available on the day.

"Do you fancy it?", he asked.

Four or five pints down, of course we did.

And so it was that the following day Marc - as the youngest of the travelling Chelsea Three - was sent to sit with our Leeds hosts while Scott and I, as the more experienced elders, headed off to try our luck elsewhere.

With little thought towards completion of a full risk assessment, we opted for tickets in the top tier of the giant East Stand on the Lowfields side of Elland Road and wound our way up its never-ending staircase while polishing our best Yorkshire accents.

Our seats were in the very top row of the stand and we'd barely had time to don our oxygen masks before Leeds raced into a third-minute lead.

None of our near neighbours paid any attention to us as they launched into song; remembering the time, when they were just little boys, that they were asked by their mothers to fetch their father's gun and shoot the Chelsea scum.

And neither did they pay much attention when Noel Whelan doubled the lead before 20 minutes were on the clock.

But it may have become noticeable, as the half progressed, that we were the only ones in our part of Elland Road not 'Marching on Together', so when a Dennis Wise penalty put Chelsea back into the game a few minutes before half-time the first few inquisitive heads turned our way despite our best poker faces.

Fearing we'd been rumbled, confirmation came in the refreshments queue at half-time when I was asked by a snotty-nosed adolescent where I was from as, to quote the old classic, 'mine wasn't a face he'd seen before'.

I mumbled some half-arsed reply about being neutral and just coming along to see a game, but my lack of confidence and his pie-flecked cynical smile confirmed that we both knew my Equity card wouldn't be in the post any time soon.

Back in our seats, and with increased anxiety, there were further chances for Leeds in the opening stages of the half before the inevitable happened... Chelsea equalised.

For the first time there was audible Chelsea / female genitalia alliteration. And it was clearly plural, so the likelihood was that it was aimed at Scott and I rather than scorer John Spencer.

Sitting in the back row meant we couldn't be clumped from behind and our immediate neighbours seemed to have no desire to dish out personal punishment, but the verbals were clear from all around.

But as the game ticked towards full-time and a share of the points, focus eventually returned to the pitch and the abuse started to ease... we were probably home and dry as long as Chelsea didn't score.

Chelsea scored. Fuck.

It was the 88th-minute when Spencer swung a foot at a half-cleared header that crept through the arms - and legs - of John Lukic to trickle into an empty net for his second of the game.

And just like that, Scott and I were swimming in a sea of sharks... and we were a very, very long way from shore.

With immediate offers to resolve the matter in hand being made from all directions, we scurried down to the exit with the intention of losing ourselves in the final-whistle crowd for the long journey down to ground level.

As we travelled down the top tier gangway towards the exit, a game of pass-the-parcel ensued with raging Leeds fans in one row pointing us out to equally raging Leeds fans in other rows to ensure everyone knew exactly who we were.

And we weren't exactly difficult to pick out in a crowd as my damaged left arm was now in a sling, and Scott had bright ginger hair.

The reality was that only CCTV and incredible good fortune had probably saved us from immediate physical attack but, on the final whistle, we knew our time was coming.

As we scrambled down the staircases behind the stand, the game of pass-the-parcel continued - "those two, Chelsea!" - and the second we hit ground level... SMACK... Scott took an almighty punch to the jaw.

To his credit, and my continued respect, he stayed on his feet as he fended off a few more body blows while I tried to pull him away with my single free arm.

Incredibly not a single blow was laid upon me as, I suppose, even in Leeds there is an honour among hooligans that looks down on slapping a bloke already sporting a sling.

But with Scott mentally preparing for a month eating through a straw, we approached a nearby member of the West Yorkshire Constabulary to enquire about the availability of first aid.

"Are you Chelsea?"

"Yes."

"Fuck off then."

"Cheers."

We duly fucked off.

Two games in though and it was two wins from two, which Chelsea made three from three with a 3-0 midweek defeat of Manchester City to chalk up their best start to a season since 1964.

Bigger tests were to come though, and next up was a visit to St James' Park to face a Kevin Keegan-led Newcastle side that also had a 100% start.

Chelsea fans were right to be anxious; despite twice coming from behind they ultimately fell short against a powerful and fluent Newcastle team that ran out 4-2 winners, with Dennis Wise seeing red for apparently saying bad words in the general direction of referee Peter Jones once the day's scoring was complete.

I haven't been responsible for launching many songs from the seats or terraces of Stamford Bridge across the years, but - while accepting hundreds of others may do the same - I'm claiming credit for an ear-splitting chorus that followed their first goal in European football for 23 years.

On a night of high anticipation Czech team Viktoria Zizkov were the visitors for the first round, first leg of the European Cup Winners' Cup when just three minutes in Minto, making his Chelsea debut, fired in a low shot that was spilled by the teenage keeper Daniel Zítka and bundled home by Furlong.

Down on the Benches, I launched into an immediate chant of 'Chelsea are back' that spread around a ground now benefiting from having the Shed-end support within kissing distance of the pitch.

A couple of minutes later it was 2-0, via Frank Sinclair heading home a Dennis Wise free-kick.

European football, it seemed, was a piece of piss…

But, of course, Chelsea never make things easy and Zizkov

had levelled ahead of half-time before an exquisite Rocastle chip in the 54th-minute settled nerves and gave fans a chance to celebrate his first goal for the club.

Chelsea desperately needed another though to offer breathing space ahead of the away leg and it came in wonderful style when Dennis Wise pirouetted 30-35 yards from goal before unleashing a thunderous left-foot strike that settled in the net after striking the underside of the bar.

Once more then: *"Chelsea are back, Chelsea are back, 'ello, 'ello'..."*

The return to league action saw a home defeat to a big-spending Blackburn Rovers team that would go on to win the title and a 1-0 win at Crystal Palace before Chelsea headed off to the Czech outpost of Jablonec nad Nisou for the second-leg against Zizkov - the game moved 60 miles north due to the hosts' home stadium in Prague being deemed unsuitable for holding the game.

Despite more suitable alternative venues being available in the capital city, the venue of the second leg was not confirmed until days before the game - ensuring maximum disruption for the majority of the travelling Chelsea support who were taking the opportunity to see their team in competitive action overseas for the first time.

Courtesy of a UEFA ruling that just three foreigners could compete in European competition - the definition of 'foreign' extending to Chelsea's not insignificant Scottish contingent - squad depth was also tested to the full, with youth team coach Graham Rix making his full Chelsea debut at the ripe old age of 36 simply due to being English.

Progress, however, was secured with a goalless encounter - Dmitri Kharine saving a first-half penalty to keep nerves at bay.

Defeat at home to West Ham and League Cup progression against Bournemouth was followed by a rampaging 4-0 dismissal of Leicester - Chelsea two to the good inside just four minutes through John Spencer and Gavin Peacock as the improved acoustics of the new-look Stamford Bridge again shone.

On the back of defeat at Arsenal the European adventure continued with a second-leg clash against FK Austria Wien - or Austria Memphis, if you prefer, rebranded as they were at the time courtesy of a deal with a cigarette company.

Austrian champions for three of the previous four seasons, Wien were an immediate upgrade on the threat posed by Zizkov and produced a committed, damage-limitation exercise in the

Stamford Bridge first leg to take a 0-0 draw back to the Austrian capital, despite being reduced to 10-men for the final 20 minutes.

Chelsea's up-and-down domestic form continued with a 2-0 defeat of Ipswich, undeserved League Cup defeat at West Ham and a share of the points at Sheffield Wednesday before the return leg in Austria was the stage for one of the most iconic goals in Chelsea's history.

After sitting out the first game, Scot John Spencer was one of the three selected foreign starters alongside Dmitri Kharine and Erland Johnsen.

Sporting a freshly-shaven head, Spencer picked up a cleared corner just outside the Chelsea box.

With all outfield Wien players committed to attack, all he had to do was run 40 yards… and then run another 40 yards… and then round keeper Franz Wohlfahrt to give Chelsea a crucial away goal.

Spenny completed the task with the calmness of an SAS commander that his new look resembled and, despite some late anxiety after Wien levelled on the night, Chelsea were through to the last eight courtesy of the away-goal rule.

With European football now parked until the end of February, Chelsea entered November in a respectable eighth spot and with an opportunity to put pressure on those sitting above them.

Reasons to be optimistic were aplenty: a defensive unit built around the likes of Erland Johnsen, Jakob Kjeldbjerg and Frank Sinclair was (*mostly*) reliable, Rocastle had settled well in midfield, and Furlong - while not exactly setting the world on fire - was finding the net often enough to still be considered an upgrade on target men of the previous couple of campaigns.

Meanwhile, along with Sinclair, the continued development of the likes of Andy Myers, Eddie Newton and Craig Burley was satisfying for those among the support who like to see the growth of players from within.

Concerns, however, centred on a lengthy injury list, the continued inability to find any league consistency and criminal court proceedings that would hang over the head of Dennis Wise for six months of the campaign.

Following the Leicester game in October Wise was among a group that hailed a black cab outside England manager Terry Venables' Kensington club before, following an in-cab disagreement with the driver, his girlfriend was injured when the taxi moved forward as she tried to get out.

Arrested and charged, the following February Wise was found guilty at Horseferry Magistrates' Court of assault and criminal damage - the prosecution stating that he smashed a glass partition inside the cab and punched 65-year-old driver Gerald Graham.

A month later he was back in court for sentencing; magistrates ordering him to serve three-months in prison and pay more than £1,600 in compensation, damages and costs.

While the prison sentence was put on hold until a successful summer appeal, it was a distraction that ran throughout the season that neither Wise nor the club needed - one direct impact being that he was temporarily stripped of the captain's armband by Hoddle in favour of Gavin Peacock.

Wise was absent as John Spencer and Jakob Kjeldbjerg scored the Chelsea goals in a 2-2 draw against Coventry City at the start of November.

Spencer then gave Chelsea an early lead at Anfield, only for Liverpool to hit back with three goals of their own, before finding the net once more in a credible 1-0 win at Nottingham Forest played out in front of a reduced away support due to City Ground rebuilding work.

As November ticked in to December a goalless draw at Tottenham was followed by a disappointing 1-0 defeat at home to Everton as the new North Stand welcomed fans for the first time.

A 1-0 win at Southampton courtesy of a late Paul Furlong goal then moved Chelsea up to seventh, but what we didn't know at the time was that it was to be the last league win until the end of February... a 10-game run that briefly dropped Chelsea to within three points of the relegation zone in a year in which four teams were set to go down as the Premier League was reduced from 22 to 20 teams.

The low points in December were 3-0 away defeats at both Norwich and Aston Villa, with the trip to Birmingham particularly dismal.

Three days after Christmas, a rain-soaked night in the grey shadows of Spaghetti Junction was compounded by a limp, lacklustre display.

Villa, firmly in the relegation battle and with just one previous home league win all campaign, rarely looked like doing anything other than romping to victory after opening the scoring within 10 minutes.

Even the presence of Villa villains Andy Townsend and Dean

Saunders failed to rouse much Chelsea passion, and an away support in desperate need of both shelter and alcohol was heading for the exits long before the final whistle.

Some respite from the league thankfully came in the form of a 3-0 FA Cup Third Round dismissal of Charlton Athletic to set up a fourth-round trip to Millwall.

It was a cup draw to set the bush telegraph, pulses and backsides of a nervous disposition racing.

The league slump continued with successive draws against Wimbledon, Sheffield Wednesday and Ipswich and a Stamford Bridge defeat to Nottingham Forest, but all eyes were on the trip to Millwall's New Den.

Chelsea's away support for the walk through the streets of South Bermondsey effectively fell into three categories - those going for pre-planned rucks, those who'd happily take a ruck if a ruck was in the offing, and those like me simply hoping to get home in one piece.

I'm a writer, not a fighter, so on that basis my collar was up and my head was firmly down as I stood outside the ground waiting to meet Stewie while trying to avoid the eyes of the locals.

'Millllllll-WALLLLLLLL.....' came the guttural cry of what seemed like every second home fan that turned the corner as the agreed meeting time with Stewie came, went, and passed into recent history.

With 15 minutes to kick-off and Stewie - in possession of my match ticket - now the best part of an hour late, a thick-set bloke who I'd nervously noticed eyeing me up finally approached.

Here we go...

Clenching a fist behind my back... just in case... I fidgeted nervously as he moved in close.

"Are you looking for a ticket fella?", he whispered, almost cheek to cheek.

"Err, yeah, maybe. Are you selling?", I replied, taking half a step back.

"Depends. What are ya? Chelsea or Millwall?"

Well, there's a question with no right answer...

After a pause for thought I put the ball back in his court.

"Depends. What are you selling?"

Now a step back from him; a fixing of the eyes, another pause, a smile, and - again quietly - the answer I was hoping for.

"Chelsea, face value, sitting next to me. Will that do for you?"

"Ha. Perfect. Cheers."

But no sooner had the deal been done and the inevitable happened - a happily-lubricated Stewie, along with my original ticket, came bounding round the corner.

My supplier saw the funny side but wasn't doing refunds, so now it was my turn to become amateur tout.

After having my parentage questioned by the first group I approached loitering on the corner of Zampa Road, my second attempt was interrupted by the dreaded black glove of the law landing on my left shoulder.

"Do you want to get nicked son?"

"Sorry officer, got a spare, didn't want it to go to waste... face value and all that. Sorry officer, very sorry. Don't worry, I'll keep it. Can I go now?"

Allowed on my way with a warning, I finally made my way to the away end and a choice of two seats for what was a scrappy 0-0 draw in which Chelsea fans renewed acquaintances with Dave Mitchell - now firing blanks for Millwall.

There were some relatively low-level clashes to the left of the away end on the final whistle and a pub missing a window or two as I returned to the car suggested some had found their desired day out, but courtesy of a huge police operation the predicted mass disorder was avoided.

The replay, however, was to prove a little livelier.

To the surprise of no-one Millwall were everywhere on the Fulham Road, ensuring pockets of trouble were consistently breaking out in the run up to kick-off.

Handed the temporary seats at the Shed end for the evening they also gathered in large numbers near the Stamford Bridge forecourt, happily slapping numerous sitting ducks trying to get past them.

Inside the ground they were their usual boisterous selves, filling the air with their 'no-one likes us' chant from the off. My sympathies were very much with Chelsea keeper Dmitri Kharine, who would spend half the evening with all 4,000 of them breathing down his neck with just a thin line of advertising boards for protection.

Mark Stein, now starting to re-establish himself in the side after missing the first four months of the season through injury, opened the scoring on the 70-minute mark but the joy was short-lived as Millwall fans spilled on to the pitch in celebration of an equaliser just 10 minutes later.

An increasingly tense period of extra-time failed to split the teams, leading to a penalty shoot-out that went to the death.

With nine penalties from nine scored, John Spencer was the fall guy when his kick was saved by Kasey Keller. The miss, and resulting defeat, confirmed a return to pre-1993/94 form for Chelsea by once again exiting the cup to opposition from a lower league.

With the police primarily focused on holding back the away end, it was Chelsea fans that would lead the charge for trouble as hundreds spilled from the North Stand. It was only the intervention of police horses on the pitch that prevented trouble escalating or - at least - delayed it until both sets of fans were back on the streets.

After the fun of Millwall came league clashes with the more familiar - but no more friendly - foes of Tottenham and West Ham.

Wise secured a late point against Tottenham before Craig Burley and Stein were the scorers in a much-needed 2-1 win at West Ham that saw Kevin Hitchcock brought on as a late replacement for the injured Dmitri Kharine.

"We're the best behaved supporters in the land, we're the best behaved supporters in the land, we're the best behaved supporters, best behaved supporters, best behaved supporters in the land...

"WHEN WE WIN!!

"But we're right nasty bastards when we lose, but we're right nasty bastards when we lose, but we're right nasty bastards, right nasty bastards, right nasty bastards when we lose...

"CHELSEA (hooligans), CHELSEA (hooligans), CHELSEA (hooligans)..."

The Dover to Calais ferry was rocking to the motion of both the waves and the sound of Chelsea fans as those travelling on the official club coaches made their way to the Belgian city of Bruges ahead of the first leg of the Cup Winners' Cup quarter-final.

The ditty about our behaviour was not coincidental, as in the run-up to the game the advanced guard of Chelsea fans that had already arrived in West Flanders was featuring in the news bulletins amid early reports of misadventure and heavy-handed policing.

While we were heading out, in fact, the first of hundreds of fans that would eventually be deported had already been sent back home.

For those on the convoy of 50 coaches that carried Chelsea's official support of around 2,000 fans across the Channel, the policing policy ahead of eventual arrival in Bruges was already obvious - those travelling on club-approved packages were to be kept under close guard at all times, while anyone else was to be considered fair game.

Delaying tactics for the journey from Calais included a circuitous route along the lesser-known roads of northern France and Belgium, a stop for coaches to be inspected by Belgian police at the border and, on eventual arrival in Bruges, lengthy detention in a city coach park that prevented those hoping for nothing more than a couple of beers from seeing anything of the city they'd paid good money to visit.

A few mostly unsuccessful attempts were made to escape the coach-park gulag, but the majority suffered in silence to avoid the risk of arrest or missing the game.

Eventual arrival at Club Brugge's Olympiastadion ground - so close to kick-off it resulted in some crushing to get in - confirmed the reports we'd heard as we saw Chelsea fans being widely detained in plastic wrist-ties on suspicion of having forged tickets, home tickets or no tickets at all.

What there wasn't at the ground was any actual hooliganism, despite water cannons and German Shepherds clearly itching to be unleashed on what the Belgian police had described as 'one of the top five hooligan sides in Europe'.

As for the game, on a muddy and uneven pitch Kevin Hitchcock kept Chelsea in the tie, making numerous saves until Gert Verheyen broke the resistance with fewer than 10 minutes remaining to give Brugge a slender advantage going into the second-leg.

Post-match the official travelling support was pointed in the direction of the coast of Kent with immediate effect, ensuring the local police could confidently sweep up any remaining English nationals roaming the streets and bars with whatever force they felt was justified.

In addition to those sent home pre-match, the final reported figures on the day of the game added up to more than 300 Chelsea fans being detained overnight in an empty warehouse before being deported the following morning - many without the opportunity to collect cars, passports and luggage that remained in Belgium.

According to news reports at the time there were just two actual, official arrests - both released without charge. Nice work.

Ahead of the second-leg the league inconsistency continued

with a 0-0 draw against Crystal Palace and a 3-0 thumping at home to Leeds, but a much-needed three points were secured via a Mark Stein brace at Manchester City - a midweek game considered low-key enough for the despised David Elleray to referee Chelsea for the first time since the previous season's FA Cup final.

The ongoing resentment felt by Chelsea fans that travelled to Belgium ensured there was a Fulham Road welcoming committee for Club Brugge supporters for the return leg; the occasional missile adding to the warm words of goodwill as their coaches pulled up outside Stamford Bridge.

It was a hostile welcome that would set the tone for one of the great Stamford Bridge European nights.

Dennis Wise - fresh from his court sentencing the previous day - was missing through injury, with David Rocastle replacing him from the first leg. Craig Burley, meanwhile, came in for Eddie Newton in another midfield change.

It was Burley that took a free-kick in the 16th-minute that Paul Furlong headed back across goal for Mark Stein to jab home in front of an ecstatic North Stand.

Then, with half-time approaching, Steve Clarke played a ball down to the right corner flag for Stein to chase. Holding off a Brugge challenge, Stein managed to bundle the ball in to the middle where Paul Furlong was arriving to side-foot home.

Stamford Bridge went... and I believe this is the only suitable adjective in the circumstances... garrity.

A goal to the good on aggregate, as the half-time whistle blew Chelsea knew they would be through to the last four as long as they didn't concede a crucial away goal.

The second half saw Brugge prod and probe but, backed by an intense home support providing continued, deafening, vocal support, Chelsea held on.

The final-whistle celebrations were loud, long and hard... while the unpopular graphite and tangerine away kit Chelsea were forced to wear for the evening instantly, and unexpectedly, took on a cult status that lasts to this day.

The semi-final draw placed Chelsea against north-eastern Spanish outfit Real Zaragoza, with Arsenal or star-studded Italian side Sampdoria awaiting in a potential European final in Paris.

If it felt too good to be true following so many years of mediocrity and malaise, it is because it was; the semi-final proving to be a step too far as Chelsea were over-run in the first-leg.

The hosts, featuring future Chelsea midfielder Gus Poyet in their starting 11, were dominant from the off to win 3-0.

It could have been five as Chelsea were outclassed; the misery compounded by vicious assaults on the away support from baton-wielding, balaclava-wearing Spanish police.

With the fat lady clearing her throat on the European adventure, league woes continued with a point at Wimbledon and a 2-0 defeat to Southampton that saw Neil Shipperley score on his return to Stamford Bridge following a January move.

Back to just four points off the drop-zone with six games left to play, potential relegation relief came in the form of a 1-0 defeat of Aston Villa to secure Chelsea's first home win in the league since October.

The goal came via one of the few moments of quality, with Paul Furlong finding Mark Stein to fire low past Mark Bosnich.

The win was followed by a credible 0-0 Easter Monday draw at Manchester United to edge further to safety but, Chelsea being Chelsea, relief on the field was starting to be overshadowed by signs of tension in the boardroom.

After initially handing over a £7.5m loan, the majority of which was to support the development of the North Stand, Matthew Harding had now become the de facto landlord of Stamford Bridge with the purchase of West Register Properties; the company which now owned Stamford Bridge and which, in turn, was owned by the Royal Bank of Scotland.

His growing influence had got the Fleet Street keyboards twitching with talk of a boardroom 'coup', and Harding seeking to replace Ken Bates as club chairman.

While both parties were happy to dismiss speculation as nothing more than paper talk, it helped further cement the reputation of Harding as the fans' favourite and future saviour. As the coming months unfolded, it would also prove that there is - indeed - no smoke without fire.

A clearance that cannoned off Paul Furlong's shoulder straight back into the net gave Chelsea initial hope of a European fightback in the return leg against Zaragoza, but a crucial away strike by Santiago Aragon killed the contest and the atmosphere with little over 30 minutes gone.

Goals from Frank Sinclair and, late on, Mark Stein, briefly resulted in abacuses being pulled from pockets to see if an incredible comeback was still on but the reality was that - courtesy of the Aragon goal - Chelsea were still two shy of their target as they exited the competition 4-3 on aggregate.

Any lingering doubts about relegation were ended courtesy of a 1-0 home defeat of QPR and an entertaining 3-3 draw on a balmy May evening at Everton's Goodison Park before - in the last game of the campaign - Arsenal were defeated 2-1 at Stamford Bridge as Glenn Hoddle made his final Chelsea playing appearance.

With visiting keeper David Seaman mocked throughout for conceding to *"Nayim from the half-way line"* in his side's Cup Winners' Cup Final defeat to Zaragoza, the game was a fun way to end a campaign that was lifted by the European adventure but failed to hide the fact that it was now 24 years since Chelsea had last won a major trophy.

Before seeing off Arsenal, however, a week earlier Chelsea had travelled to an already-relegated Leicester City for the penultimate game of the season.

Working on the morning of the game I was unsure if I'd make it to Leicester but had teed up a weekend with Yvette, at that point studying in the city, should the gods of news deadlines allow me to get away in time.

On a gloriously hot day I raced up the M1 just in time to discover two things - firstly, Celine would also be joining us for the weekend and, secondly, my rapidly-assembled weekend bag contained shorts and a T-shirt but no change of shoes.

Having never been to a game of football in a suit I didn't intend to start now, so it was on with the shorts and T-shirt and to hell with the black work shoes that would attract bemused looks throughout the day from people who clearly thought I was on a day out with my two carers.

'Look at that poor bloke; they could have at least bought him a pair of trainers...'

Following an uneventful 1-1 draw, post-match the three of us headed into the city centre for a relaxed beer and food before heading back to Yvette's digs.

As we walked past the train station it was clear we had narrowly missed some serious disorder; a pub's soft furnishings had been casually rearranged on the pavement, police vans lined the streets, and a small assortment of some familiar Chelsea faces were being interrogated by Leicestershire's boys in blue.

One copper, however, clearly feared he was still one arrest short in that day's sweepstake so - from the opposite side of the street - he ran across the road, pulled out his baton, jumped some railings, and told me to stay where I was.

Before I knew what was happening, he was in my face and threatening me with arrest.

The situation was thus... I was more than a mile from a football ground; it was at least two hours after the final whistle; I wasn't wearing any football colours; I wasn't drunk; I wasn't disorderly; I wasn't engaging in any way with the disorder.

But I was a young male that *may* also have been a football fan... so, unless I was about to be handcuffed by the fashion police, that was all the evidence he needed to try to arrest me, put me in front of the local magistrates, and potentially end my fledgling career.

Thankfully - after a period of debate - the outrage of Yvette and Celine finally encouraged second thoughts, but it left a bitter taste on the day.

Back at Yvette's digs the three of us drank wine late into the evening and contemplated the dangers of wrongful arrest before settling down to sleep in the same room.

And it was at that point, as she lay by my side while wearing only my T-shirt to protect her modesty, that I had the first flutter of a previously unknown - and somewhat disturbing - feeling...

CHAPTER TEN
FA CUP SIXTH ROUND

Portsmouth v Chelsea
Fratton Park
Sunday, March 9, 1997

Portsmouth: Knight, Pethick, Thomson, McLoughlin, Perrett, Awford, Hall, Simpson (Igoe, 72), Bradbury, Svennson (Burton, 60), Hillier.

Chelsea: Grodas, Petrescu, Leboeuf (Johnsen, 76), Clarke, M Hughes, Wise, Di Matteo (Burley, 63), Minto, Sinclair, Zola, P Hughes.

Referee: Jeff Winter (Stockton-On-Tees)
Attendance: 15,701

Labour had crushed the Tories in the Wirral by-election the previous week, with the seat vacated by the death of Conservative MP Barry Porter now in the hands of Ben Chapman courtesy of a huge 18-per-cent swing.

It meant that once again the Tories no longer held a majority in the House of Commons; the latest indication in a long line of indications that - when eventually called - the May General Election would result in a Labour landslide.

It had been 24 years since Labour had last won a General Election; not quite the 27 years since Chelsea had won the FA Cup but close enough to get the superstitious among us believing that football and political fortunes may be intertwined... two once dominant institutions now back in business after almost two decades in the wilderness, the long road to recovery from respective election and relegation humiliations in 1979 now almost complete.

A tortuous comparison? Maybe. But the comeback from two down against Liverpool, the controversial late penalty in the replay win against Leicester and a favourable sixth-round draw were all being evidenced as fortune favouring Chelsea.

In addition, if they could navigate a route past second-tier Portsmouth only two of Sheffield Wednesday, Wimbledon, Derby County, Middlesbrough, Chesterfield or Wrexham would stand in the way of Wembley success.

No Manchester United. No Arsenal.

Not even a Tottenham, Everton, Newcastle or Leeds.

Ignoring the fact that both Wednesday and Wimbledon remained above them in the Premier League, Chelsea were 7/4 favourites, Chelsea the name that stood out from the crowd.

As we cleared away the Sunday lunch plates it was a fact that made Simon nervous, still unsure if my threat to propose should Chelsea win the cup was serious and still unsure, therefore, if he'd shortly have a wedding to pay for as step-father of the bride.

"What happens if you win today then?" he said. "How many more games will you have to play?"

"Just the two Simon," I said, "just the two..."

The truth is I could barely eat lunch. That's no reflection on the fine standard of Sue's cooking but a nervousness created by the game ahead, which was due to kick-off at 1.30pm and was awaiting me on television as soon as I could make my escape with as little offence caused as possible.

The fact that I'd be watching on TV also created a sickness in the stomach; my failure to lay my hands on one of the limited number of tickets available meaning - just like for the replay in the last round - Chelsea would have to do this one without me.

When I turn down dessert and finally get away, muttering apologies, I turn on the TV to see the cameras are panning across a Fratton Park crowd decked out in full quarter-final splendour - scarves, flags and tin-foil cups, the whiff of cup upset in the sea air.

As they pan across I think how my day should have been panning out; not forcing down an early roast but stepping off the train at Fratton Station, turning left on to the main road that's a mix of retail, residential and industrial, and then turning left again on to the terraced street that leads to the ground.

I think about how much I love Fratton Park. I love its Archibald Leitch main stand with its mock-Tudor entrance. I love the despair of the narrow alleyway behind the away end with its residential garages to the right and concrete wall to the left, all covered in graffiti of mixed quality and offensiveness.

I even love the Victorian-standard toilets that are nothing short of a health hazard, catching out all those trying to protect their box-fresh Adidas Gazelles from the overflowing piss of their fellow fans.

And last of all I love the atmosphere generated by the home support, an old-school menace that always lets you know you are in for a game regardless of the respective qualities or league positions of the two sides.

As the cameras pan across the crowd I also wonder if she's there.

I don't remember her name, she certainly wouldn't remember mine, but I still wonder if she's there - the Pompey fan that led me up the garden path.

On that occasion, two or three years previously, I'd gone down to Portsmouth with some work mates to see a former colleague who had moved to the city; the intention to have a Friday night on the town and watch the Fratton Park side play whoever they were due to play the following day.

Wedged into the middle of the back seat for the car journey down - chatting, laughing, drinking - I paid no attention as to where we were when we pulled up outside his flat in a nondescript street, dumped our bags, jumped in a cab and immediately hit the town.

We went from pub to pub and on to a club, where I quickly got lucky with the aforementioned local girl who - after a couple of hours of tonsil-tennis - said the magic words... "do you want to come back to mine?".

I caught the eye of a mate across the dancefloor.

I pointed at myself, I pointed at her, I gave a thumbs up and I pointed to the door.

"See you tomorrow," I mouthed.

We walked through the city centre; a cut through here, a cut through there, along the main roads, down terraced streets. We walked for a mile, two miles, three, and then four; we left Portsea, headed under the M27 and into more terraced streets.

Eventually we made a final turn; a suburban street of solid, semi-detached family homes with small front lawns, low brick walls and reliable estate cars waiting to be washed on Sunday.

"This is me," she said, smiling as she opened the gate and walked up the path.

"I'm really sorry, but my parents wouldn't approve. Have a safe trip home."

And without as much as a final kiss goodbye, she was gone.

It was around 3am, and as I turned to begin the long walk back - coming to terms with the unexpected rejection - I came to the startling realisation that I had no idea where I was going... I didn't know the name of the street in which I was staying, and I didn't have a contact number for my host. I was hopelessly lost in a city I didn't know.

I headed back in the direction of the city centre, passing back under the M27, sobering up, hoping for inspiration, when the final humiliation came - a driving, horizontal, freezing rain that soaked me within seconds.

Walking, walking, walking, arms folded, chin tucked into chest, heading towards the sea, planning to work my way back out from the pubs I'd visited hours earlier in what I hoped was vaguely the right direction.

Down one street, down another, looking for anything familiar, anything that would give me hope of finding my designated floor for the night.

One hour became two, two became three, and still the rain came down.

I startled a milkman walking out of a dark alley.

"I'm lost mate, wondering if you can help?"

"Where are you trying to get to?"

"Errr, not sure..."

"Right. Good luck with that then."

Back I went to walking the streets and then, still raining, the sun started to rise.

And then, eventually, after going round and round, unknowingly circling my destination, relief. Parked on a side street, outside a flat above a shop, was the only thing I recognised - the car I'd travelled down in.

It was pushing 7am when I banged on the door, waking a travelling companion.

"You jammy bastard", he said, immediately turning and returning to where he'd come from without seeking possession of the facts.

After a few hours of desperate sleep the comedy became a farce when I woke to be told the game we were due to attend was off due to a waterlogged pitch. Apparently, the lads told me, it had been pissing down all night.

As the cameras pan across the crowd I hope she is there, because - represented by Chelsea - I owe her. I owe her big time.

The Chelsea team contains one surprise, with Paul Hughes

making just his third start in midfield in place of the injured Eddie Newton.

The highly-rated 20-year-old made a goal-scoring debut from the bench in January and progression has been encouraging, but it's still a surprise to see him given a start in such a big game, a potential risk to he see him selected for a banana skin tie against a side that hasn't lost in nine matches, is pushing for promotion and has already claimed the scalp of top-flight Leeds in the cup.

Clichés are only clichés because they are true, and as the game kicks off the cliché here is about silencing the crowd, getting a foot in the game.

And it's what we do. Portsmouth start strong but Chelsea stand tall, with Leboeuf leading the way, controlling the defence, chucking a fire blanket over any early threat, building a way into the game.

As the game moves past the 20-minute mark I look at the away end to the right of my TV screen and think of those I know who are there, another pang of envy striking through my heart, and I think of how far Chelsea have come in the past two to three years.

There's a new professionalism about Chelsea now. Started by Hoddle, continued by Gullit, cemented by the higher calibre of players that we now sign with every passing year.

The Chelsea teams of '92 or '93 would have lost this game, of that I have no doubt, but I don't think the current crop will as there is a calmness about their play, a professionalism and confidence absent in the not too distant past.

And as if to prove my point, pulling my thoughts back to the game, Chelsea take the lead.

A long ball from Leboeuf finds Mark Hughes on the edge of the box where, without breaking his stride, the Welshman fires across Alan Knight on the half-volley.

It's a classic Hughes goal, the type of strike on which he has built his career. He's a winner, Mark Hughes, and he's making winners of those around him.

The goal has the expected effect on the atmosphere, sucking energy from the home crowd, inspiring the away end, and Chelsea look in the mood.

Standing up to Portsmouth's physicality with physicality of their own, they look keen to kill this one off; probing, prodding, searching for the next goal.

And two minutes before the break, it comes.

Mark Hughes wins a free-kick 25 yards from goal which Zola

floats across to the opposite corner of the six-yard box, where Steve Clarke - the unlikeliest of scorers - is waiting to head home.

Alan Knight half-blocks the effort but it's still going in when Dennis Wise storms in to get the final touch on the line. I laugh, unable to feel anything but a little sorry for Clarke who hasn't scored for five seasons and may never do so again.

He doesn't seem too bothered though, racing off with his arms in the air in celebration, knowing he has just put Chelsea within touching distance of the last four.

I open a beer at half-time, already confident enough to think the game is all but won, and again I think back to FA Cup quarter finals of the past.

In my lifetime this is the fifth time Chelsea have reached this stage, but for the first time it feels comfortable.

Tottenham in the early '80s didn't really count as Second Division Chelsea were clear underdogs, but in recent years we've had the Sunderland horror of '92, Wolves and Wimbledon. Each were tight affairs, decided by the odd-goal or after a replay, but we're in control here.

As the second-half gets under way the biggest threat to progression seems to be the weather, with a heavy mist rolling in off the nearby sea and covering Fratton Park in a cloak of grey.

But in the gloom Di Matteo curls a ball past the far post as Chelsea continue to dominate and then, minutes later, Portsmouth's Andy Awford misjudges a clearance, Mark Hughes runs into space down the right and crosses for Di Matteo to touch it on to Zola who - unmarked - passes it into the net. It's all too easy, it's game over. I don't think Frode Grodas in the Chelsea goal has had a save to make.

With fewer than 10 minutes to go Portsmouth finally get a breakthrough - substitute Deon Burton thumping home a Paul Hall cross - but it's an insult to the gulf in class, to Chelsea's superiority.

And as if to prove the point Chelsea go back up the other end and immediately get a fourth; Wise capitalising on an Alan Knight error to combine with Mark Hughes and virtually walk the ball into the net.

"Flying high up in the sky, we'll keep the blue flag flying high, from Stamford Bridge to Wem-ber-ley, we'll keep the blue flag flying high."

"CHELSEA (clap, clap, clap), CHELSEA (clap, clap, clap), CHELSEA..."

As the cameras pan back across the crowd I wonder if she's there.

'Safe trip home', I think with a smug smile.

FA Cup Sixth Round results

Chesterfield 1 Wrexham 0; Portsmouth 1 Chelsea 4; Sheffield Wednesday 0 Wimbledon 2; Derby County 0 Middlesbrough 2.

CHAPTER ELEVEN
1995/1996

Two days on from my near arrest at the Leicester game at the tail-end of the previous campaign, the UK was given a Bank Holiday to mark the 50th anniversary of D-Day.

On a beautiful May Monday the sun was shining, the mood was celebratory, and I joined Yvette, Celine and other friends to take advantage of the day off to visit Stratford-upon-Avon.

It was on a rowing boat, in the middle of the River Avon, that it happened.

As we all took to the water, she offered to take the oars.

At her first attempt to navigate under a bridge... bang, straight into one of its ancient arches.

Second attempt, bang.

Third attempt, bang.

Fourth attempt, with an amused crowd now starting to gather, bang.

Fifth attempt, bang.

Sixth attempt, and now under threat of taking on water, bang.

"For Christ's sake..." I said, with increasing bewilderment, "it's 70% air, just row straight."

Not one to take criticism lightly, she quietly and gently lifted an oar from the water.

She then turned, glared, and smacked it squarely round the side of my head.

Had I been a gap beneath the bridge she'd obviously have missed but, with a crushing blow to the temple, the unexpected realisation I'd tried to shrug off two days previously was confirmed...

I was hopelessly in love with Celine.

That night I gave her a lift back to Birmingham, where she was spending a few weeks on a teacher-training programme.

We sat on a window ledge into the small hours, sharing a bottle of vodka and a packet of cigarettes before finally enjoying a much-anticipated kiss and spending a first night together.

By the time I was awake she had already left for her day's work, so I left her a note and then drove home deliriously happy... but also deeply confused.

Celine was captivatingly pretty. She was funny, she was intelligent. She loved a laugh and she liked a pint. But despite getting to know her better over the previous year or so, I never considered her anything more than a friend. A beautiful friend, in every sense of the word, but just a friend.

So with my heart saying one thing and my head trying to say another, I spent the next few months being a total arse... happily taking whatever opportunity was available to progress the relationship, but refusing to commit to an actual relationship.

I didn't deserve her patience and she didn't deserve my indecision, so it was entirely understandable when she finally called my bluff by proving two could play the same game.

It was decision time. I had to commit or lose her. I committed.

There still remained though one *'other'* winning my affections across that summer of 1995, and permission to spend quality time in the company of this one was non-negotiable if Celine and I were to have any form of future.

Ruud Gullit was a European Championship-winning, double European Cup-winning, Dutch legend.

A footballing God, he was in the right place at the right time as the Bosman ruling allowing players to move for free at the end of their contracts started to open up new opportunities across Europe.

Signed at the end of his contract with Italian side Sampdoria, he was attracted to Chelsea ahead of offers from Turkey, Germany and Japan due to London's cosmopolitan lifestyle, its easy access to family in Amsterdam and white socks... our new hero claiming he always won things playing for teams in white socks.

To look at it another way, teams in white socks always seemed to win things when Gullit played for them - but if the great man said it was the other way round, then who was I to disagree?

With his dreadlocks, balance and poise, Gullit was first introduced to his new followers in a sell-out pre-season friendly at Gillingham before making his first appearance on the Stamford Bridge turf in a benefit match for the now-retired Paul Elliott that ended in 1-1 draw against FC Porto.

Also making his first appearances in a Chelsea shirt across the same pre-season was the second major signing of the summer -

former Manchester United and Barcelona striker Mark Hughes.

A niggly forward with an eye for spectacular finishes who was universally despised by opposition fans, Hughes - like Gullit - was arriving in SW6 the wrong side of 30 but, all being well, with enough left in the tank to be a significant upgrade on what went before.

With the early talk about challenging for league European spots and one of the two domestic cups, Gullit and Hughes were both in the starting 11 for the opening day league game against Everton... a 0-0 draw that failed to ignite despite the roasting temperatures.

They retained their spots for another 0-0 draw in a midweek trip to Nottingham Forest, and for a 2-0 defeat at Middlesbrough's new Riverside Stadium.

Three games, no wins, and not a single goal scored. Chelsea; pissing on bonfires since 1905.

The first goals of the new campaign finally came against Coventry City at the end of August; Dennis Wise scoring from the spot after Gavin Peacock was upended in the opening stages before - minutes later - Gullit and Hughes combined to finally deliver on expectation.

Gullit received the ball from Wise on the right touchline just inside the Chelsea half. With three touches of the ball and a lifting of the head, the Dutchman used the outside of his right foot to thread the ball through the eye of a Coventry needle for Hughes to use his strength to hold off a challenge, take it wide of the keeper and slide home. It was a goal of beauty... and one that secured Chelsea a point as sloppy defending allowed Coventry to hit back for another disappointing draw.

The overdue first win finally came at West Ham, with a last-minute goal by John Spencer - made by Gullit - adding to an earlier strike by the Scot and a second of the season from Wise in a 3-1 win.

And Gullit's first goal came the following Saturday against Southampton. And what a goal it was.

With Chelsea one to the good through defender Frank Sinclair, time was ticking down as Hughes headed into Gullit's path to volley past former Blue Dave Beasant in front of an adoring North Stand. Moments later we were celebrating again, with Hughes connecting with a volley of his own to wrap up a 3-0 win.

The League Cup campaign got under way at second-tier Stoke City, where a full-strength Chelsea side was held to a 0-0 first-leg draw at an atmospheric Victoria Ground, before the return to league action took us to Newcastle for a 4pm Sunday kick-off.

While I was fighting my feelings for Celine, over the course of the summer Scott and Yvette had made an alliance of their own so - not fancying completing the furthest domestic trip of the season in a single day - we'd asked the girls if they wanted to make a romantic weekend of it.

With a hotel booked, we made our way up the final stretch of the A1 on the Saturday afternoon listening to radio reports from around the grounds and, in particular, talk of a Tony Yeboah wonder-goal for Leeds at Wimbledon.

Bringing the ball under control on his chest about 30-or-so yards from goal, the Ghanaian international dropped it on to his left thigh, then on to his left foot... then, cutting to his right, took out a couple of Wimbledon midfielders before, still about 20 yards from goal, unleashing what has been most accurately described as a 'thunder-bastard' in to the top corner with a thumping swing of his right peg. It was, it has to be said, quite the goal.

The plan on arrival at the hotel was to dump our bags and head into the city to savour the sights and sounds of the Bigg Market, but Scott and I gave each other a look, gave each other a nod, and headed off to our respective rooms with an unspoken understanding that we'd see each other in the morning.

And so to the next morning, and as the girls filled up their orange juice at the breakfast bar we took the opportunity to compare notes.

"Get any sleep...?"

"Nope, you...?"

And on it went... several minutes of increasingly exaggerated and dubious sexual boasts, world-class lovers that we both clearly were, before the killer question was asked:

"... did you see Yeboah's goal??"

We both confirmed we had; proving - despite our fanciful claims - that football still, ahem, came first.

The other conversational highlight of the weekend came inside the ground when Scott and I got chatting to a local Chelsea fan attending the game with his son, who was no older than six or seven years of age.

Talk turned to a former Chelsea player with connections to the North East.

Our new Geordie friend, though, wasn't a fan and regaled us with a tale of the time he met said player - whose name I'll withhold in respect of the libel laws - and introduced him to his son; now standing alongside us and listening to every word.

"I'm sure he can be a lovely bloke," said Geordie, "but he was a disgrace that day."

"Really? Why's that?" we asked.

"I'll fucking tell you why," he said, with some unnecessary anger. "Despite the fact I had the bairn standing right next to me, as fucking close as he fucking is now, he was the most foul-mouthed fucking c*nt I've ever met in my fucking life..."

Lifting our jaws back into place, we took our seats for a 2-0 defeat.

And now, a brief interlude to talk about Nigel Spackman.

First signed from Bournemouth in the summer of 1983 as part of manager John Neal's re-building of a side that narrowly avoided relegation to the Third Division, Spackman was a near ever-present, hard-working midfielder who made a significant contribution to Chelsea's subsequent promotion campaign and successful return to the top flight.

Moved on to Liverpool in 1987 following a falling out with Neal's replacement, John Hollins, he won the title at Anfield before, via Queen's Park Rangers, joining Glasgow Rangers to win further honours.

His unexpected return to Stamford Bridge came in 1992 and despite missing the majority of his first two seasons through injury he recovered to be a near ever-present in the 1994/95 campaign; his experience particularly beneficial in the European journey as he became one of Hoddle's most-trusted lieutenants.

His second spell at the club, however, will always be most fondly remembered for a spectacular strike against Arsenal.

With a Mark Hughes shot through a crowded goalmouth giving Chelsea a 1-0 advantage in a feisty London derby, the game was entering its final moments when Spackman went up for an aerial challenge with Arsenal's Martin Keown in the centre of the park.

An easy footballer to dislike, Keown went up with a leading arm and a handful of Spackman's shirt... and went down with a right-hook to the back of the head.

To the delight of all Chelsea fans present, the normally mild-mannered Spackman took the Arsenal man out with a single punch that saw him receive an immediate red card.

After leaving the pitch to a standing ovation, Spackman was told by Hoddle that he'd be punished "severely"... which was hopefully code from the boss to say they'd be having a whip-round to pay his FA fine.

Ahead of the Arsenal game Robert Fleck finally achieved a permanent escape route from Stamford Bridge - returning to Norwich for less than a third of the £2.1m paid for him three years previously - but the spirit of his incompetence remained as Chelsea exited the League Cup at the first hurdle with a 1-0 second-leg defeat to Stoke. Part of a strong line-up, Gullit played the full 90 minutes to add his name to the lengthy honours' board of Chelsea players to lose cup games to lower-league opposition.

A solitary Dennis Wise goal got Chelsea back to winning ways at Aston Villa, before back-to-back defeats against Manchester United and Blackburn Rovers gave a clear indication of just how big the gap between Hoddle's team and genuine title challengers remained.

United - with Eric Cantona making his first appearance in London since being banned for his infamous 'kung-fu' kick at Crystal Palace the previous January - were as dominant in their 4-1 win at the Bridge as Chelsea were negligent in the following week's 3-0 defeat at Blackburn.

Life at this stage had settled into a very satisfactory routine of staying at Celine's Oxford university digs 2-3 nights per week, drinking with work colleagues of similar mind for the rest of the week, and heading to wherever Chelsea took me at the weekend.

Such was my excess volume of time, youth and cash, I'd think nothing of heading to places such as Blackburn even if - as was so on this occasion - no-one was available to join me.

It was, though, a grim day out. Cold, and a bloody long way with just a crackling radio for company, I didn't even bump into any familiar faces on arrival, as I would have expected at the time.

Despite suffering an indifferent start to the campaign, Blackburn were defending champions and it showed as Tim Sherwood, Alan Shearer and Mike Newell bagged the goals in a performance that was far too easy for the hosts.

It was also a game that highlighted as much as any that - with the notable exceptions of Hughes and Wise - too many were not yet on Gullit's wavelength.

Thankfully Hoddle saw the same, and ahead of the following week's 0-0 draw at home to Sheffield Wednesday another era-defining transfer was completed.

A member of the Steaua Bucharest squad that reached the 1989 European Cup final, Dan Petrescu continued his development with Italian sides Foggia and Genoa and shone as part of a talented Romania side in the 1994 World Cup before making his first impression in England in a single season at Sheffield Wednesday.

While not eligible to play against his most recent employers on the day he was unveiled, the £2.3m man had been bought in with the specific objective of playing as an attacking wing back on the right-side of Hoddle's sweeper system.

A much-needed round peg for a round hole, if you will.

A week later another round peg joined the ranks when Chelsea signed Irish international Terry Phelan - *'whoa, whoa, that Terrrry Phelan'* - to run, run, run down the left side and offer balance to Petrescu on the right.

While Phelan - signed for £750,000 from Manchester City - had to wait for his debut, Petrescu went straight into the starting 11 for a 1-0 defeat at Leeds in which Chelsea were denied the services of Gullit due to an injury that would keep him out for six weeks.

With 20-year-old centre-half Michael Dubbery coming in to make just his second start following a debut at the end of the 1993/94 campaign, Chelsea held on until Tony Yeboah scored with little over 10 to play despite appeals for a foul on Dmitri Kharine in the build-up to the goal.

Ahead of the following midweek clash against Bolton Wanderers - a 3-2 win in which the home-growns of David Lee, Gareth Hall and Eddie Newton took scoring responsibility - the increasingly fractured relationship between Ken Bates and Matthew Harding was again to the fore in the national press, before Bates used his programme notes to challenge his boardroom rival to offer "precise details" of the "crock of gold" he intended to produce.

By this stage there appeared to be little middle ground between the two men.

Harding remained the man of the people, drinking Guinness alongside fans in The Imperial Arms on the King's Road with a deep well of both cash and goodwill.

But Bates retained the keys to the castle.

Harding had friends in the media, who were hinting at his intentions to take the top job and suggesting Hoddle may not extend his contract if the current chairman remained.

But Bates was telling fans he was going nowhere, and that the rent of £1.5m per year paid to Harding was putting £3 on every ticket.

Harding had come to the rescue when cash was needed, and

was said to be worth around £140m.

Bates had saved the club from possible extinction and secured the future of the ground, but was not in obvious possession of Harding's deep cash reserves.

Harding wanted to build Chelsea FC; investing in new players.

Bates wanted to build Chelsea Village; investing in hotels, flats and restaurants.

In summary, by the time Tottenham Hotspur visited Stamford Bridge for a 0-0 draw at the end of November Harding had been banned by Bates from the directors' box due to "behaviour related to heavy drinking both home and away".

"Never mind," Harding replied, "I'll go and sit in the North Stand... after all, I did pay for it."

The vast majority of fans were with Harding but, whichever side of the fence they sat, there was no denying it was a disruptive affair threatening to undermine much of the good work from both men that had gone before.

With Bates absent due to illness, Harding returned to the directors' box at Manchester United to see long-serving defender (and occasional midfield genius) Gareth Hall make his last Chelsea appearance in a 1-1 draw, before a much-needed temporary ceasefire saw the pair lunch together ahead of the next home match - a 1-0 defeat of Newcastle United in which Phelan made his debut and Petrescu scored his first goal.

Following a 1-1 draw at Arsenal and a 1-0 win at Manchester City that saw the return of Gullit in a midfield role, I spent a very pleasant Christmas night having the run of a country hotel ahead of a Boxing Day clash against Wimbledon.

Relatives of Celine were duty managers of the hotel which was closed over the festive period but still required people on site for security purposes. So rather than rattle around on their own, they invited various family members to stay with free access to all rooms, drink, food and leisure facilities.

Quite frankly, it would have been rude to say no.

I had previously been told that Anton, a cousin of Celine by second marriage, was a Chelsea fan but I'd been introduced to people the same way before and it normally turned out that their definition of 'fan' was very different to mine.

Anton, though, was different; a season ticket holder for a number of years he'd done the hard slog of the '80s and early-'90s and immediately earned the right to be placed alongside those I classed as 'proper Chels'.

Bonding over games of snooker and Chelsea chat, another new friendship was launched that would see us become regular match-going companions in the following years.

But as if to prove he was the better man, the next morning Anton was up and off down the M40 for the midday 2-1 defeat to Wimbledon while I was still in bed; controversially opting to put a free luxury hotel suite and Celine ahead of Robbie Earle and Mick Harford.

In the loyal supporter stakes Anton had taken an early lead, but I can say without any fear of contradiction that I had more fun.

The year ended at Stamford Bridge with two goals from Liverpool's Steve McManaman cancelling out two by John Spencer, before 1996 got under way with a 2-1 win at Queens Park Rangers - a last-minute Paul Furlong goal giving Chelsea the points.

Focus then returned to Newcastle, with the league leaders making their second trip to Stamford Bridge in a month to get the FA Cup campaign up and running.

Gullit was again on the treatment table, but to everyone's surprise Chelsea largely dominated and - with Duberry shining at the back - led through a Mark Hughes goal until one lapse in concentration from Dmitri Kharine allowed Les Ferdinand to level with seconds left.

Mark Hughes then saw red in an otherwise uneventful 1-1 draw at Everton before Chelsea headed to St James' Park for expected defeat in the cup replay.

The script was being followed when Philippe Albert put the hosts in front with a deflected free-kick in the first half, but Chelsea were both level and a man to the good when Dennis Wise scored from the spot after Darren Peacock was dismissed for a foul on John Spencer.

Level, that is, for two minutes, as almost from the restart David Lee sent Paul Kitson to the ground and Peter Beardsley put Newcastle back in front from 12 yards.

With the game approaching 90 minutes and Newcastle looking ahead to the fourth-round, John Spencer crossed from the left, Dubbery knocked it down and Gullit was on hand to prod it home at the far post. With a race to the delirious away fans in the corner, it was enough to send the game to extra-time and penalties.

In the shoot-out, Beardsley and Steve Watson missed for Newcastle while Lee, Wise, Gavin Peacock and Eddie Newton all scored for Chelsea for a surprise win.

Gullit, Petrescu and Wise again stood out in a hard-fought win over Nottingham Forest, secured through a solitary John Spencer goal, before cup progress continued with a nervous win at QPR.

In control of the tie through Gavin Peacock and Paul Furlong, Chelsea fans were ultimately left whistling for full-time after Nigel Quashie volleyed the hosts back into the game before Bradley Allen spurned a chance from the penalty spot.

One of the highlights of the league campaign came on the first weekend of February against Middlesbrough, with Hoddle's work across the previous two-and-a-half years clicking into place for a mesmerising 5-0 win.

Peacock volleyed home a half-cleared corner to put Chelsea one up on the half-hour, before Spencer latched on to an exquisite pass from Petrescu to make it 2-0 and Gullit squared for Peacock to make it three before the break.

In the second half Petrescu was again the provider as Furlong made it four, and Peacock was then on hand to score the first Chelsea hat-trick for nearly six years with more than half an hour still to play.

The day had one final delight in store when Hammersmith-born Jody Morris came on to make his debut at the age of 17, proving there was still a route to the first team for those with necessary talent irrespective of how many European superstars we signed.

On the back of the best league performance of the season Chelsea, naturally, lost 1-0 at Coventry, 2-1 at home to West Ham and narrowly avoided an FA Cup fifth-round upset at Grimsby.

Making their first visit to Blundell Park since securing the Second Division title on the southern banks of the Humber Estuary in May 1984, Chelsea had to dig deep to take the tie back to Stamford Bridge.

Second-tier Grimsby had already seen off Premier League opponents in the form of West Ham in the previous round and, despite Gullit again taking up a midfield role, they had the better of the chances - Steve Livingstone (he who played a full 35 minutes for Chelsea back in 1993) among those who came close to breaking the deadlock.

The replay - which came on the back of an enthralling 3-2 win at Southampton - was a much simpler affair as Duberry, Hughes, Peacock and Spencer saw Chelsea book another quarter final place with a 4-1 win.

Chelsea would welcome Wimbledon in the last eight, but first the sides met in a 1-1 league draw at Selhurst Park the week ahead of the game - making it a Wimbledon fortnight, so to speak, but with an FA Cup dream rather than strawberries and cream.

It would be wrong to say familiarity breeds contempt for a club as starved of success as Chelsea at the time, but when the cup game came around the mood was very much one of 'job to be done' when compared to the nervous anticipation of the quarter-finals against Sunderland and Wolves in recent seasons.

That, in its own right, was progress of sorts, but Wimbledon had the best of the opening period - quicker, sharper, stronger and twice going close through Robbie Earle and Chelsea old boy Mick Harford, who hit the post.

Harford, scorer of a credible 11 goals in 33 appearances in his single season at Stamford Bridge, was a continued nuisance to the home side along with another returning old boy - Vinnie Jones.

Jones took the free-kick that was headed in by Earle to give Wimbledon the lead and, finally, inspire Chelsea into some form of life.

First, an effort from the outstretched leg of Paul Furlong rebounded off the post to the feet of Mark Hughes to level before, with less than 10 to play, a Gullit free-kick was deflected off Jones to give Chelsea the lead.

The celebrations lasted less than a minute... Dean Holdsworth heading home a free-kick to set up a third FA Cup replay of the season, and again put the chances of progression in serious doubt.

Gullit created his own space to score a spectacular drive in a 1-1 draw against Manchester City before Chelsea went into the Wimbledon replay on the back of a 2-0 defeat at Liverpool.

Of all Gullit's appearances as a Chelsea player, it is the cup match at Selhurst Park on a murky Wednesday night in March that arguably stands out above all others.

With Chelsea fans making up the vast majority of the 21,000 crowd, the dreadlocked-genius was a man on a mission after overcoming a bout of pre-match flu - and in defence, midfield or up front, with grace or guts, he dominated the game.

Starting in the middle of the park he went toe-to-toe with the Wimbledon scrappers to put down a marker that led to Chelsea taking the lead on 20 minutes when Dan Petrescu fired in to the roof of the net from a tight angle.

Mark Hughes, another ideally suited to the heavy pitch, forced a good save from Neil Sullivan before a surging run from Petrescu was ended by a tug from Alan Kimble to give Dennis Wise the chance to double the lead from the spot.

Wise missed; his weak shot saved by Sullivan to indicate this one would be going the distance.

Gullit again went close, hitting the post, but Wimbledon levelled six minutes before the break through a John Goodman header. It had been coming, as they say.

Sitting along the side of Selhurst Park, we were getting increasingly nervous as the game edged towards the final stages and Chelsea failed to regain the advantage despite the continued efforts of Gullit and Hughes.

Relief, though, finally came with little over 10 to play when Michael Duberry headed home a John Spencer cross before, five minutes later, Gullit drove down the left to pull back for Hughes to bundle home.

The record books would show a 3-1 win, but it was a score-line that looked significantly more comfortable on paper than it was in reality.

With just 11 days and a 1-1 home draw against QPR separating the quarter and semi-finals, tickets for the last-four clash against Manchester United were secured via an overnight trip to Stamford Bridge before we all headed off to the neutral venue of Villa Park, Birmingham, in our thousands.

I've always found the home of the Bullring and the Balti to be a strange place, uncomfortable with its status as England's second city.

Despite growing up surrounded by friendly Brummies who moved the 45 miles to my home town as part of a 1970s' overspill programme, it's a city for which I have struggled to ever find any affection.

Although vastly improved in recent times, its New Street station was previously a good representation of the city itself; over-crowded, grey, and polluted.

In recent years I've also worked in the city and made many good new friends, so while I'm now able to finally acknowledge it contains various pockets of pleasure it doesn't hide the fact that it continues to have some particularly unsightly boils on its arse.

And right near the top (or bottom) of those is Aston, home of Villa Park.

Not too many years ago I was having a quiet pre-match pint with my brother in the courtyard of a pub on the Witton Road when a woman approached and said, with a degree of confidence, "you two aren't Villa".

Confirming that she was correct, we absolutely were not Villa, we politely asked how she knew and why she felt the need to point it out.

Her response?

"You look too clean."

Now, I'm no Brad Pitt, but there you go; a Villa fan not just happily, but almost proudly, identifying two blokes as being from out of town on the basis that they'd had a shower.

As I said, it's a strange place.

But back to 1996, where we found ourselves in a particularly grim estate pub around 20-minutes from Villa Park.

It was the type of establishment anyone of sound mind would normally avoid - all plastic glasses, adverts in ashtrays and threadbare pool tables - but on this occasion it at least had the consolation of being full of Chelsea buzzing with confidence ahead of the clash with United.

There was no specific reason for being overly optimistic but we owed Alex Ferguson's side for the 1994 4-0 Wembley humiliation, we'd beaten three Premier League teams in a tricky cup run, and we had Ruud Gullit - a man born to take centre stage in an FA Cup semi-final if ever there was one.

And above all else, it just *felt* right in a way it had never felt right before.

The only point of concern was that Dan Petrescu would be missing through injury; a huge loss based on the impact he'd had in his brief time at the club.

Coming in to the side would be the hot-and-cold Andy Myers, playing alongside Steve Clarke and David Lee as part of a back three, with Phelan on the left and Michael Duberry moving out to fill the gap left by Petrescu on the right.

With Gullit, Craig Burley and Dennis Wise filling the midfield slots, it would be left to Mark Hughes, supported by John Spencer, to lead the line against his former club.

As for Manchester United... apart from David Beckham, Roy Keane, Lee Sharpe, Ryan Giggs and Eric Cantona, there really wasn't anyone to particularly worry about.

Chelsea fans filled their allocation in the main stand and half of the massive Holte End, revelling in the opportunity to attend a traditional FA Cup semi-final at a neutral club ground.

In keeping with the atmosphere, the game was full-blooded.

On a sandy pitch Beckham was the first to go close when he thundered a Giggs cross on to the post within five minutes.

Duberry responded by also curling one on to the woodwork before, after a period of pressure, Chelsea took the lead 10 minutes before half-time - Gullit's dreadlocks floating in the West Midlands air as he headed home a Hughes cross from close range.

Half-time was filled with nervous chat.

It was going to plan, it still *felt* right, but we knew better than to think too far ahead...

And rightly so, because all half-time hopes were shattered within 15 miserable, heart-breaking minutes at the start of the second period.

First, with Chelsea having already lost Steve Clarke to injury in the first half, Phelan pulled up with a thigh strain mid-sprint but was curiously deemed fit enough to stay on the pitch.

And almost immediately, running into space that Phelan should have been protecting, Gary Neville charged down the United right and crossed for Cantona to head back across the box for Andy Cole to knock home.

And then, well, then... minutes after the restart Craig Burley got the better of Giggs on the half-way line before - faced with a multitude of better options - trying to scissor-kick the ball back towards the Chelsea goal for an attempted back-pass.

It was a single rush of blood for which Burley, despite his undoubted talents, will forever be most remembered by Chelsea fans.

The attempted pass fell well short of its intended target, leaving a lame Phelan to chase a thoroughbred Beckham who joyously gobbled up the gift.

Chelsea almost equalised immediately, but John Spencer's volley was headed off the line by Cantona and we knew the game was up.

Phelan was finally substituted about 10 minutes too late and Gullit went close again when he fizzed one over the bar, but the clock soon ticked down to make it 25 years since Chelsea had last won a major trophy.

It was a miserable way to lose and there was no consolation in again getting so close, no joy to be found from pushing the best team in the country to the limit.

There was just emptiness, anger and frustration; emotions that spilled on to the streets with random and - in some cases - quite vicious attacks on departing United supporters from Chelsea fans struggling to find either a sense of humour or perspective.

"We're right nasty bastards when we lose..." etc, etc.

With the season now over bar the formalities, all that was left to resolve was the future of manager Glenn Hoddle.

England - looking for a replacement for Terry Venables at the end of the forthcoming Euro '96 tournament - had been sniffing around for a while and, as the season entered it final stages and others linked with the national job fell by the wayside, Hoddle was yet to sign an extension to his Chelsea contract.

After first being offered a new deal in September it was deferred to December, and then February, then March, and then April...

Aside from the England job, other complicating factors included the dispute between Bates and Harding.

While a bid to find compromise was now being held behind closed doors rather than on the back pages, the ongoing uncertainty could hardly have been conducive to Hoddle making any long-term commitments.

On the back of the semi-final defeat Chelsea lost to Aston Villa and Bolton, celebrated a Hughes hat-trick in a 4-1 return to winning ways against Leeds, and drew 0-0 at Sheffield Wednesday ahead of the final away game of the season at Tottenham.

At the conclusion of another draw - 1-1, courtesy of Hughes - Hoddle told the press that talks over a new contract "could be resolved by next weekend, but then again it could take another month".

It was the former, as by the time the final game of the season arrived eight days later we knew he'd be the new boss of England.

Hoddle would leave Chelsea as he arrived three years earlier, with a home defeat to Blackburn Rovers.

But despite the cup near misses, mid-table league finishes and the lack of progress against teams from northern mill towns, there was no reason to be anything other than grateful to him.

He had transformed attitudes to diet, training and fitness, he'd reached two major semi-finals and one final, and he'd improved the quality of the squad with each passing season. As a result, he left the club in a more confident - and certainly more professional - position than he found it.

The single challenge for Bates and the board was to now progress, not regress, and that would largely depend on who they appointed to become the 20th permanent manager of Chelsea Football Club.

Media speculation pointed to former Arsenal boss George Graham as being among the favourites for the job, but Chelsea fans had other ideas.

"*You can stick your George Graham up your arse*," they sang with passion and meaning throughout the Blackburn game, before even more loudly revealing the name of the man they wanted in charge… "*Ruudy, Ruudy, Ruudy.*"

Over to you Ken…

CHAPTER TWELVE
FA CUP SEMI-FINAL

Wimbledon v Chelsea
Highbury
Sunday, April 13, 1997

Wimbledon: Sullivan, Cunningham, Kimble, Jones, Blackwell, Leonhardsen, Earle, Ekoku, Gayle, Perry, Ardley (Holdsworth, 63).

Chelsea: Grodas, Leboeuf, Clarke, Hughes, Wise, Burley, Di Matteo, Johnsen, Sinclair, Newton, Zola.

Referee: Gerald Ashby (Worcester)
Attendance: 32,674

304 Holloway Road, London.

A run-down, four-storey building covered in the exhaust fumes of the traffic that runs past its exterior - a never-ending barrage of cars, cabs, motorbikes and lorries chipping away at its Victorian brickwork.

At ground level, a retail unit in a row of retail units, an identikit collection of cut-price mini-marts, takeaways and bookmakers that could be any filthy-busy north London street.

The scene contradicts a Tory General Election manifesto built on a strong economy and family values as the lonely, the homeless, the lost and the drunk also pass the door of 304 Holloway Road; people on the edge of society, camouflaged by the cards they have been dealt in life.

They don't give it another glance because there is nothing to avert the glance, nothing special about 304 Holloway Road.

Except there is.

From 1961 to 1967, the accommodation above what was then a leather store on 304 Holloway Road was the home of pioneering music producer Joe Meek.

It was while living there in 1962 that Meek - a complex character who was blackmailed over his homosexuality and was said to be in dispute with the Krays - wrote and produced the ground-breaking Telstar.

Written for the Tornadoes it was the first British record to top the US singles chart, plugging in to the space-race fascination of the 1960s. An 'otherworldly instrumental' that created a futuristic sound with the electronic circuitry of a clavioline, you'll know it as soon as you hear it.

But it was also while living in 304 Holloway Road, London, that Meek - at the age of 37, on February 3, 1967 - shot his landlady Violet Shenton dead with a single-barrelled shotgun and then turned the weapon on himself.

For a brief period of time, 304 Holloway Road was the most notorious address in all of London.

Aidy opened the door that led up to the flats above, telling me and Scott of the history of the building that for the past few months had been his latest student home.

I wasn't particularly familiar with the story, but my first thought was that the flat looked almost untouched since the bodies of Meek and Shenton were removed - peeling wallpaper, damp, and rotting window frames doing little to disguise its grisly past.

We spent the night sitting, drinking; three best mates all back together for the first time in months, each the victim of a spell of piss-take before the baton was passed to another.

When not pushing Aidy for any information on where the fatal shots may have been fired, we climbed a stepladder that led to the flat-roof of the property.

From there - across the neighbouring rooftops, across the East Coast railway line that hurries passengers in and out of London, across a plot of light industrial units hemmed in by the tracks at Ashburton Grove - we could see Highbury, the venue for the next day's FA Cup Semi-Final.

In the fading evening light it brought immediate butterflies to the stomach.

We could see the flags flying on Highbury's East and West stands, we could see a glimpse of the red seats that fill the North Bank and Clock End.

And as we looked, we wondered... 'what will tomorrow bring?'

And as we looked we talked about how much we were looking forward to Chelsea invading Highbury, massively outnumbering the Wimbledon fans and filling the North Bank.

And mention of Chelsea and the North Bank in the same sentence set off the inevitable earworm so I sat there, beer in hand, looking at the stand as the terrace chant played through my mind...

"Chelsea in the North Bank, Chelsea in the North Bank, la, la, la, la, oi, la, la, la, la, oi; Chelsea in the North Bank, Chelsea in the North Bank, la, la, la, la, oi, la, la, la, la, oi..."

In the days before seats replaced the North Bank terrace it was a soundtrack that would feature at almost any Chelsea visit to Highbury, a soundtrack that would normally accompany a gap appearing on the terrace as those invading the home end 'did their job' with the encouragement of those watching on from the away terrace.

But there were more innocent moments too, and Scott and I reminisced about our visit in '92 when a mural featuring thousands of faces of Arsenal fans covered the building site creating the new two-tier seated stand we were looking at.

One of the Chelsea fanzines - Red Card or the Chelsea Independent, I don't now remember which - handed out thousands of pieces of card with faces printed on them, and throughout the game we waved them in the air and again sang the familiar tune...

"... Chelsea in the North Bank, la, la, la..."

It was juvenile, knock-about stuff aimed at mocking the Arsenal mural but, as was so often the case in those early '90s days, it was still more entertaining than what we were watching on the pitch.

As the night passed by and darkness fully fell we made further trips to the rooftop to see Highbury bathed in its own soft light as final preparations for the game continued.

Taking one last look before calling it a night, a darker thought - a thought far more serious than the game - entered my mind.

That thought was terrorism.

With the General Election now less than a month away and the future of Northern Ireland a key part of the discussion, the previous weekend's Grand National was postponed due to an Aintree bomb threat.

It had dominated the headlines for days and one week on, with the Chelsea-Wimbledon game taking place at the same time as the London Marathon, there was a nervousness about the level of threat potentially facing the capital on a big day for sport.

"Be careful," my mum had said when I spoke to her before

setting off for the weekend; saying it without saying it.

I'm up and about early.

The game kicks off at noon and our decision to spend the night at Aidy's is already paying off.

The first task of the day is a full English on the Holloway Road followed by a read of the Sunday papers which 30 years previously would have reported on the death of Joe Meek in the flat in which we now sit.

As always it's the sports pages and, specifically, the semi-final previews that we turn to first as we tick down the clock for the 10-minute walk around the corner to Highbury.

When me and Scott eventually stroll to the ground, we can see everyone else is already there.

On Avenell Road they are meeting and greeting, chatting and laughing, killing more time before Arsenal Stadium's glorious Art Deco East Stand sucks us in for the trials and tribulations ahead.

There's Gaz, Paul and Ken. There's Anton, Alan and Steve. There's Mary, Paul and their girls. There's Stewie saying a quick hello before heading to the North Bank, and there's Wendy, Feisal and Brian. And then - best of all - there's Dad and my brother Andrew who, like the others, have travelled down this morning and made good time.

The group includes those still at primary school, those approaching retirement; those committed to the church, those committed to the clubs; blue collar, white collar; settled and single.

They are my family and friends. They are all Chelsea.

The sun is shining and confidence is high as I go through the turnstile, pushing waist against iron, that beautiful sound… 'click, click, click'… the opening credits to each new Chelsea drama.

Scott and I are sitting with Gaz and his clan, and Mary and hers. The seats are perfect, just to the left of the Chelsea bench, almost within touching distance of those who won't be in the starting 11.

Dad and Andrew are further down the stand, closer to the Clock End with which I am more familiar.

I don't know it now, but I'll later learn that Dad - under the same 'be careful' instruction that I received from Mum - is the cause of some temporary alarm.

Taking in his surroundings he looks up at the structure supporting the stand's upper tier.

There, hidden among the maze of beams, he spots a single, sizeable, cardboard box.

He tries to brush it off but curiosity eventually gets the better of him.

"Excuse me, any idea what's in that box?" he says to a passing steward.

"Don't know mate. Sure it's nothing to worry about."

"Well... if you don't know, don't you think you should check?"

The steward relents and asks a senior steward, who is also in the dark.

The senior steward calls the head steward, and the head steward summons people in suits.

They look up, they point and they get out walkie-talkies.

It takes time, but eventually the answer comes.

"Apparently sir [*it's 'sir' now, not 'mate'*], it contains spare floodlight bulbs - thank you for alerting us."

And while all that's going on, emergency evacuation of Highbury narrowly avoided, the teams are coming out.

Chelsea run to our right, the yellow away kit they are wearing glowing in the sunshine as they are welcomed by a wall of noise... the famous *Highbury Library* raucous for one day and one day only.

Grodas, Leboeuf, Clarke, Hughes, Wise, Burley, Di Matteo, Johnsen, Sinclair, Newton, Zola.

Eleven men with our dreams at their feet.

There is a strong confidence among the Chelsea support but it's time to focus, because this is Wimbledon... and Wimbledon will always be Wimbledon.

Just one place behind Chelsea in the Premier League, previous winners of the FA Cup, and last season's battling quarter-final opponents that pushed us so close, they are perennial over-achievers who will fancy their chances against their London neighbours.

And they are quick to lay down their marker, with Neil Ardley booked for crunching into Steve Clarke after just 10 seconds.

Minutes later Zola is on the receiving end, a bit of afters resulting in a knock to the face in a 50-50 duel.

But we knew it would be like this and so, thankfully, did Ruud Gullit, who has set up his team accordingly.

As is always the case when I'm more focused on launching into song at the start of the game, it takes me a few minutes to work out the formation but, when I do, I'm reassured that our Dutch leader has dispensed with our usual back three and wing-backs for a flat back four.

From left to right it's Frank Sinclair, Erland Johnsen, Frank Leboeuf and Steve Clarke; four old hands with enough experience and muscle to stand up to the inevitable intimidation ahead.

As the game settles we note that it's a scrappy and uncultured start, but suggest that if Chelsea can hold their own in the physical battle then skill may win out in the end. We'll see...

For now though, just like at Portsmouth in the last round, Leboeuf is the early stand-out performer. Winning headers, snuffing out Wimbledon's early threat, the Frenchman is helping his attacking colleagues build a foothold in the game.

And as Chelsea settle Hughes and Wise both fire in shots, but it's Zola that goes closest when he beautifully cuts back on the edge of the six-yard box to fire low into the hands of Neil Sullivan.

The Wimbledon threat remains though, and with half-time approaching the always under-rated Robbie Earle puts hearts in mouths with an overhead kick that requires Grodas to be alert in the Chelsea goal.

They may be significantly outnumbered, but for the first time Wimbledon's fans are making themselves heard.

The truth is that Chelsea could do with half-time and we all agree that we will take 0-0 at the break.

Looking to my immediate right I can see Gullit in conversation with his backroom team, working out what he's going to say in the interval and what tweaks need to be made to turn toe-to-toe combat into match-winning glory.

While I'm distracted those around me lift from their seats.

I turn to see Wise overlapping down the left before lifting in a cross from the edge of the box.

He puts it right in the mixer, as Wimbledon would say, where Craig Burley tries to touch it goal-bound but is blocked by Alan Kimble.

As the ball bounces Chelsea get lucky and it ricochets off Hughes, who is left with the simplest of tasks to smash it into the net.

It's a scrappy goal, a Wimbledon-type goal, but that's irrelevant... coming just two minutes before half-time we go appropriately loopy and the celebrations merge into the whistle that signals the break.

And now it's time to breathe and calm down. The mid-day sun has been beating down since kick-off and it has been exhausting just watching.

But thoughts immediately turn to last season's semi-final

against Manchester United when we also led 1-0 at the break, also felt confident, only to suffer misery in the second-half.

We try not to mention it but we can't help it, picking at a scab that refuses to heal.

We say that we hope lessons have been learned, we say that we hope Craig Burley doesn't attempt a back-pass from the halfway line and we say that we hope a more open Wimbledon - who must now show more ambition to get back into the game - allows Chelsea's more creative players to get more space.

Wimbledon boss Joe Kinnear is biding his time though, sending out the same 11 to start the second half that had come so close to reaching its initial target in the first.

As a result the game continues in a similar vein with Chelsea struggling for width with the absence of wing-backs and Wimbledon pushing, looking for that one free-kick or one misjudged defensive clearance to find a way back into the match.

Just after the hour Kinnear finally twists when he brings the dangerous Dean Holdsworth off the bench to look for another way through the Chelsea rear-guard.

Within seconds of his arrival, still dishing out instructions to his teammates, Holdsworth looks on as Chelsea's Wise takes delivery of the ball 35 yards from goal.

From the left Wise lays off a simple square pass to Di Matteo, who is in space further infield.

With a touch to control, Di Matteo then plays another simple ball to Zola who has burst to the edge of the penalty area 'D'.

Dean Blackwell has him covered as the ball arrives, but our little magician is fleeter of foot and quicker of mind.

With a quick flick of the inside of his right foot - a flick that looks so simple when delivered by a genius - Zola turns 180 degrees.

Blackwell is bamboozled, now in a different postcode to the man he was shadowing just a split-second earlier.

Everything is now in slow motion and we instinctively rise to our feet, already in half-celebration of a goal that is yet to come.

Zola, with that one quick flick of the inside of his right foot, has given himself the freedom of Highbury.

As our arms lift to shoulder height, then head height, Zola takes one more touch to take it even further from Blackwell... and then fires right-footed past the despairing hand of Neil Sullivan.

As the net rustles we are hugging our nearest neighbours, falling over one another in joyous celebration.

Amid the chaos Zola, arms outstretched, is jigging in front of the North Bank before blowing a double-handed kiss to an adoring crowd united in adulation, united in song…

"ZOLA, LA, LA, LA, LA ZOLA, LA, LA, LA, LA ZOLA…"

We know immediately that it is one of the greatest goals the FA Cup has ever seen, and as the match restarts we also know that it's game over, that there's no way back for Wimbledon - for all their hustle, bustle and muscle they have no answer for our blue ballerina.

With 25 minutes still to play we can't stop smiling, can't stop singing.

It's a lunchtime party in the North London sun and we serenade Zola time and time again.

We cheer every tackle and applaud every pass.

With the game entering injury time there is one more delight still in store as a long ball skims off the head of Chris Perry to leave Mark Hughes all alone and bearing down on goal.

With one touch followed by the briefest of pauses, he hammers it in to the roof of the net from six yards.

Chelsea 3 Wimbledon 0.

"QUE SERA SERA, WHATEVER WILL BE WILL BE, WE'RE GOING TO WEM-BER-LEY, QUE SERA SERA…"

FA Cup Semi-Final results

Chelsea 3 Wimbledon 0; Middlesbrough 3 Chesterfield 3; (Replay: Middlesbrough 3 Chesterfield 0).

CHAPTER THIRTEEN
1996/1997

Before the semi-final joy of 1997 came the heartbreak of 1996.

On April 1, 1996, the very day after that FA Cup semi-final defeat to Manchester United, I started a new job - moving from Northampton to become News Editor for a series of weekly newspapers based in Buckingham.

The irony was not lost on me that it was April Fool's Day, but as I sulked and moaned my way through my first day and the following few weeks - appearing generally disinterested in anything and anyone - my new boss would have been forgiven for thinking he'd made a terrible mistake.

I obviously explained the reasons for my low mood but only Barry, the genial sports editor who was a lifelong Luton Town fan, had any understanding of my suffering. Everyone else, quite naturally, simply marked me down as an immature, petulant child.

Not that I cared. That was their problem, not mine, I would have been thinking as I ripped into junior reporter after junior reporter for dropped intros or incorrect usage of the Oxford comma.

On the back of the previous FA Cup flirtations that were cut short in Sunderland in '92 and at Wembley in '94, the Villa Park defeat of '96 felt like the deepest cut of all.

Quite simply, it appeared it was time to admit defeat; if a team with that much potential and talent fell short, I had to finally accept I'd backed the wrong horse.

It was time to acknowledge Chelsea had done their best; they'd got closer than I could have ever imagined in the dying Darren Wood days of the '80s or the painful Porterfield period of the early '90s but regardless of who Chelsea signed or how well they played someone, somewhere, would always kill the dream.

Memories of league and cup success stories, it seemed, would forever be for those - and only those - fortunate enough to have served on the Stamford Bridge terraces from the mid-'50s to early-'70s.

'Born after 1971?'

'Unlucky son; enjoy the second division promotions and Full Members' Cups because it will never get better than that.'

Even the confirmation of Ruud Gullit as Chelsea manager immediately after Hoddle's departure in May initially struggled to lift my mood.

While I was delighted he'd got the job, and while I knew he'd bring optimism and charisma to the role, he had no coaching experience and it is common knowledge that great players rarely make great managers.

For all we knew, he could be bloody useless. Fast forward a few years, and Newcastle fans would tell you he was.

But over the summer of '96 Gullit signed highly-rated French centre-half Frank Leboeuf... and he signed Italian midfielder Roberto Di Matteo from Lazio.

And - hold still my beating heart - he also signed Gianluca Vialli.

Against my better judgement, Ruud Gullit again injected me with hope. The bastard.

Those who were saying their farewells to Chelsea included Paul Furlong, who weighed up the chances of securing a starting spot ahead of Vialli and wisely headed straight to Birmingham.

Also on their way out were Anthony Barness, who had spectacularly failed to live up to early expectations and returned to Charlton Athletic, and Nigel Spackman - the midfielder leaving Stamford Bridge for a second time.

With Celine by my side, my first sighting of Leboeuf and Di Matteo came against Nottingham Forest on the first day of the Umbro Trophy - a four-team pre-season tournament held across a baking-hot August weekend on the banks of the River Trent.

The first sighting of Vialli came the next day, with the Italian introduced as a second-half substitute to the delight of a large Chelsea support as goals from Dennis Wise and Dan Petrescu saw Gullit's team lift the trophy with a 2-0 defeat of Ajax.

The new league campaign got under way with a 0-0 draw at The Dell in Southampton, in which Vialli hit the post with an overhead kick, followed by a 1-0 defeat of Middlesbrough in a midweek Stamford Bridge opener - an evening best remembered for an iconic celebration which saw scorer Di Matteo joined by Jody Morris, Dennis Wise, Dan Petrescu, Frank Leboeuf and Erland Johnsen to sit in front of the West Stand.

Coventry were dispatched 2-0 on the following Saturday with goals from Leboeuf and Vialli ensuring all three new men had now opened their Chelsea accounts, before a Highbury humdinger kept the unbeaten start going courtesy of some late drama in front of Arsenal's North Bank.

Leboeuf (6, pen), 1-0 Chelsea, get in; *"VIALLI, VIALLI, VIALLI"* (30), 2-0, my word; Merson (44), Keown (64), Wright (77), 2-3 Arsenal, bollocks; Wise (90), 3-3, away end bedlam.

So then, Gianluca Vialli...

Just a few days before his free transfer to Chelsea he had lifted the European Cup with Juventus and, at 31, still had plenty to offer.

In 325 Serie A games for Cremonese, Sampdoria and Juve he had scored 123 goals, in addition to the 16 he'd netted in 59 Italian appearances.

Just like Gullit the year before, he was a gold-standard signing attracted by the cosmopolitan lifestyle of west London as he chose Chelsea above a more lucrative financial offer from Glasgow Rangers.

With his puppy-dog eyes and penchant for a cheeky fag round the back of the stand, he was everything we could have wanted in a new hero and his two goals in four games had helped put Chelsea in fourth spot as they travelled to early leaders Sheffield Wednesday.

Dating back to their toe-to-toe promotion battle in 1983/84, Chelsea and Wednesday had largely followed similar trajectories - the odd spell competing at the top end of the top flight, followed by relegation, followed by another promotion to the top flight.

The only difference was that the Yorkshire club had put their hands on silverware - winning the League Cup in 1991 - but on September 7, 1996, goals from Craig Burley and Andy Myers gave Chelsea a solid 2-0 win and the two sides have rarely been on a level playing field since.

The Wednesday win moved Chelsea up to second before it was revealed that one of the greatest players of all time, Diego Maradona, was due to visit Stamford Bridge for the visit of Aston Villa.

In London at the invite of Vialli, the late Argentinian hand-ball merchant was set to watch the game from the stands but, surrounded by autograph hunters, quickly headed off to find entertainment elsewhere - a decision of particular disappointment for Villa's Andy Townsend, who for a brief period looked like being only the second-most despised man in the ground upon his latest return to Stamford Bridge.

The game ended 1-1, with Leboeuf again on target in reply to a Townsend free-kick, before Chelsea faced two games in the north-west in the space of four days.

A 4-1 first-leg win at Blackpool got the League Cup campaign off to a strong start, but if a reality check was in order then it came in a return to league action at Liverpool - a 5-1 defeat at the hands of one of the title favourites giving pause for thought.

The hiccup continued when League Cup embarrassment was narrowly avoided with a 3-1 second-leg defeat to Blackpool - an inauspicious start for new Norwegian goalkeeper Frode Grodas as Chelsea hung on to win 5-4 on aggregate - before I was given a clear indication that times were changing with the league visit of Nottingham Forest.

With redevelopment of the Shed end continuing and capacity capped at 28,000, we arrived to buy tickets around three hours ahead of kick-off only to discover the sold-out signs were already up. It meant, for the first time in my Chelsea-supporting life, that I was locked out for a league game. What a liberty.

Rewind 10 or 15 years and I could clearly recall a childhood fear of missing out if Chelsea were ever successful - 'FOMO', as it's now known by youth who haven't got time to type full words.

I'd look at what appeared to be sell-out crowds for league or cup winning sides at Anfield, Goodison Park or Old Trafford and wonder, with genuine childhood concern, if there would be room for me if ever we were them.

My dad would do his best to reassure, crushing my dreams with a reminder it wouldn't be something I was likely to have to worry about, but here we were - the first sign of a Chelsea side with genuine title-winning potential and I was standing miserable and ticketless outside Stamford Bridge.

Access was finally secured courtesy of a late deal with Fulham Broadway touts, but we found ourselves sitting at the top of the East Stand surrounded by what we now know as 'football tourists'.

"Where were they when we were shit?" we asked of many of those around us who - when it came to Chelsea - didn't know their Harris from their elbow.

The other sign of the growing popularity of football came in the form of Forest substitute Jason Lee, who at the time was best known for being the target of a song driven into the nation's consciousness by comedians David Baddiel and Frank Skinner.

From their studio sofa on their Friday night TV show Fantasy Football - a show launched on the back of the increasing gentrification of the national game - the pair had ridiculed the dreadlocked Lee's failings in front of goal with a song stating he had a 'pineapple on his head'.

For sketches that should never have seen the light of day, Baddiel would paint his skin black and wear the tropical fruit on his bonce to get laughs at the Forest man's expense.

It was hardly Bafta-winning comedy and Baddiel has since gone on record to apologise for his involvement, but it struck a chord with football fans and meant Lee was subjected to the song at every ground he visited.

By the time he made the trip to Chelsea Lee had shaved off his dreadlocks and was introduced as a second-half substitute. Naturally - with Chelsea season-ticket holder Baddiel almost certainly in the ground - it was his intended cross in the last minute that looped into the net to earn Forest a 1-1 draw. He who laughs last, etc, etc...

Away from Stamford Bridge, life around this time continued to move on at pace with the now-graduated Celine and I renting our first house together in south Northants.

One of four cluster homes that backed on to each other in a square block, it was - to be generous - intimate.

One highlight was a neighbour in her mid-30s who kept herself to herself, other than on Tuesday evenings when a bloke dressed in football training kit would call regular as clockwork to... smut alert... loudly knock some balls about. Twenty-five years on I like to think there is still a 60-year-old somewhere in south Northants popping out at 7pm every Tuesday - shin-pads and training bib tucked under his arm - as his wife suggests it's probably time he took up bowls...

But I digress.

Chelsea bounced back from the blips against Liverpool, Blackpool and Forest to win 3-1 at Leicester - Eddie Newton making his first appearance since a February leg-break as Vialli, Di Matteo and Hughes scored - but were immediately put back in their place by Wimbledon.

On the back of six successive wins, the Dons were dominant from the off and moved up to second in the table with a deserved 4-2 win; the likes of Marcus Gayle and Efan Ekoku getting the better of Frank Leboeuf and co before attention turned back to the League Cup and a tie at Bolton Wanderers.

"You're 40 now. In ten years' time when you're 50..."

"If still alive!"

"... do you envisage being chairman of Chelsea Football Club? Does the idea excite you?"

"I haven't really thought that far. If at some point the position was open and I was the right man for the job, then yes, I would consider it. Ken keeps threatening to outlive me anyway!"

The questions were being posed by Ross Fraser, editor of the Chelsea Independent fanzine.

The answers were being provided by Matthew Harding in an interview ahead of the 1994 FA Cup Final.

Just over two years later - as the night of Tuesday, October 22, 1996 ticked in to the early hours of Wednesday, October 23 - the words took on chilling new significance with the sudden and tragic death of Harding.

'If still alive'...

By the time he took his fatal helicopter journey home from the 2-1 defeat at Bolton, Harding - aged just 42 - had committed in the region of £26.5 million to Chelsea Football Club and had become vice chairman as he and Ken Bates continued to work towards a more united front.

The North Stand built with Harding's money was completed, and the development of the South Stand to replace the Shed terrace was under way.

On the pitch we were revelling in a team of established internationals purchased from across Europe - Italians, French, and a Romanian to name just a few.

Bates wanted to build Chelsea Village, Harding wanted to build Chelsea FC... the sad irony was that, despite the very public fallings out over control and direction, both men were on the path to fulfilling their ambitions.

Harding's chartered helicopter came down on farmland near Middlewich, Cheshire, just off the M6.

Also on board, also killed, was pilot Michael Goss, 38, and Harding's friends Raymond Deane, 43, John Bauldie, 47, and Tony Burridge, 39.

Five young lives lost; husbands, sons and fathers mourned.

Debris from the crash was spread across 400-yards, but a charred piece of paper with the word 'Burnden' written on it gave emergency services an immediate indication of the earlier movements of those on board - the 'Burnden' in question being the name of Bolton's home ground.

By the time the majority of Chelsea fans rubbed sleep from their eyes on the Wednesday morning the news had been confirmed; Matthew Harding - vice chairman of Chelsea Football Club and one of the 100 wealthiest people in the UK - was dead.

Every Chelsea fan of the time will remember where they were, and what they did, as the news was delivered.

I, stunned to the core, drove into work listening to radio reports and then spent the majority of the day taking calls from Chelsea friends in an act of shared grief.

If there was any doubt about Harding's standing not just at Chelsea but also in the wider game and the country, it came in the form of tributes from both Prime Minister John Major and opposition leader Tony Blair - Labour being the party of which Harding was both a supporter and significant benefactor.

Closer to home, Ruud Gullit spoke of his "depression", adding: "He [Harding] was a guy who wanted to be a player also, one of us, and was more like a supporter really than a director.

"He wanted it that way. I knew him for a short time but I will remember him for his laugh, happiness after a game and his enthusiasm about the club. He was really a Chelsea fan and this is something I would like to treasure."

Harding's friend and former manager Glenn Hoddle said: "It is almost unbelievable that the game should lose somebody who had so much to offer, who was so young and in such circumstances.

"Matthew made a considerable contribution to football and to Chelsea in particular, and still had a huge contribution to make in the future.

"He had a great enthusiasm for life, for football and Chelsea but he always said he wouldn't have done it for any other club. He'd only do it for Chelsea. If success is round the corner, the energy he put into the club will be a massive reason for it."

And Ken Bates, treading a tricky path based on their relationship, quickly announced the North Stand would be named in Harding's honour before adding: "Matthew's death does not, and will not, affect our future plans. Such was his devotion to the club that he ensured his promised financial commitments were totally in place, evidenced by the southern complex [of the stadium development] which is rising as we speak.

"It's the next phase of achieving his and all Chelsea fans' dream of having a world-class team and world-class stadium."

Harding's premature death came just days before a home game against Tottenham Hotspur, a fixture which the players agreed to fulfil in honour of his memory.

It was 100% the right decision.

First we went to the Stamford Bridge forecourt to view the sea of flowers, scarves and other tributes that had been placed in the preceding days in memory of one of our own. And from there we moved to the Ferret & Firkin in the Lots Road; pints of Guinness in honour of one of our own.

Among those in the pub being comforted by friends was Harding's partner Vicky, who would later take a seat at the front of the North Stand now named after him. In the director's box of the East Stand, meanwhile, would be Harding's wife Ruth.

The moments before kick-off were unlike anything anyone inside Stamford Bridge was ever likely to have witnessed at a football game before.

With Harding's smiling face adorning the front of the match programme, wreaths from both clubs were laid in the centre circle and a pint of Guinness was placed on the centre spot.

Dennis Wise and Steve Clarke carried out a floral message reading "Matthew RIP" and placed it in front of the Matthew Harding Stand.

The minute's silence was perfection, the ground not just silent but completely motionless; Tottenham fans as respectful and dignified as anyone wearing blue.

It was followed by a chorus of *"One Matthew Harding, there's only one Matthew Harding"* as, across the ground, tears flowed from many an eye.

But then the first whistle blew, and a team and ground raw with emotion gave it everything they had for Matthew.

He would, without question, have loved it.

Manager Gullit, making his first league start of the season as a player, led from the front - physically and mentally - before opening the scoring shortly before the half hour. A Roberto Di Matteo cross was headed onto the foot of the post by Mark Hughes and Gullit swivelled to knock the rebound beyond Ian Walker.

Chris Armstrong capitalised on a Kevin Hitchcock error to equalise, but a David Lee penalty and near-post sliding finish from Di Matteo gave the day the only result it deserved.

The one cloud on a near-perfect performance was a serious injury to the likeable Lee shortly ahead of the third goal; a leg-break that would keep him out for the season and effectively end his Chelsea career.

First rising to prominence in the 1988/89 promotion season, the defender and occasional midfielder was largely popular with the fans but struggled to hold down a regular spot as loan moves came and loan moves went before he finally found a mentor in Hoddle.

The appointment of Gullit, though, again stalled progress and it was the collision with Tottenham's Sol Campbell that would have the crucial last word - a great shame for a player that deserved more for his loyalty and commitment to the club.

Lee's injury, though, remained the sub-plot in post-match interviews as attention rightly turned back to tributes to Harding.

"It had nothing to do with getting three points. It was a perfect tribute to Matthew," Gullit said. "There was a special feeling and everyone responded in their own way."

Captain Dennis Wise, meanwhile, said: "We've just got to win something now, simple as that. We've got to go out and make his dream come true."

And so said all of us... RIP, Matthew Harding.

Next up for *"Matthew Harding's Blue and White Army"* was a trip to Manchester United to witness an iconic Vialli goal.

With Chelsea already one to the good through a Michael Duberry header, a ball over the top from Leboeuf found Vialli free in the United half.

With a little skip, and a little hop, he slid the ball through the legs of Peter Schmeichel before running to ecstatic Chelsea fans already working on the words of a new love song for their majestic number nine.

"When the ball hits the back of the Old Trafford net, it's Vialli...

"When his goals light the sky there's a tear in my eye, oh Vialli..."

United pulled one back, but it was of little relevance. On the back of two draining weeks following the death of Matthew Harding, Chelsea had responded in the best possible way with back-to-back wins.

Rarely, it has to be said, had there been such love or connection between team and fans... but there is always room for one more legend in a team of growing legends so, to the tune of Lola by the Kinks, away we go:

"If you want to know about taking the piss, go down to West Ham and ask Julian Dicks about Zola... la la la la Zola, la la la la Zola..."

Sitting alongside Scott and Stewie in the Upper Tier of the Matthew Harding Stand, I was directly in line as Gianfranco Zola picked up a pass from Mark Hughes 40 yards from the Shed-end goal; the shaven-headed Julian Dicks offering immediate attention.

Zola, eating up the yards, controlled it with the inside of his right foot, turned east and sent Dicks west.

Dicks... compass spinning, blood twisting, back-to-goal, face-to-goal... tried to square up again.

This time it was Zola that went west, flicking the ball between the legs of his punch-drunk opponent before drilling the ball past Ludek Miklosko.

The fleet-footed featherweight had floored the blundering heavyweight, and Stamford Bridge rose in joyous recognition of one of the great Chelsea goals of all time from what would become one of the great Chelsea signings of all time.

Zola had signed from Palma for £4.5 million in the days after the Old Trafford win in November but made a deceptively slow start, with a debut in a 1-1 draw at Blackburn followed by another draw at home to Newcastle and defeat at Leeds.

His first goal - a glorious 25-yard free-kick in a 2-2 home draw against Everton - gave confirmation of the talent we'd signed, but a heavy 3-0 defeat at Sunderland meant Chelsea picked up just three points from his first five games.

But then came the West Ham goal - the second in a 3-1 win which saw a young player named Frank Lampard come on as a late substitute for the visitors.

Zola made it four goals in four games with both in a 2-0 Boxing Day win at Villa Park and then - despite being man-marked by Peter Atherton - scored and created as Chelsea threw away a two-goal lead at home to Sheffield Wednesday.

"I prefer my wife," Zola told the press when quizzed about the close attention of Atherton, proving world-class talent doesn't always have to come at the cost of charm and personality.

But while Zola was taking the lead role, quietly departing Chelsea throughout November and December were a clutch of favourites of the recent past as John Spencer and Gavin Peacock made the short trip to Queen's Park Rangers, Mark Stein returned to Stoke City on loan and Terry Phelan headed back north to Everton.

Each had helped Chelsea on its upward curve across the past couple of seasons and each went with our best wishes, but each also knew - as much as we did - that as we entered a new year, we were also entering a new era.

And talking of new eras...

"So then, when are you going to ask me to marry you?"

Leaning back - pausing only to take a brief sip of a pint and a drag on a Marlboro Light - the response came naturally:

"I'll marry you sweetheart when Chelsea win the FA Cup."

There were several witnesses...

New Year's Eve was spent at a fancy dress party on the Isle of Wight at the invitation of Laura, Celine's best friend from university, and - despite being 'sort of Tottenham' - one of the kindest, warmest and most beautiful human beings you could ever wish to meet.

It was a brilliant night in brilliant company - a strong group of friends at the peak of their powers and all loving life - but waking early with a heavy head, any thoughts of potential proposals had already been cast aside as attention switched to the continuation of Chelsea's league campaign with the visit of Liverpool.

Aidy joined Scott and I on a freezing trip back across the Solent to witness a largely low-key, but well-earned, 1-0 defeat of the league leaders courtesy of a goal from Di Matteo.

Of most note, though, was the continued absence of Vialli for what was now a fifth successive league game as Gullit continued to put his faith in a Zola-Hughes partnership - a decision that would become a 'three into two often doesn't go' sub-plot for the remainder of the campaign as the relationship between manager and superstar striker became increasingly strained.

Vialli was again benched for the 3-0 FA Cup Third-Round defeat of West Brom, a 2-0 defeat at a struggling Nottingham Forest, and a 3-1 home defeat of Derby County for which he remained unused as Wise, Leboeuf from the penalty spot and latest youth team graduate Paul Hughes scored the goals.

With it now being eight games since the former Juve man had started a game the main headline from the routine win, the third goal coming after Derby were reduced to 10 men, came via a message from Wise to Vialli - the captain racing towards the bench following his goal to lift his shirt and reveal a message on his vest: "Cheer up Luca, we love you."

No-one among the 28,000 crowd was in disagreement.

Fast-forward a week though and Vialli was back in the starting 11 for the FA Cup Fourth-Round clash against Liverpool; a game in which he missed the best of the home side's few first-half chances before regaining favour for his central role in the stunning second-half comeback.

But while his part in one of the most joyous 45 minutes ever witnessed at Stamford Bridge confirmed there was room for him alongside both Hughes and Zola, Gullit benched the Italian once more for the return to league action at Tottenham.

So while Vialli was captured by the television cameras having a cigarette in the White Hart Lane tunnel, it was Di Matteo that caught the eye with a stunning 30-yard strike that was becoming his trademark.

The screamer - doubling Chelsea's lead after Sol Campbell had bundled a Zola free-kick into his own net in the first minute - sparked delirium in the away end as the swingometer of football powerhouses further continued its graceful glide from north to west London.

Across a thin line of segregation to my right, the *see you outside*' and throat-slitting gestures from the home support were met with derision; the Tottenham fans again failing to realise that the only thing we enjoy more than beating them is laughing at them.

But back to Di Matteo.

A Swiss-born Italian international, the classy midfielder was a key part of the clockwork that made this Chelsea team tick.

Possessing strength in the tackle, vision for a pass, and an eye for a spectacular goal, the £4.9m former Lazio man was again on target as Chelsea let a two-goal lead slip in the FA Cup Fifth Round at Leicester before he lined up for a much-anticipated visit of latest league leaders Manchester United at Stamford Bridge.

A capacity crowd of 28,336 was present at the Bridge for the clash against Alex Ferguson's team, but I wasn't among them.

I can't now remember why I didn't get a ticket, but it must have been for good reason being - as it was - one of only a handful of games I missed throughout the season.

What I do recall, however, is that whatever was initially deemed so important to keep me away was no longer an issue as the game approached because, on the day before the match, I was frantically calling round mates in an unsuccessful bid to pick up a spare ticket.

As a fruitless Friday drifted into a stressful Saturday I was getting ready to travel down regardless when - playing on my lack of will-power - Celine fluttered her eye-lashes, whispered sweet nothings and persuaded me to spend the day with her instead.

So, with the first 10 minutes of the day satisfactorily accounted for, it was then a question of what to do next...

"Let's look at buying a house," said Celine.

"I don't want to buy a house."

"I've seen a lovely cottage, let's see if we can get a late viewing. It will be fun."

"It won't be fun. And I'm not buying a house…"

"Let's just look…"

"I'm not buying a house."

So as Gianfranco Zola spectacularly blazed Chelsea into a second-minute lead - pulling back the ball on the byline to send Dennis Irwin into the Shed-end building site, dance through what was left of the dazed United defence and fire in at Peter Schmeichel's near post - I was knocking on the door of an 18th-century, stone-built, two-up two-down with 'a compact courtyard and period features'.

By the time United equalised in the second-half through a stunning David Beckham volley, an offer for the £48,000 asking price had been submitted and Celine was already measuring for curtains.

We'd bought a house. Which in turn meant that fewer than two years later we'd be key witnesses in criminal court proceedings, I'd be fighting in the street, and we'd be looking to move on again.

I'll fill in the blanks later, but for now take my advice…always go to Chelsea - it keeps you out of trouble.

FA Cup progression was secured with a fortuitous extra-time defeat of Leicester to put Chelsea in the quarter finals for the fourth time in six years, before - mortgage application now under way - I saw Chelsea drop to seventh in the table with a 3-2 defeat at Derby's Baseball Ground.

While the loss meant Chelsea remained on the outer fringes of the European qualification places, of greater concern was an ankle-injury to Gullit that threatened to rule him out for what remained of the season.

Coming on as a second-half substitute for Vialli, who had replaced Zola in the starting line-up, the player-boss lasted little over 15 minutes before limping off a joke of a pitch lacking the basics of grass.

With Eddie Newton also picking up an injury ahead of the game in the East Midlands, the priority was no further loss to the treatment table as a 1-1 home draw to Blackburn started a run of six games in 18 days.

That one small requirement was, at least, successfully met in order to provide Chelsea with enough fit options for a trip to

Portsmouth's Fratton Park for an FA Cup last-eight clash.

On a foggy day on the south coast, Chelsea brushed past a Pompey team chasing promotion to the top flight with unexpected ease - the 4-1 win offering further evidence of the new-found confidence and expectation running through the club.

With an FA Cup semi-final spot secured for the second-successive year the league inevitably became of secondary importance... but that didn't prevent a couple of classics, followed by a worrying dip in form.

First, Chelsea lost a five-goal thriller at West Ham.

A Mark Hughes equaliser in the 87th minute looked to have secured a share of the spoils before debutant goalkeeper Nick Colgan was beaten by Paul Kitson in the dying seconds - the goal sparking much bubble-blowing delight for the relegation-threatened, Lonsdale-loving East End supporters.

Zola, Frank Sinclair, Dan Petrescu, Mark Hughes (twice) and Di Matteo then found the net as Sunderland were dismissed in a 6-2 romp that saw England 1990 World Cup wing-back Paul Parker begin a brief stay at the Bridge as a second-half substitute, before Zola was again on target in a 1-0 defeat of Southampton.

But then came the bump...

Back up to the fifth-place spot that would secure European qualification via the league, the predictable unpredictables imploded - losing 1-0 at fellow FA Cup semi-finalists and relegation-threatened Middlesbrough, 3-0 in an 11.15am home humbling to Arsenal, and 3-1 at Coventry City.

Kick-off was delayed for the midweek game at Coventry's Highfield Road with referee Dermot Gallagher declaring Chelsea's royal blue strip clashed with the sky blue/navy blue stripes of the home side.

When the teams did eventually appear Chelsea found themselves in the home side's away shirts of red and navy checks; the reason for the visitors being told to wear the Coventry kit rather than the home side simply swapping colours remaining as much a mystery today as it did then.

Paul Hughes became the first and last Chelsea player to score for Chelsea while wearing the colours of Coventry, but Dion Dublin, Paul Williams, and Noel Whelan put the home side in control with three quick second-half goals.

Even the introduction of substitute Vialli, who had asked for "human respect" from Gullit following criticism of his performance in the Arsenal game, failed to spark any life into a struggling

Chelsea side who were due to face Wimbledon in a Highbury FA Cup semi-final just four days later.

"You're shit, and you know you are," taunted the Coventry support.

"We're shit, cos we're in your kit," replied the away fans; the humour failing to disguise the fact that, in reality, the home support had perfectly summarised the evening's performance.

But we of little faith...

The losing run came to an end as Wimbledon were swept aside in stunning fashion in the north London semi-final sunshine; the 3-0 win secured with limited cause for concern as Chelsea booked a place in the FA Cup Final for the fifth time in their 92-year history and second time in four seasons.

With lowly Middlesbrough or the even lowlier Chesterfield meeting in the second semi-final, the feeling as we celebrated long after the final whistle was that we'd never get a better chance to add to our single 1970 cup success.

And just as in '94 when I'd wanted to face Manchester United in the final ahead of the potentially more winnable option of Oldham, this time I was hoping for Middlesbrough rather than Chesterfield.

The north Derbyshire minnows had been on a headline-grabbing cup run but - just like Oldham - they were not a team I'd ever dreamt of beating in an FA Cup final.

To be fair, neither were Middlesbrough, but with their own foreign legion of Italian Fabrizio Ravanelli and Brazilians Juninho and Emerson, they felt like a more enticing prospect when compared to all the focus being on the Chesterfield 'fairy tale'.

And, that aside, even the very thought of losing the final to a team from the third tier would have been enough to consider a weekend break at Dignitas...

As it turned out the Swiss-based death squad would have to wait another day for my business, but it was a close-run thing - Chesterfield having a legitimate goal ruled out in a 3-3 draw hours after Chelsea had secured their spot in the final, before losing the replay 3-0.

With fans' focus turning to securing a much-valued Wembley ticket, Chelsea then turned in an 'after the Lord Mayor's Show' performance to lose 3-1 at Newcastle and effectively cancel the insurance policy of qualifying for European football via the league route.

The first league points in five games finally came with a 2-1 win against Leicester before Wimbledon were seen off once more via a 1-0 Chelsea win at Selhurst Park.

That left just a 0-0 draw at home to Leeds United and a final-day 2-1 win at Everton ahead of the biggest game, and potentially the biggest decision, of my life…

CHAPTER FOURTEEN
FA CUP FINAL

Chelsea v Middlesbrough
Wembley Stadium
Saturday, May 17, 1997

Chelsea: Grodas, Petrescu, Leboeuf, Clarke, Hughes, Wise, Di Matteo, Minto, Sinclair, Newton, Zola (Vialli, 89).

Middlesbrough: Roberts, Pearson, Emerson, Mustoe (Vickers, 29), Juninho, Ravanelli (Beck, 24), Fleming, Blackmore, Festa, Stamp, Hignett (Kinder, 74).

Referee: Steve Lodge (Barnsley)
Attendance: 79,160

Martin was peeling potatoes.

It was five hours before the biggest Chelsea game in a generation, and Scott's Uncle Martin was sitting in front of the television casually peeling a huge bowl of potatoes.

It struck me as odd.

I'd spent the week bouncing around like a toddler on acid, unable to focus on anything - literally anything - other than the countdown to 3pm on Saturday, May 17; the countdown to Chelsea v Middlesbrough; the countdown to the 1997 FA Cup Final at Wembley Stadium, London.

I'd become obsessive-compulsive about my ticket, hiding it in a safe place that non-existent burglars wouldn't find but then constantly checking it was still there, and then checking again to check I hadn't lost it when I last checked it was still there.

On the Wednesday, a whole three days before the game, I started placing post-it notes around the house with a single word written on each - 'Ticket'. The notes were a reminder not to forget that priceless piece of paper amid the gut-wrenching anxiety of the morning of the game.

And there was Martin casually peeling potatoes.

But, in fairness, he had been there before.

He was a member of the lucky generation above that had seen Chelsea win major silverware.

He had his memories, albeit from the Seventies, when Ossie and Co restored our pride.

He was already a Chelsea cup winner, already in possession of ribbon-wrapped stories to pass on to children and grand-children.

And at that precise moment, the only thing I wanted from the world - absolutely the only thing I wanted - was to finally have what Martin had.

We'd called at his Acton home to leave Scott's car in a safe place for the weekend.

Martin would later make the short trip from home to Wembley by bus and tube, but we were heading into London to give the day the full Cup Final treatment - drinks, mates, tube to Wembley Park, and the cliched, but unmissable, walk up Wembley Way.

Celine and Yvette were with us for the weekend and they would be watching the game at Stamford Bridge while we headed off to Wembley, so our first stop after leaving Acton was to dump bags at a hotel we'd booked for the night near Paddington station.

And from there it was to Great Portland Street, where the serious business of the day would begin.

As we travelled through London there was a huge feel-good factor in the air.

It was a glorious day with the temperature in the mid-20s. Labour - as expected - had won the General Election at a canter just over two weeks previously and, just two days after that, the UK had even won the Eurovision Song Contest for the first time since 1981.

Love Shine a Light by Katrina and the Waves wasn't exactly to my taste, but it captured the positive spirit sweeping the country in the May of '97 - the Cool Britannia period now at the peak of its powers; a feeling that the Great was back in Britain.

'Love shine a light in every corner of my heart
'Let the love light carry, let the love light carry
'Light up the magic in every little part
'Let our love shine a light in every corner of our hearts'

As we walked through the doors of the Greene Man, Stewie was already there. As was Jan and his brother Kim, and other recognisable faces from across the years. All old enough to have suffered the pain, all young enough to still be seeking the same debut trophy dream.

We settled the nerves with drink - just enough to enjoy the experience, not too much to cloud our focus on the day ahead.

And then one of our group revealed the banner; perhaps 15ft in width, 3ft in height, with four yellow words sewn onto its royal blue background.

It simply said: 'WIN IT FOR MATTHEW'

As we stood outside posing for pictures with the banner, the banner made in honour of Matthew Harding, a bride and groom walked by.

Her dress and his suit were adorned with red and white in honour of their support of Middlesbrough.

"Some people will do anything to get on the telly," Stewie shouted after them to laughter from us.

But the moment made me feel temporarily uncomfortable, and I turned to Celine to see if I could gather her thoughts.

What began as a cheap gag from me had for the past few weeks been at the centre of conversation with family and friends, and everyone had the same question:

"Seriously, if Chelsea do win, are you going to propose?"

With two hours to kick-off, the honest answer was that I still didn't have a clue.

But, as we prepared to say our goodbyes, I did know one thing... every single thing about Celine was perfect...

Her flowing hair, her green eyes, her electric smile and her luscious laugh... the point on her neck that makes her giggle when kissed... the dimple in her nose that housed a former piercing... and the single, lengthy hair wrap that had survived the transition from student to teacher. Now decorated blue and white, it was a personalised Chelsea bar scarf that she'd modified just for me.

"You're gorgeous", I half-said half-sang, quoting the Babybird song that had become one of ours.

And with that, I disappeared into Great Portland Street station.

We jump on the northbound Metropolitan line and everything immediately steps up another gear.

The number of fans multiplies, the number of police watching our every move intensifies, the decibels rise.

It's just three stops: Baker Street, Finchley Road and Wembley Park.

And then we pile out of the tube, heartbeats rising, singing our songs.

"FLYING HIGH UP IN THE SKY, WE'LL KEEP THE BLUE FLAG FLYING HIGH; FROM STAMFORD BRIDGE TO WEMBER-LEY, WE'LL KEEP THE BLUE FLAG FLYING HIGH."

We walk out the station concourse and down the steps; we step on to Wembley Way, at the top of which the Twin Towers stand tall, looking over the day's adventure.

I think of Arsenal, Leeds, Sunderland and Liverpool. Of West Ham, Southampton, Manchester United and Ipswich Town. Of Tottenham, Everton, Coventry and Wimbledon... Coventry and bloody Wimbledon... two of the 12 different teams that have lifted the cup in the 27 years since Chelsea's only success.

I can't contemplate the thought of Middlesbrough making it an unlucky 13. Today's day simply has to be Chelsea's day. It simply has to be.

As we walk up Wembley Way the magnetic forces start to pull red and blue apart, Chelsea easing to the right and 'Boro to the left as we prepare to make our way around the stadium to our respective turnstiles. As we separate both sets of fans become braver, the songs and gestures edgier through the safety net of unofficial segregation.

It's a reminder that we've got history with 'Boro.

They relegated us in '88 in a game that ended with a pitch invasion and violence, and they clashed with us again at the tin-pot Zenith Data Systems Cup Final in 1990.

Lose today, I think, and there will be trouble again.

But then I refocus on the matter in hand.

At the top of Wembley Way I hug Scott, wish him luck and arrange where to meet after the game.

Our respective tickets aren't together. I'll be with Stewie, which is great, but I won't be with my best mate - a thought that saddens me but is quickly brushed aside as I move on to head through the turnstiles.

Inside the concourse is heaving. Wembley is a ground built for pre-war football that is glamorous in name only, but it's still the ultimate English football experience and we force our way through the singing, swinging, drink-happy Chelsea fans to move back out of the shadows and into the sunlit colosseum.

Block 133, row eight. Our seats are low, a little too low for my liking, to the right of the post behind the goal; bucket seats amateurishly bolted on to terrace in the post-Taylor Report rush to convert Wembley to an all-seater stadium.

But what we now have is no safer than what went before. The

total opposite in fact, because these backless 'seats' aren't designed for sitting so we'll probably be standing all game, standing on thousands of man-made trip hazards where once a much safer terrace stood.

And we are standing on the seats at 2.45pm, holding aloft the 'WIN IT FOR MATTHEW' banner, when Sir Cliff Richard leads us in traditional Cup Final hymn.

"Abide with me; fast falls the eventide.

"The darkness deepens; Lord, with me abide..."

And we are standing on our seats roaring at 2.50pm when Ruud Gullit and Bryan Robson lead the Chelsea and Middlesbrough teams on the long walk from the Wembley tunnel to sing the National Anthem... *"God save our gracious Queen, Long live our noble Queen..."* and to be presented to Their Royal Highnesses the Duke and Duchess of Kent.

The presentation, much to our amusement, is made to a backdrop of protests from the 'Boro end as their fans vent their collective spleen at the FA over a three-point penalty for failing to fulfil a Premier League fixture which ultimately led to their relegation.

And we are still standing on our seats at 3pm when referee Steve Lodge puts the whistle to his lips and signals for Middlesbrough to get the game under way, attacking the end in which we are gathered.

Fabrizio Ravanelli is first to touch the ball, knocking it back to Brazilian midfielder Emerson.

From there, four successive balls across the 'Boro back-line before a long ball down the right from Clayton Blackmore to Juninho, the Teessiders' talented answer to Gianfranco Zola.

But Steve Clarke gets there first; the first Chelsea touch of the day putting the ball out for a throw.

From the resultant ball back into play 'Boro put two or three short passes together before Dennis Wise dispossesses Robbie Mustoe.

We give a little cheer, the first minor duel of the day won by Chelsea.

Wise plays square to Di Matteo on the edge of the centre circle, in the Chelsea half, not Middlesbrough's.

From behind we can see Di Matteo running into a gap that has opened up.

One touch, two touches, three then four, gracefully eating up yards of Wembley turf ...

Twenty-five yards from goal he looks set to take a fifth, but reconsiders and pulls his right boot back for a hopeful early shot.

But as ball leaves boot we realise it's not hopeful, it's looping.

And in the Middlesbrough goal Ben Roberts looks in trouble.

He leaps with both hands, back arched, but he can't get a touch.

We're watching from afar, eyes wide open, waiting to see what happens next.

And what happens next is the ball thumps the underside of the bar, drops, and hits the back of the Wembley net.

And then... nothing, absolutely nothing.

For a split second everything goes blank.

Everything is blank until I become aware of Stewie screaming in my face.

I scream back, a look of disbelief from us both followed by laughter and swearing; quite a lot of celebratory swearing.

I don't know how long the celebrations last, but when I next look at the pitch the game is back under way.

I run my hands through my hair, try to compose myself and look at the scoreboard... which says 'Chelsea 0 Middlesbrough 0'.

"Chelsea 0? Eh? What? Eh?"

I look around for confirmation. Was the goal given?

"Yes, yes..." people say, "yes...well, I think so..."

I continue to stare at the scoreboard, and then - with a single digital click - it changes.

'Chelsea 1 Middlesbrough 0'.

Another cheer, a cheer of relief, followed by a song of belief:

"When Wise goes up, to lift the FA Cup we'll be there, we'll be there," we bellow en masse.

The game is passing me by in a blur, I can't focus on what's happening; head spinning, heart beating trying to remind myself that there is a long way - a very long way - to go, but then I'm stretching in anticipation again as Scott Minto goes close, latching on to a Di Matteo through-ball that Roberts blocks.

"Carefree wherever you may be, we are the famous CFC..."

Everything still seems to be 100-miles-per-hour, but someone with a greater capacity than me to think straight draws comparison between Di Matteo's shot and one from Gavin Peacock in the 1994 final against Manchester United.

On that occasion Chelsea were on top when Peacock, from pretty much the same spot as Di Matteo, hit a near identical looping shot at the same goal with the score at 0-0.

That one hit the bar and came back ahead of a 4-0 defeat; this one hit the bar and went in.

The difference between glory and failure, he accurately notes, is about three inches.

Another difference between glory and failure is good fortune, and on 25 minutes 'Boro produce their first chance when Ravanelli tries to get on to the end of a dangerous Juninho ball but is blocked by Frank Sinclair.

But as he is blocked he's already signalling, telling the Middlesbrough bench that he can't continue as he suffers a re-occurrence of a back problem that threatened his place in the starting 11.

We cruelly cheer his misfortune, our good fortune, with realisation that their dangerous front man is to be replaced by the slightly less dangerous Mikkel Beck.

But even as Ravanelli is being treated Chelsea go close again, with Dan Petrescu looping an effort that is cleared from beneath the bar.

Hands back through hair, the pace refusing to relent, I think that we should already be out of sight.

It's too early for negative thoughts, but it's the default setting for any Chelsea fan.

"I want another before half-time," I say.

As I speak there is another boost for Chelsea with Robbie Mustoe going off injured to be replaced by Steve Vickers, the second forced change in five minutes.

"COME ON CHELSEA, COME ON CHELSEA, COME ON CHELSEA..."

'Boro's game-plan is having to be re-written, but the changes disrupt Chelsea too and the next significant action is not until the stroke of half-time when Zola goes close with a free-kick.

From the resultant Chelsea corner, easily gathered by Roberts, 'Boro quickly break forward and force a corner of their own. Half-cleared it falls to Stamp, whose cross to the back-post is headed home by an unmarked Festa.

Roars from the 'Boro end, but from the Chelsea end too - the linesman flags early and we see it go up before the ball hits the net. We know the goal won't stand.

It is close though, far too close for comfort in a game that could already be over.

Half-time is much welcomed, and as we gather our thoughts we talk of Di Matteo's goal.

Is it the quickest FA Cup Final goal ever? No one is sure, but we can't think of a quicker one.

"What a fucking goal though," we laugh, finally having the time to give it our full consideration.

But then we start to worry again. Despite being relegated and losing the League Cup final just a month earlier, this is a decent Middlesbrough team that won its most recent league clash against Chelsea.

There's a danger, we still feel, that the football Gods owe them a favour after a disappointing campaign. And they may have lost Ravanelli but they still have Juninho, their Brazilian boy wonder playing his final game - a headline in the making.

And as the second half settles it is Juninho that brings the first moment of note, breaking into space towards the edge of the penalty area before he is brought down by Di Matteo.

It's a yellow for the Chelsea man and a worthy one, bringing the danger to an end at the expense of a free-kick that leads to nothing.

I don't like the way it's going though, and I want Chelsea to retake control, show more composure.

I'm clearly not alone as the songs have eased off now, the atmosphere has dipped; everyone too nervous to focus on anything other than the game.

As we go past the hour-mark Leboeuf stumbles on a long throw into the box and Festa pounces, knocking the ball narrowly wide.

"Fucksake Frank," half of Wembley quietly but nervously mutters.

It's a warning, but Leboeuf redeems himself with a late tackle to extinguish another 'Boro threat and then Clarke is called into action to do the same.

I can't take much more, nerves shredded. We're less than 20 minutes now from winning the cup, that lifelong dream of winning the cup.

But in an increasingly rare attack Zola weaves through the 'Boro back line, beats three, gets to the byline and cuts back....

"Go on Franco, go on Franco..."

He gets his shot away, but this time it's not to be and Roberts blocks at the near post.

Now there's just over 10 to go. Middlesbrough have replaced Craig Hignett with Vladimir Kinder for their final switch of the game and stewards are starting to line the front of the stands.

I don't care about a second now. I'll be happy - ecstatically happy - to let the record books show the score of the 1997 FA Cup Final as Chelsea 1 (Di Matteo, 1) Middlesbrough 0.

But 'Boro are now taking greater risks and Juninho plays a quick free-kick to release Vickers who, one on one, is thwarted by the legs of Frode Grodas in the Chelsea goal.

Chelsea need our support and we try to roar them over the line...

"CHELSEA, CHELSEA, CHELSEA, CHELSEA, CHELSEA, CHELSEEEA, CHELSEA..." is the ageless war cry that we offer from the stands before it fades out and rolls into another songbook classic.

"CAREFREE WHEREVER YOU MAY BE, WE ARE THE FAMOUS CFC..."

But as the songs ease off again Eddie Newton continues a brief period of Chelsea possession by picking up the ball in the centre of the park.

Moving forward he pushes it right to Dan Petrescu just inside the box.

The Romanian, who has had such a good game, floats a cross to the far post.

And there, as if by magic, unseen to us and unseen to 'Boro, is Zola who - ice cool in the heat of battle - flicks the ball in to the heart of the six-yard box with the back of his right heel.

And now our mouths are open, ready for the moment, as we can see that continuing his run to meet the bouncing ball is Newton - our local lad, Chelsea since a boy - to bundle it home with the inside of his left foot.

And that, just like that, is that.

Chelsea, for the first time in my lifetime, for the first time since 1971, have won a major trophy.

Chelsea have won the 1997 Football Association Challenge Cup.

To my surprise though, this time my celebration is, if anything, a little muted.

I manage to stay on my feet, hug Stewie, hug an unknown woman in the row behind, but it's all too overwhelming.

As Zola, Newton and Wise celebrate right in front of us, I'm like a marathon runner that has stumbled across the winning line; bent double, hands on knees, gasping for breath.

But as I pull myself back up straight - shoulders back, chest out, looking up to the blue sky above - I can feel the ghosts of past failures already starting to rise into the air.

It's a mental cleansing, a reset button.

Everything will be better now, the future will be brighter, and our smiles are beyond wide as we break into our first song as cup winners.

"We love you Chelsea, we do, we love you Chelsea, we do, we love you Chelsea, we do, oh Chelsea we love you..."

And on the back of that, for the first time with certainty rather than hope:

"When Wise goes up, to lift the FA Cup we'll be there, we'll be there..."

And then, goosebumps visibly rising on my arms:

"We shall not we shall not be moved, we shall not we shall not be moved, until we win the FA Cup we shall not be moved..."

And then, again, but louder:

"WE SHALL NOT WE SHALL NOT BE MOVED, WE SHALL NOT WE SHALL NOT BE MOVED, UNTIL WE WIN THE FA CUP WE SHALL NOT BE MOVED..."

Meanwhile, down on the bench, Ruud Gullit is instructing Gianluca Vialli to get ready for action.

We spot it in the stands and roar our bald-headed hero's name.

"VIALLI, VIALLI, VIALLI, VIALLI..."

It's a nice touch by Gullit. His relationship with Luca has been strained but he knows what this means to him, and he knows what it means to us.

And when he does come on, he replaces Zola - Italian God replacing Italian God.

Again, it's a nice touch by Gullit, allowing us to show our appreciation to both men, men that we adore, before the final-whistle group celebrations overshadow individual talents.

The game is still going on in front of us, but no-one is paying any attention as we count down the seconds to the final whistle and sing it again.

"WHEN WISE GOES UP, TO LIFT THE FA CUP WE'LL BE THERE, WE'LL BE THERE..."

And after the final whistle has gone and after we've thrown our arms in the air and after we've cheered and after we've hugged and after the players have celebrated in front of us, Wise does go up to lift the FA Cup.

And we are there.

Cup in arms, blue and white ribbons wrapped around its handles, the players then come back to jump and dance and jig some more, and the celebrations go on, and on, and on.

For 15 minutes, 30 minutes, 45 minutes, perhaps an hour, we party into the late afternoon Wembley sunshine.

We sing *'Blue is the Colour'* and *'Chelsea, Chelsea',* the magnificent cup final song penned by Chelsea fan Suggs.

"We've waited so long, but we'd wait forever,

"Our blood is blue and we would leave you never,

"And when we make it, it'll be together...

"Oh oh oh...

"Chelsea, Chelsea; Chelsea, Chelsea,

"We're gonna make this a Blue Day..."

The perfect song for the perfect day, when Robbie and Co restored our pride.

And then, finally, we walk out of Wembley as cup winners.

I walk around to the top of Wembley Way and meet Scott, his dad, and his brother Sean. Ken, Paul and Gaz are there too, and Paul and Mary.

We hug, we pat backs, we celebrate the moment, everyone buzzing; everyone talking across one another but pretty much making the same excited comments.

I take a moment to think of Dad and my brother Andrew. They couldn't get tickets and I now realise how much I'm missing them as I am surrounded by friends celebrating with their families.

They are watching at home with my Uncle Des, the man who first took my Dad to Stamford Bridge back in the 1950s. All three deserve to be here but have missed out due to thousands of tickets being given to the wider 'football family' that the FA so loves on Cup Final day.

As I pull myself from my moment of melancholy we take photos beneath the Twin Towers and then set off for the tube back to Stamford Bridge.

It's a celebratory journey with the tube packed all the way, but as we get closer to SW6 the ice is broken and the question on everyone's lips is finally asked.

"Got the ring ready then Jase?"

"Maybe," I say, trying to laugh it off, to brush it aside, but also knowing - for want of a better phrase - that shit has just got real.

We pull into Fulham Broadway and walk on to the street.

It's a heaving mass of celebration.

However many fans we had at Wembley, there are three, four, perhaps even five times as many here.

We walk down the Fulham Road and past Stamford Bridge, the new home of the FA Cup winners.

We turn right down Holmead Road and left on to the King's Road, briefly pausing to take a look at the Imperial Arms so loved by Matthew Harding.

"One Matthew Harding, there's only one Matthew Harding," we sing not for the first or last time today.

The Imperial, like every other familiar pub we pass, is heaving with well-oiled punters spilling out the doors and on to the streets and it's clear those of us returning from Wembley will be playing catch-up into the evening.

Now desperate to see Celine - and desperate for my first celebratory pint - I finally turn on to the Lots Road and make the walk down to the Ferret & Firkin pub that sits beneath the shadow of the power station.

There, waiting for me outside, fresh from watching the game in Drake's bar at Stamford Bridge and looking even more beautiful than she did when I left her six hours earlier, is the love of my life.

"I've just won the cup!" I say. "Give me a kiss."

As we catch up on our respective days and have a first drink, one by one everyone else arrives - those I was with at Wembley and those friends I'd missed.

And as each individual arrives they nod in my direction and ask the same question: "Has he done it yet?"

As one pint leads to four the only person not to mention it is Celine, the only one that matters.

It's all good natured, jovial banter that I knock back for as long as I can, but as the sun starts to set on the celebratory scene I know the time has come... I need to get Celine on my own.

I wait until she next gets up to go inside the pub.

"Back in a minute," she says, opening my door of opportunity.

Giving her a couple of seconds to walk ahead, I then get up and follow.

And as she steps through the door I tap her on the shoulder, the two of us alone for the first time.

"Wait there," I say, "I want to say something."

She stops, and those gorgeous green eyes look straight at me with expectation.

As nervous as I have ever been in my life, I search for the right words.

"You know I love you, don't you..."

A nod of confirmation.

"And I think you know that I want to spend the rest of my life with you..."

A half smile and tilt of the head, less confident than her response to my first statement.

"...well, I do," I continue, "and... so...but... here's the thing..."

Deep breath.

"I'm not going to ask you to marry me; not today, not yet."

She looks without response.

It's clear she wants more, I'm going to have to keep talking.

"I just, I just don't think it's fair on you," I mumble like a poor man's Hugh Grant, now not sure what's going to come out of my mouth next.

"Because when I do ask you, and I'm sure I will ask you, one day, I want it to be special... just you and me...

"And...and... to be honest, I don't want to be that bloke who proposed just because Chelsea won the cup. That's, well, that's a bit pathetic... Isn't it...??"

The question hangs in the air, our eyes locked, but eventually she speaks.

"Well... it was you that said you would..."

Ouch.

"But OK, I think I know what you are trying to say. Now... I'm going to the loo so go and get me another drink."

She smiles as she goes but she's a little hurt, that much is clear.

I feel terrible. I've misjudged the moment, and to avoid making it worse I now desperately need to tell the others to knock it on the head to spare further embarrassment.

I need to tell them it's not happening tonight, tell them I've spoken to Celine, and politely ask them to please stop asking.

As I return from the bar I see that Celine is already back outside, sitting on the kerb.

I approach but then notice Sean standing in the middle of the road, calling for silence from everyone gathered around.

"What's he doing?" I ask, as I sit down next to Celine.

But I don't have to wait for an answer...

"This man," he says, pointing at me.

"Told this woman," he says, pointing at Celine.

"That he'd ask her to marry him if Chelsea won the cup..."

Oh. For fuck's sake.

FA Cup Final result

Chelsea 2 Middlesbrough 0

CHAPTER FIFTEEN
1997/1998

She said yes.

Still sitting on the kerb in the Lots Road, Celine declared that the man she wanted to spend the rest of her life with was the drunken fool kneeling in the gutter with a fresh pint in his hand.

She declared that the man she wanted to spend the rest of her life with was the idiot who only moments earlier had told her this wasn't going to happen.

Any other woman would have said no.

But playing to the celebrating crowd filling the street, her acceptance came to a backdrop of cheers, sprayed beers and song offering guidance on the use of celery as a sex aid.

"Celery, celery, if she don't cum then tickle her bum with a lump of celery…"

A more ridiculous proposal you will struggle to find but, if nothing else, with thanks to Sean it was more original than the banks of the Seine.

Drink was thrust upon us by friends new and old; a bottle of champagne - also, I think, thanks to Sean - among the many pleasant surprises to appear.

The revelry lasted into the night when, without explanation, it was brought to an abrupt end by the police - the Met deciding that the best way to disperse the thousands of happily celebrating fans in the bars and streets around Stamford Bridge was to close all the pubs.

It was a ridiculous decision, only ever likely to incite trouble rather than prevent it but - despite the protests - the majority eventually dispersed peacefully rather than end the greatest of days on a sour note.

For Celine and I, along with Scott and Yvette, it was back to the hotel where we'd dumped our bags many hours previously to continue the celebrations.

At this point I think it's worth pointing out that I have three basic life rules that have largely served me well over the years. You'll thank me, I promise.

First, always have a coat to hand when there is an 'R' in the month. The temperature can fluctuate even in September or April, so it's better to be safe than sorry.

Secondly, never drink in a flat-roofed pub. This should require no further explanation, but if your local lacks the basics of a pitched-roof then I am afraid it is unlikely we can ever be true friends.

Finally, and most importantly, never sleep anywhere that requires you to put your shoes on to take a piss.

This is a rule primarily aimed at ensuring I never go camping - a pastime I will never understand as long as we have easy access to accommodation with clean bedding and running water in any destination of sensible choice.

It also, however, sets a minimum standard when staying in hotels.

On which point, here follows a brief review of the Paddington hotel which accepted our booking for the night of May 17, 1997...

Located on a garden square surrounded by Grade II Listed Edwardian buildings, it looked perfectly respectable from the front and the reception area caused no undue reason for alarm when we paid a fleeting visit to dispose of our bags at the start of the Cup Final day.

It was, though, a pig in lipstick as our room consisted solely of - in no particular order - a flea-bitten bed, bars on the window, a single paper napkin on the pillow (sans case) and a shower with cold-running hose but no head.

It was immediately obvious that our mistake had been booking for the night, not the hour.

For the first time in my life the 'shoes/piss' test had spectacularly failed, so Celine and I spent our first night as an engaged couple fully clothed with one eye open checking for rats.

We said we'd laugh about it one day. And perhaps one day we still will.

The following morning saw a sleep-deprived return to the Fulham Road where, at the junction of Harwood Road and Fulham Broadway, we stood on tip-toe to catch another glimpse of the cup and sing more songs in honour of our Chelsea heroes as they took an open-top bus to Fulham Town Hall.

In the week that followed Celine and I joined my family for a few days in Bournemouth where, with the essential ingredient of a ring now in my possession, I proposed again... just the two of us, alone, under the light of the moon.

It still wasn't the banks of the Seine, but it was a step up from a Lots Road gutter.

And then, one week on from the FA Cup Final, I was joined by Celine and my family for a quick return to Wembley where we met Aidy for Northampton Town's Third Division Play-off Final against Swansea City.

Whereas Chelsea had scored after 42 seconds a week previously, a Northampton team backed by 32,000 fans had to wait until the last kick of the game to secure a 1-0 victory - the lesser-known John Frain firing a retaken free-kick into the same Wembley net that Di Matteo had so gloriously rattled.

The goals - one in the first minute, one in the last - made for the most fabulous bookends on what remains one of the greatest weeks of my life; repellent Paddington hotels aside.

I continued to walk on air throughout the summer, and by the time August came around there was another reason to smile as - for the first time - I was a Chelsea season ticket holder.

Despite doing, perhaps, 80%-90% of all Chelsea home games across the decade and as many away days as I missed, I'd never gone down the season ticket route because - quite frankly - there was little point.

Accessing a Chelsea ticket for any game - home, away or even Wembley - had very rarely been a problem, but in the previous season we'd started to realise such things could no longer be taken for granted.

The FA Cup win was obviously only going to amplify demand so there was little other option than to secure my own little piece of Stamford Bridge, regardless of whether life would allow me to attend all the games I'd paid for or not.

It felt good though. And after 18 years of active attendance at Chelsea matches, my first as what some still only accept as a 'proper supporter' would come at home to Southampton at the end of August - a delayed start to the home campaign to allow for the completion of the new all-seated Shed end and demolition of the West Stand as the redevelopment of Stamford Bridge continued.

Prior to that though I'd make my third trip to Wembley in four months to watch Chelsea appear in the Charity Shield.

That ended in a penalty shoot-out defeat to league champions Manchester United, a poor game in which Chelsea briefly led through Mark Hughes, before the league campaign opened with a trip to Coventry City.

Coventry's Highfield Road was always a personal favourite away trip, primarily because it was only 30 minutes from home but also because it was a 'proper football ground' surrounded by terraced houses with unique character of its own.

Through the '80s and '90s it was also a ground to which I'd make the odd visit for a football fix if Chelsea or Northampton weren't available Saturday options.

Off the top of my head Liverpool, Manchester City and Southampton were among the teams I watched as a neutral, with the Saints game being the one that stands out for providing the greatest entertainment.

We're talking the mid to late-'80s, and standing alongside us in the away end was well-travelled goalkeeper John Burridge... who spent an entire half shadowing the movements of England goalkeeper Peter Shilton in the Southampton goal.

Well known for his eccentricities, 'Budgie' would move left, right, forwards and backwards in time with the movements of the national team's number one - only stopping short of diving full-length on the concrete terrace or turning to pick the ball out of the net.

Among those watching on, meanwhile, were two blokes in full wedding suits.

Perhaps disheartened by Burridge attracting most of the attention, at some point in the game one turned to the other, pulled back a fist and smacked his mate square in the mouth to ensure both were evicted in time to get to church.

I have no recollection of the score, but it was a highly-enjoyable afternoon's entertainment.

In August '97 though, Burridge was elsewhere as Chelsea lined up at Highfield Road with four new summer additions.

In goal, replacing one-season wonder and FA Cup winner Frode Grodas, was Dutch international Ed De Goey.

In midfield, last seen playing against Chelsea in the Cup Winners' Cup for Real Zaragoza, was Uruguayan Gus Poyet, while on the bench was beanpole striker Tore Andre Flo - a Norwegian with high potential signed for a bargain £300,000.

Completing the quartet of new boys, meanwhile, was a returning old boy - Graeme Le Saux.

When Le Saux departed for Blackburn in March 1993 Chelsea were on the fringes of the relegation battle, attendances were regularly below 15,000, and Stamford Bridge was a windswept bowl with crumbling stands and terraces.

He returned to the FA Cup holders, capacity crowds and a stadium undergoing continuing transformation.

Of his first spell, Le Saux later spoke of the "macho, masculine archetypes" that filled the dressing room and of a "bullying culture".

Of his return, he later told the Chelsea website: "The atmosphere was different; everything seemed more positive and professional."

Of the squad he left behind, only a small number - including Steve Clarke, Frank Sinclair, Eddie Newton and Dennis Wise - had shown the necessary professionalism and ability to survive.

Le Saux, who had picked up a league title, established himself as an England regular and completed his transformation from promising attacking midfielder to trusted full-back during his years away, signed for a record £7million 24 hours ahead of the Coventry game.

For the Chelsea fans it was the perfect conclusion to an exciting few months of transfer business.

In addition to the four that would make league debuts at Highfield Road, Nigerian defender/midfielder Celestine Babayaro was waiting to make his first start after signing from Anderlecht the previous April, and French defender Bernard Lambourde had joined from Bordeaux for £1.5million.

Making room for the new arrivals was the defensive quartet of Erland Johnsen, Jakob Kjeldbjerg, Paul Parker and injury-prone Scott Minto. While Kjeldbjerg had not been seen in the first team for a couple of years and Parker had only been a short-term solution, Johnsen and Minto both moved on despite making significant contributions to the cup-winning campaign.

Also heading through the exit door was Craig Burley, the Scottish midfielder moving to Celtic for £2.5m.

A player of undeniable talent, Burley's most significant contributions were his role in the run to the 1994 FA Cup Final, in which he played in every round and contributed three goals, and - even more memorably - his fatal back-pass that gifted Manchester United the winning goal in the 1996 FA Cup Semi-Final.

It was also the FA Cup that signalled the end of his Chelsea career when he was omitted from the squad for the 1997 final amid rumours he had fallen out with Ruud Gullit on the morning of the game.

So with the squad changes putting expectations at an all-time high, a significant number of Chelsea fans celebrated from the home seats as Frank Sinclair got the season's scoring under way at Coventry - the defender dropping his shorts in celebration to ensure he got himself on the back pages on the day of the expected birth of his daughter.

The day though was to belong to future Homes Under the Hammer TV presenter Dion Dublin, who levelled within two minutes, levelled again after substitute Flo had put Chelsea back in front, and then - to give the home fans full return on their Highfield Road investment - completed the scoring and his hat-trick with two minutes to go.

Gianluca Vialli had started the new campaign as he had ended the last one by being out of favour with Gullit, but responded in style when handed a start at the expense of Mark Hughes for the trip to top-flight new boys Barnsley - firing four of six that Chelsea scored without reply, before starting again in a routine 2-0 win at Wimbledon.

With Vialli back on the bench for the long-awaited first home game of the campaign against Southampton, I took my seat as a first-time season ticket holder - Matthew Harding Lower, Block 14, Row FF, Seat 121 - to see Dan Petrescu become the first player to score in front of the new Shed when he chipped in off the post after just seven minutes.

By half-time Chelsea were in full control as Leboeuf, Mark Hughes and Wise made it four after Kevin Davies had briefly put Southampton back on level terms.

Chelsea old boy Ken Monkou reduced the deficit in a second-half that saw Frank Sinclair sent off for flinging an arm at Andy Williams, but three wins from four did nothing to dampen hopes of a title push before league football paused for an international break.

England's forthcoming World Cup qualifier against Moldova, however, would quickly become the least of the nation's concerns.

Celine and I stayed at my parents' house on the night of the Southampton game.

It was about 8am on the Sunday morning when Dad burst through our bedroom door - failing to knock to protect our privacy - to wake us, at some volume, with two never-to-be-forgotten words: "Diana's dead".

With that he turned, shut the door and walked down the stairs, before finally pausing to shout back some additional information... "and Dodi".

Celine and I, wondering if we were having some weird shared

dream, rapidly pulled on some clothes and headed downstairs for confirmation.

Living just 15 minutes from Diana's Northamptonshire family home we then took some time to watch - and try to digest - the breaking news reports from Paris before heading over to Althorp House and its neighbouring village of Great Brington to witness the world's media descend.

I considered phoning my former daily newspaper employers in Northampton to see if they needed an extra pair of hands, but I knew they would already have all current staff through the door and I also knew my energy would be required for coverage on my own Buckingham-based titles over the coming days.

Six days later, after an intense week of work, I was on duty to report on proceedings as the Diana funeral cortege pulled off the M1 at Northampton for the final leg of its journey from London to Althorp for her burial.

It was a surreal moment; an almost carnival atmosphere created by the gathered crowds as the procession travelled past the less-than regal setting of Northampton Town's Sixfields Stadium on the outskirts of the town.

With quotes and pictures that would feature in that week's papers captured, I jumped into the car to follow the procession to Althorp.

As a lowly regional journalist there would be no special access or privileges for me on arrival, but I had to capture the scenes and be witness to a global news story on my doorstep.

By the time league football returned the following week - quietly, almost apologetic - the country was still in shock, still mourning and still dealing with the fall-out of the death of Diana and its potential long-term impact on the Monarchy.

I'll admit to having limited recollection of the game that came next, but the record books show that goals from Mark Hughes, Leboeuf (pen) and Le Saux gave Chelsea a 3-0 win at Crystal Palace before a 2-0 first-leg defeat of Slovan Bratislava got the European Cup Winners' Cup campaign under way.

Gullit's team were now dining at football's top table, but a true test of how close they were to seriously competing for the title would come in a run of successive league games against the previous season's top four - Manchester United, Newcastle United, Arsenal and Liverpool.

First up was the team that finished third, Arsene Wenger's Arsenal.

On a topsy-turvy afternoon at Stamford Bridge Poyet opened the scoring, Dennis Bergkamp struck twice to give the visitors the advantage, Zola equalised immediately and - cruelly - Nigel Winterburn scored late, late on from long range to give the visitors the points just as Chelsea looked likely to hang on after the dismissal of Leboeuf for a second yellow card.

Bernard Lambourde made his debut in a feisty 2-2 draw at Manchester United that saw him among eight players booked as Chelsea were twice pegged back after leading, before Poyet was on target again for a 1-0 defeat of Newcastle.

So it was lost one, drew one, won one with Liverpool away still to come...

On the back of securing European progress with another 2-0 win against Bratislava, a game that saw Babayaro make his first appearance, disciplinary problems were again to the fore as Lambourde became the third Chelsea player of the campaign to be sent off in the trip to Anfield.

Zola had put Chelsea level within two minutes of Patrik Berger giving Liverpool the lead before, already booked, Lambourde was dismissed for bundling Steve McManaman to the ground with more than an hour still to play.

Berger - whose annoying habit of scoring against Chelsea began with a brace on his Liverpool home debut a year earlier - took full advantage to score another two before Robbie Fowler and a late Poyet penalty concluded a 4-2 score-line.

Blackburn were beaten on penalties to get the League Cup campaign off to a winning start and Leboeuf almost burst the net with the only goal of the game against Leicester before Chelsea headed to the Arctic Circle for a farcical first-leg tie in the second round of the Cup Winners' Cup.

While on paper the game should have been an easy win for Chelsea, on snow it was a different matter... Arctic blizzards, as the book of football clichés should perhaps note, being a great leveller.

Often forgotten though is that the pitch was still green when Norwegian opponents Tromso raced into a surprise two-goal lead in the opening 20 minutes, with the heavy snow only causing issues in the second-half.

By the time the game entered its final five minutes the pitch was effectively unplayable, but Vialli swept numerous challenges aside to reduce the deficit - only for Ole Martin Arst to immediately restore the hosts' two-goal advantage.

Vialli was now warming to the task though, and snow ploughed through once more to score the last of the night's five goals and ease pressures for the second-leg a fortnight later.

On the back of a 1-0 defeat at Bolton and 2-0 win at Aston Villa that left Chelsea in fourth spot in the league, Petrescu and Vialli gave Chelsea the early advantage in the Tromso return leg as quality finally began to shine through.

The Norwegians briefly levelled the aggregate score, but Zola made it three and a Leboeuf penalty took it to four. Viall then completed his hat-trick with the fifth and sixth before Petrescu got the seventh of the night.

"Win when it's snowing, you only win when it's snowing..." the Chelsea fans merrily sang as their team booked their place in the last eight of European competition for the second time in just four seasons.

Europe, though, would now be on hold until the spring, allowing Chelsea to focus on the domestic schedule and the realistic chase for trophies on three fronts.

With a third of the league campaign complete, a trademark Zola free-kick and Rio Ferdinand own goal gave Chelsea a 2-1 home win against West Ham to leave the Blues just three points off leaders Manchester United with a game in hand.

In the League Cup, meanwhile, only Dennis Wise and Frank Sinclair retained their starting spots from the West Ham game as progression was secured with a 2-1 extra-time dismissal of Southampton - the depth of talent in the squad highlighted by the win against a full-strength Saints side, a debut for midfielder Nick Crittenden, and a start for young striker Mark Nicholls.

Progress was temporarily stalled by a 1-0 defeat at third-placed Blackburn, but penalties for both Wise and Zola in a 2-0 defeat of Everton and a Zola hat-trick in a 4-0 rout of Derby moved Chelsea up to second ahead of a mouth-watering trip to Tottenham.

Chelsea's record since they last tasted defeat at White Hart Lane in 1987 was a thing of delight - nine games played, five won, four drawn, none lost; 17 scored, just seven conceded.

But on December 6, 1997 the best was about to come.

Ruud Gullit again changed a winning side, bringing in Tore Andre Flo ahead of Mark Hughes, and the move paid dividends when - in 40th minute - Zola centred perfectly for the Norwegian to head home.

Relegation-threatened Spurs, playing their first home game under new boss Christian Gross, levelled within minutes through

Ramon Vega before Chelsea took control - and the piss - in the second-half.

Three minutes after the restart Zola released Petrescu, who centred for Di Matteo to head past Ian Walker - 2-1.

Leboeuf then played a long ball into the box for Petrescu to delicately lift it over Walker - 3-1.

Just after the hour Zola dinked it to Flo to fire home right-footed - 4-1.

In front of an increasingly giddy away support, Zola was again the provider for first-half substitute Mark Nicholls to tap in - 5-1.

And, in the closing minutes, Flo beat the offside trap to chip Walker and simultaneously complete his hat-trick and the humiliation - 6-1.

"We shall not, we shall not be moved, we shall not we shall not be moved, until we win the Premier League, we shall not be moved," sang the jubilant away end which, for the first time in a generation or more, genuinely believed that we could... until, that is, a run of just three wins in 11 league games and the sacking of Ruud Gullit.

There was no cause for immediate concern when Chelsea failed to break-down a stubborn Leeds United side - the visitors escaping with a 0-0 draw after being reduced to nine men before the break - or when they rediscovered their shooting boots in a comfortable 4-1 win at Sheffield Wednesday.

But a 1-1 Boxing Day draw at home to Wimbledon followed by a one-goal defeat at Southampton meant Chelsea had picked up just five points from 12 since the White Hart Lane rout, dropping seven points behind leaders Manchester United in the process.

Suggesting that not all was well, Gullit said he "didn't recognise" his team at Southampton, adding "the way they played makes me angry".

In the meantime...

What have David Beckham and a gold ring got in common?
Comedic pause...
They both come in a Posh box.

The joke was one of a number doing the rounds as Manchester United poster-boy Beckham and Spice Girl Victoria Adams - aka Posh Spice - became the UK's number one celebrity pairing throughout 1997.

The couple were on the cusp of announcing their engagement when Manchester United travelled to holders Chelsea for the third round of the 1998 FA Cup, and the game would be played to a continued backdrop of taunts from the home crowd enquiring about the sexual preferences of the future Mrs Beckham.

But while the United midfielder failed to confirm - or, for that matter, deny - if his intended allowed for the occasional extra-curricular activity, he certainly wasn't hitting a bum note on the field.

Beckham revelled in the taunts and scored twice as United embarrassed Chelsea by racing into a five-goal lead with more than 15 minutes still to play.

Le Saux and Vialli, with two, reduced the deficit to restore a sense of respectability, but the three late goals could not disguise United's superiority or Chelsea's growing loss of direction under Gullit.

The concerns were only mildly eased four days later as focus switched from the FA Cup to League Cup, with Chelsea requiring another penalty shoot-out to progress to the last four after letting a two-goal lead slip at second-tier Ipswich Town.

One of the accusations aimed at Gullit was inconsistency in selection and formation; fine when you are winning 6-1 at Tottenham, but open to inspection when the cards fail to fall.

Against Coventry Chelsea found themselves a goal down at the break with four at the back, but pulled Paul Nicholls from the bench and switched to a three-man defence to run out eventual 3-1 winners - a Nicholls double supported by a Di Matteo strike.

A week later though it was back to a back four and, with Wise injured and Zola dropped, back to defeat with a 3-1 loss at Everton.

With the Sardinian joining Vialli in becoming the latest to fall out of favour, it was clear the rotation policy was starting to cause concern.

"To say it how Wisey would say it, I was very pissed off," Vialli would later say when quizzed about the period. Quite.

And beyond the playing squad there was additional friction, with Gullit's contract talks becoming worryingly protracted as the club failed to announce a deal that would extend beyond June.

Storm clouds were gathering... and all would come to a head in a three-part play centred on Arsenal.

Act 1 saw Chelsea travel to Highbury for the semi-final first-leg of the League Cup.

With Roberto Di Matteo and Frank Leboeuf away on international duty, and Wise still absent, Chelsea threatened to implode in a first-half horror show.

The Gunners dominated and were worthy of so much more than a 1-0 half-time lead; the goal conceded when Gullit himself was guilty of a weak header that was picked up and dispatched by Marc Overmars.

The gulf in quality was given a more realistic reflection when Stephen Hughes drove past Ed de Goey straight from the restart, but the introduction of another Hughes - Chelsea's Mark - brought hope; the Welshman's close-range header from a restored-Zola cross giving Chelsea something to play for in the second leg.

Ahead of that Chelsea claimed three points with an immediately-forgettable 2-0 defeat of Barnsley at Stamford Bridge, before returning to Highbury for the second game of the Arsenal three.

This time, in the Premier League, there would be no consolation goal to disguise the difference in quality.

With Zola back on the bench Arsenal again dominated and Stephen Hughes was again on target, this time with both in a 2-0 defeat that was to be Gullit's final game as manager.

The axe fell four days later.

While the sacking was officially due to failure to agree on the Dutchman's contract demands, it came against the backdrop of reported unrest regarding tactics and selection - a 'rebellion' against Gullit's dictatorial methods being led by, according to reports from the time, a small group of 'senior, mostly foreign players'.

The 'rebellion' - it should be said - was denied by all those Gullit left behind, but what was on the record was that the club said it was prepared to make Gullit the best paid manager in the league but that he forced their hand with excessive demands of £2million a year 'netto'.

In return an angry Gullit claimed he first saw confirmation of his sacking on Teletext, was only asked to attend one meeting in six months to discuss a two-year contract extension, and fully expected to be negotiated down on his initial wage demands.

"They are using that as a stick to hit me with," he said at the time. "I want to know the real reason."

More than 20 years later, writing for the BBC website, he would reveal more - claiming deliberate diversion tactics were put in place to prevent him talking to a potential new signing as his future was being decided.

"The day before I was sacked, I was playing golf with one of my coaches, Gwyn Williams, and a couple of the players, Franco

[Zola] and Kevin Hitchcock," he said.

"I was trying to contact [Brian] Laudrup during our round but I couldn't get hold of him, which was weird.

"It turns out Gwyn, who was one of my closest friends and who had helped me a lot, knew exactly what was going on and that they were going to fire me. He was just playing golf with me to keep me away, to make sure I didn't go to any of the places where Laudrup was.

"That was the worst thing anyone had ever done to me, in my career or in my life."

Glasgow Rangers' Danish midfielder Laudrup, meanwhile, had indeed met with Chelsea representatives to talk about life in London - those representatives including managing director Colin Hutchinson, Gullit's golfing pal Gianfranco Zola... and, pulled from the bench, new player-manager Gianluca Vialli.

Hutchinson said the meeting went ahead with Gullit's knowledge; the outgoing manager clearly felt otherwise.

Either way, it was all very Shakespearean.

For his part Gullit has since gone on record as saying he attached no blame to Vialli but, amid all the claim, counter-claim and conspiracy, one thing was clear... the Dutch impressionist had been cast aside for an Italian's renaissance.

First approached about the potential of becoming manager on the Monday after the Arsenal defeat, confirmation of Vialli's appointment came on the same day Gullit was sacked.

"This is the most unbelievable thing that's happened in my career," the managerial novice said. "But I'm just a beginner and I know it's going to be different from being a player. The supporters have been unbelievable with me over the past two seasons and I would just ask them to keep supporting the club and the team."

The supporters of which Vialli talked found their emotions torn between the loss of one legend and appointment of another, but there was never any doubt about their support for the new man.

Vialli's first task was to overturn the League Cup last-four deficit to Arsenal and - naming himself in the starting 11 while restoring Zola from the bench - he shared a pre-match glass of champagne with those now under his charge.

With more reason than most to raise a glass was Mark Hughes who, earlier in the day, had collected an MBE from the Queen before returning to the Bridge to take his place in the front line and give Chelsea the advantage after just 10 minutes.

On an atmospheric night under the lights, Hughes picked up a

Di Matteo pass to turn from 15 yards and level the tie on aggregate.

With no further goals in the first half, the game and the tie was effectively decided in a rapturous 10 minute-spell at the start of the second period.

First Arsenal's Patrick Vieira was sent off for a second yellow and then - in the blink of an eye - Di Matteo struck a 30-yard rocket and Petrescu, creating his own space from a Zola corner, extended the advantage to 3-0 on the night, 4-2 on aggregate.

When Vialli was withdrawn with 10 minutes to go, it was to a standing ovation and a red-hot atmosphere that even a late Dennis Bergkamp penalty couldn't cool.

So, with Gullit gone, Vialli's first day in office had seen him take Chelsea back to Wembley.

De Koning is dead, long live il Re...

Often overlooked on the back of Vialli's League Cup success, however, is that his start in league management was somewhat less memorable.

Of the five league games that separated the League Cup semi-final and the late March final only one - a 6-2 romp against bottom-side Crystal Palace in which Vialli and Flo both scored twice - bought any points.

Other than that, it was defeat to Leicester, Manchester United, Aston Villa and West Ham and a drop from a league high of second to a low of fifth.

Fortunate, then, that during the run of league defeats Chelsea also moved into the last four of the Cup Winners' Cup with an impressive two-leg win against Spanish side Real Betis.

Flo was the star man in the quarter-final first-leg trip to Seville, scoring twice in the opening 15 minutes in a 2-1 success, before Frank Sinclair, Di Matteo and Zola secured progression in a 3-1 second-leg win at Stamford Bridge.

"Score in a minute, we're gonna score in a minute..."

Ten months on from the 1997 FA Cup success we were back at Wembley, and back facing Middlesbrough - this time in the League Cup final, a competition won just once by Chelsea way back in 1965.

And with players preparing to kick-off, Chelsea fans were quick to remind the 'Boro support of Di Matteo's first-minute screamer back in May.

As it turned out though, on this occasion we had to wait a bit longer for a goal - all the way, in fact, to extra-time.

A Middlesbrough team containing Paul Merson, Andy Townsend and - from the bench - Paul Gascoigne proved harder to break down than they did in the FA Cup Final despite Zola hitting the bar and Di Matteo and Hughes also going close.

Ultimately, with Vialli leaving himself out of the squad, it was left to Frank Sinclair to break the deadlock.

Playing in what would turn out to be his last Chelsea appearance ahead of a summer move to Leicester, Sinclair headed home from six yards after Dennis Wise crossed. It was a deserved reward for a player who had proven his value to six successive managers across eight seasons after first breaking through from the youth team.

Ten minutes later it was game over when Di Matteo hooked home a Zola corner to bag another Wembley goal against Middlesbrough.

Victory meant that just five weeks into the job Vialli had become just the fifth Chelsea manager to win major silverware, but his next challenge was to see if he could become the first to win two pots in a single season by going all the way in the European Cup Winners' Cup.

It would be a little incredulous to claim that last-four opponents Vicenza were - or ever have been - a powerhouse of Italian football, but having produced some legendary names such as Paolo Rossi and Roberto Baggio they were not to be underestimated.

And so it proved in a tricky first leg in the Stadio Romeo Menti that came just five days after the League Cup final.

Vicenza attacked from the off and De Goey had already made one good save before the hosts took the lead with the game a little over 15 minutes old; attacking midfielder Zauli getting the better of both Eddie Newton and Frank Leboeuf to beat the Dutchman in goal.

Chelsea suffered another blow when a yellow card ruled the influential Di Matteo out of the second-leg, but were relieved to leave north-east Italy with just a one-goal deficit as Vicenza missed the best of the game's remaining chances.

Two weeks separated the two legs, in which time Chelsea won 1-0 at Derby, lost 3-1 at Leeds and pushed Tottenham to within one point of the relegation zone as Flo and Vialli secured a 2-0 win at Stamford Bridge.

The home leg of the Vicenza tie had numerous direct comparisons to the memorable European night against Club

Brugge three years previously.

Just like in 1995 Chelsea trailed by a single away-leg goal; just like in 1995 they simply couldn't afford to concede at home; just like in 1995 they would be playing the home game in their away kit; and just like in 1995 the pre-match atmosphere was at fever pitch.

Unlike in 1995, however, fears around conceding proved justified - Pasquale Luiso beating De Goey in front of the Matthew Harding Stand to give Vicenza a two-goal aggregate lead after 30 minutes.

Spinning away in celebration he put his finger to his lips to suggest he'd silenced us but, while that may have been momentarily true, the reality was that the act of arrogance simply served to notch up an already hostile atmosphere another level or two.

And the comeback began just three minutes later when Gus Poyet, starting for the first time in six months after a cruciate knee ligament injury, followed up a saved Zola drive to beat keeper Pierluigi Brivio.

Game back on…

The maths were simple at the start of the second half - Chelsea needed two to progress, another Vicenza goal would effectively kill the tie.

Just six minutes into the second period the requirement for two became one when Vialli sent in a perfect cross from the right for Zola to bullet home with his head.

With 20 minutes to play and Chelsea still pushing, still searching, they rolled the dice with a double switch in search of the crucial third goal.

Making way was Eddie Newton and Jody Morris. Coming on was Frenchman Laurent Charvet, on a short-term loan from Cannes, and Mark Hughes - past provider of miracles from the bench.

Six minutes later Vicenza broke through the middle, but the half-chance was shut down when De Goey slid out to gather at The Shed end.

From his hands the keeper launched a long-kick down field.

Hughes, back to goal, won an aerial challenge under close attention from a defender.

Spinning, he steadied as the ball bounced once on the left-hand edge of the area… and then, as fans in the stands held their collective breath, flashed a sumptuous left-footed half-volley into the far corner.

Boom. Stamford Bridge exploded.

A raucous final 15 minutes saw Chelsea survive just one genuine scare when a brilliant De Goey save denied Luiso a late tap-in before, following ecstatic post-match celebrations, two thoughts hit home as I walked emotionally drained from the ground.

First, Chelsea were in a European final - something that was beyond comprehension when I was watching the Blues in the second division, in front of 4,000 in the Full Members' Cup, or losing 7-0 at Forest.

And secondly, with a wedding on the summer horizon, there was the bubble-bursting realisation that I couldn't afford to go.

The Vicenza glory was followed by a 1-0 win against Sheffield Wednesday and a 4-1 defeat of Liverpool as Chelsea moved above the fading Merseyside outfit into third, but for both games my mind was elsewhere.

With the Cup Winners' Cup Final due to be held in the Swedish capital of Stockholm, travel with the club - the only way of guaranteeing a ticket if Ken Bates was to be believed - had been confirmed as an eye-watering £450 for an overnight stay, or £350 for the pleasure of a simple day trip.

Both were well beyond my budget as, even, was the £250, 1,200-mile cattle truck option of coach and boat.

Despite dreaming of success for so many years, I was already starting to think there was perhaps a lot to be said for being shit...

Ahead of the trip to Stockholm Chelsea wrapped up domestic proceedings with a 1-0 defeat at home to Blackburn Rovers, a 3-1 loss at Newcastle and a 2-0 final-day win against relegation-threatened Bolton Wanderers that confirmed a fourth-placed finish - the highest since 1970.

The Bolton game turned into a festival of fun, with the visitors receiving the unexpected backing of the home support as, at 1-0 down after a 73rd-minute Vialli goal, news came through that an equaliser would secure their top-flight status at the expense of Everton - the Toffees being pegged back in their own game against Coventry.

"Let them score, let them score, let them score..." we chanted in support of the visitors, before Jody Morris - the massive party pooper - scored a 90th-minute second to confirm their relegation.

To show how much we really cared the goal was met with mock boos and laughter; an irrelevance when compared to the planned Chelsea invasion of Sweden three days later.

Reports suggested up to 25,000 Chelsea fans would be making the trip. The only unanswered question was, would I be among them...?

CHAPTER SIXTEEN
EUROPEAN CUP WINNERS' CUP FINAL

Chelsea v VfB Stuttgart
Råsunda Stadium
Stockholm
Wednesday, May 13, 1998

Chelsea: De Goey, Petrescu, Leboeuf, Clarke, Poyet (Newton, 80), Vialli, Wise, Duberry, Di Matteo, Granville, Flo (Zola, 71).

VfB Stuttgart: Wohlfahrt, Berthold, Yakin, Hagner (Ristic, 79), Haber (Djordjevic, 75), Balakov, Bobic, Schneider (Endress, 55), Akpoborie, Soldo, Poschner.

Referee: Stefano Braschi (Italy)
Attendance: 30,216

Four weeks separated the semi-final defeat of Vicenza and the cup final date against German side VfB Stuttgart in Stockholm.

The first week was spent doing sums. How much can I afford? Are there cheaper ways to travel? Can I do it if I don't renew my season ticket? Can I do it if (puts tongue in cheek) I postpone the wedding?

The second week was spent sulking; trying to be mature, trying to accept that adult life gets in the way, trying not to be bitter as one-by-one most of my mates - Stewie, Gaz, Anton and others - confirmed their plans.

The only consolation was that Scott was in the same boat as me - struggling to justify the cost and getting married in the autumn. At least we'd be missing out together.

And then, in the third week, potential salvation from the most unlikely of sources...

'*Cheap Ryanair flights to European destinations*' screamed the promotion on the front page of The Sun newspaper. '*Collect your vouchers today*'.

Surely not... still, worth checking... where do these flights go then?

St Etienne, nope... Carcassonne, nope... Pisa, nope... Venice, would have been bloody handy for the semi-final, but nope... Rimini, nope... Kristianstad...

"Kristianstad? That sounds Scandinavian. Where the hell is Kristianstad?"

A quick flick through the paper, and there was the answer - southern Sweden; beautiful, glorious, sumptuous, southern Sweden...

Ryanair had just given itself a free pass to lose my luggage for life.

Hopefully joining me on the flight to Kristianstad and the (not insignificant) 350-mile onward journey to Stockholm would be Scott, Sean and, the grown-up among our potential travelling group, Paul.

A few years our senior, Paul was brought up a decent goal kick from the gates of Stamford Bridge and attended his first game in Division Two in '62. While continuing to attend the occasional game as family-life became the greater priority in the '80s, he had been enticed back on a more regular basis in the Hoddle, Gullit and Vialli era.

The first hurdle for our trip, booking the flight tickets, was my responsibility - a bargain £40 each secured following the collection of the necessary number of vouchers and, just days ahead of the game, a nervous phone call from my desk while pretending to be working.

And then Paul came into his own to sort match tickets, arrange car hire, and even tap up a Swedish business contact to find us a floor to sleep on after the game.

All in, the trip came in at less than £150 each. And that, by any measure, was too good to be true. Almost too good to be true...

While I was thinking only of Stockholm, my much-loved grandad - or 'Pap' as his large collection of grand-children called him - was in the final stages of life in hospital.

I knew time was short, but I didn't know how short until - as I visited the night before heading to Stockholm - I was told it would be hours, rather than days.

In the blink of an eye the past few weeks of selfish self-interest for a simple game of football paled into insignificance.

I couldn't go now. I'd phone Scott, offer my apologies, tell them to have a beer for me and bring the cup home.

And I meant it but, of course, family said what they always say in such circumstances.

"He'd want you to go."

"What are you going to do if you stay here?"

"Go, think of him, enjoy yourself."

"You'll never get the chance again..."

Although the last statement worked both ways they were, of course, correct and I did know - deep down - exactly what he'd have told me to do had he had the capacity to do so; he'd have told me to enjoy life.

So with that, knowing he'd be surrounded by love, I said a private goodbye and prayed I'd get another chance on my return.

After an emotional night the alarm clock went off before 4am for the drive to Stansted, an early 90-minute flight, and a further seven-hour drive to get to Stockholm for an 8.45pm kick-off.

It was going to be tight, and it needed everything to go to plan.

What it didn't need was Stansted departure boards awash with two words - 'flight delayed'.

With the airport rammed with Chelsea fans waiting for official club flights, there was an air of chaos as heavy fog grounded all flights; all flights, that is, with the exception of one - the Ryanair flight to Kristianstad.

My new-found love for Ireland's favourite budget airline moved up another notch as we walked to the departure gate on time, the glares of hundreds of delayed Chelsea fans burning into the back of our heads, and up even further on discovery that we'd be travelling in comfort with, perhaps, no more 30 people on the flight.

In terms of Chelsea representation there was just us and another couple of groups who would be entering Sweden via the back door.

Kristianstad is a small town no more than 60 miles from Denmark, and its airport is appropriately humble with just a single strip of runway and a terminal no larger than a small-town UK railway station.

As we step from the plane though we still have a welcoming committee, with a gathering of Swedish police and sniffer dogs on hand to give us a friendly once over and check we're not a sub-committee of a major Chelsea firm.

I've never been to Scandinavia before and as we leave the airport I'm excited to be seeing something of Sweden.

It will largely be dual-carriageways and service stations through the windows of our small hire car, but it's better than a brief coach trip from Stockholm airport and I'm looking forward to the long drive north.

As we pass through the first small town I find myself looking at the high number of low-level apartment blocks. In design they resemble concrete compounds of eastern Europe, but pastel palettes of yellow and blue give them a warmer glow.

And then it's into the countryside, where apartment blocks first give way to family homes with ample plots of land and then to mile after mile of evergreen trees.

Infinite wire fencing separates trees from road to keep wildlife on one side and traffic on the other, but we still note with curiosity the number of signs warning us to be aware of wandering elks.

These horned beasts pose no obvious threat during daylight hours, but we'll have to be more alert the following morning when we'll be driving back at sunrise and they'll be out for an early-morning stroll.

As we continue our journey the trees finally give way to Lake Vättern, the sixth largest in Europe according to a service station information board.

We hug its shoreline for 30, perhaps 40, miles before bearing right for the final push to Stockholm.

The towns we bypass become larger in size as we head towards the capital. First Linköping, then Norrköping and then Nyköping. Ping, ping, ping... the miles and towns racing by before, mid-afternoon, we hit the suburbs of Stockholm.

Paul is in control of the directions as, first, we seek out the office block in which our Swedish host for the night will hand us the key to her apartment; an apartment which, we are told, is right next to the ground.

As we wait outside the office, keen to make progress, Paul calls us in.

"You better come and say hello," he says. "I think she's made us a smorgasbord."

And she has. As we self-consciously walk through an office of Swedish workers in our Chelsea replica shirts, awaiting us is a traditional spread of meat, fish and salad along with a few bottled beers to wash it down with.

It's a wonderful gesture, greatly appreciated, and we tuck in with enthusiasm.

But as we do so we are looking at each other, all keen to make a move.

The clock is ticking and we are desperate to track down fellow Chelsea fans to crack on with some more familiar pre-match traditions of our own.

Paul reads the signals, offers heartfelt thanks on our behalf, and suggests we better let her get back to work.

Back out to the car, into the late afternoon traffic, following the signs to Råsunda Stadium; to the north of the city centre in the suburb of Solna.

When we park we discover the apartment is, as promised, directly behind the stadium - no more than 150 metres from front door to turnstile.

Above a bar named The Dick Turpin - so-called, presumably, because the price of a beer is daylight robbery - it is on a small square that is heaving with Chelsea.

Paul, it has to be said, has played a blinder.

We dump our bags and immediately make our way back downstairs, quickly finding friends from home among the thronging crowd.

Some have been here a few days enjoying the city, while others have tales of woe about delayed club flights that have eaten into their day. But none have ever seen Chelsea - the club we have adored and endured - in a European final, and we are giddy with excitement.

As we sing and drink a football is being thrown around among the crowd; a game of about 300 per side threatening to break out with kick-off now less than two hours away.

Up goes the ball, and "wheyyyy" shouts the crowd.

Up, "wheyyyy", up, "wheyyyy", up, "wheyyyy", up, "wheyyyy".

It goes on and on until the inevitable happens... an over-enthusiastic punt is followed by the unmistakable sound of ball breaking glass.

Paul, Scott, Sean and I look at the smashed window, then look at each other.

To misquote Humphrey Bogart... of all the windows in all the towns in all the world, it has gone straight through one in the apartment in which we are staying.

Bollocks!

"What are you going to do about that then?", we ask of Paul, trying not to laugh.

The decision, we quickly decide as a group, is nothing because to take ownership would require action and kick-off is fast approaching.

The Råsunda is a traditional English-style ground with all four sides hugging the pitch.

The venue for the 1958 World Cup final, it is best known by England fans for being the venue in which Graham Taylor's side departed the 1992 European Championships to the host nation.

The majority of the fans are housed in large two-tier stands behind either goal, and as we find our seats the size of the Chelsea support becomes immediately apparent.

Outnumbering the dismal Stuttgart following by perhaps seven or eight to one, Chelsea fill three of the four tiers behind the goals as well as the two smaller stands down either side - including the East Stand in which we are sat.

"Chelsea here, Chelsea there, Chelsea every fucking where..."

Right on the halfway line we've got the perfect view, but at £45 per ticket - the only ones we could get once flights were confirmed - it's the most expensive part of our trip.

That's now of little concern though, and for the extra cost we discover we're sitting right behind some of the non-playing members of the Chelsea squad.

Among those just a couple of rows in front of us is David Lee, who has made just one start all season following his leg break against Tottenham in the previous campaign.

Lee was injured on the back of one of the best spells of his Chelsea career and it's a reminder of how fragile a footballer's lot can be... without that leg break there is a reasonable chance he would now be playing in a European final, but instead it looks like his time at Chelsea is coming to an end.

Tonight, like us, he is just one of 25,000 cheering on the team.

The starting 11 is pretty much as expected.

Zola - struggling in recent weeks with a groin injury - is left on the bench in favour of Tore Andre Flo, while Danny Granville starts on the left of defence.

A £300,000 signing from Cambridge United a little over 12 months earlier, Granville's first team chances have been limited but a late-season injury to Graeme Le Saux has thrust him into the European spotlight.

We know little about the Stuttgart team but recognise internationals Thomas Berthold and Fredi Bobic, as well as keeper Franz Wohlfahrt - last seen being rounded by John Spencer following his 80-yard solo run in Vienna.

But despite our limited knowledge of their starting 11, we still know they are a step up on anyone else we have faced in the competition having finished fourth in the Bundesliga under respected young manager Joachim Löw.

The teams emerge to a wall of blue and a pitch unbecoming of a showpiece final; rutted and with bare patches we fear it is bound to impact on the quality of play.

And as the mystifying choice of the Star Wars theme tune blares out across the stadium, both sides line up directly in front of us for pre-match presentations before Flo touches the ball to Vialli to get the game under way.

It's Chelsea v Stuttgart. It's England v Germany. It's a European final.

Just 10 years on from Chelsea's last relegation it is, quite frankly, all a little surreal.

But while our top-price seats provide the best view, they don't provide the best atmosphere and in the opening moments I can't help looking to my right with envy as the first *'ten men went to mow'* of the night from the main Chelsea support reaches its crescendo.

On the pitch, though, Chelsea start bright, winning an early free-kick that comes to nothing as the support turns its attentions to rivals watching from home.

"Fuck 'em all, fuck 'em all, United, West Ham and Millwall," spreads around the ground, *"cos we are the Chelsea and we are the best, we are the Chelsea so fuck all the rest..."*

Meanwhile, the early Chelsea pressure continues and Gus Poyet flicks a ball to the feet of Roberto Di Matteo just inside the 18-yard box.

Less than five minutes into the game Di Matteo - the scorer of the first goal in last year's FA Cup Final, the scorer of the second in this year's League Cup Final - looks perfectly placed to complete a cup final hat-trick...

We're on our feet thinking he must score, but the ball bobbles on the hard pitch and Di Matteo drags it wide with his left foot.

We look at each other with wistful smiles, a group acknowledgement of how close we were to another perfect cup final start.

The Germans also know it's an early let-off, and they quickly seek to capitalise with a couple of chances of their own.

First there is panic in the Chelsea box as Krassimir Balakov and others seek space, and then Steve Clarke mishits a pass to the feet of Bobic to shoot across goal when he should have done better.

We're still only 15 minutes into the game and Dan Petrescu is the next to lift us from our seats when he wins the ball 20 yards from goal before firing over. And then it's Stuttgart again as danger man Balakov fires in another shot that requires Ed de Goey to be alert.

It's a frantic start but both sides are struggling to come to terms with the pitch, both lacking the composure to capitalise when it counts.

Flo is the next Chelsea player to step into the half-chance saloon, creating his own space by flicking up a ball from a long free-kick before narrowly heading over from six yards.

It's close but, like all that has gone before, it's not controlled enough to be close enough.

As the players' struggles with the pitch continue, Chelsea fans - arms stretched wide, gently swaying side-to-side - are now taunting the Stuttgart support with the Dambusters tune.

"Derr-der-der-der-der-de-de-der-der; der-der-der-de-de-der-de-der; der-der-der-de-der; DER-DER-DE-DE-DE-DERRR..."

It's a bit of inevitable World War piss take, something to briefly pass the time while the ball bobbles around in midfield.

I momentarily join in, but it startles me into thoughts of home and my Burma-veteran Pap in his hospital bed.

He might see the funny side but I doubt it, so I pull my arms down, shut my mouth and take a moment's reflection, try to show some personal respect.

Dambusters morphs into a chant of *"En-ger-land, En-ger-land, En-ger-land"* and then *"Chelsea, Chelsea, Chelsea..."* and finally I get back on my feet to sing while a game of head tennis breaks out on the rectangle of green below me.

The game continues to struggle to find a controlled rhythm but hopes are raised again when, first, Poyet has a rasping volley parried away by Wohlfahrt and then Granville - looking more than capable at this level - is brought down on the corner of the box on the stroke of half-time.

The free-kick is headed clear, but only as far as Wise on the edge of the box who fizzes a right-footed volley just wide of the post. It's the closest we have come, and I'm leaping in the air thinking it is curling in to the top corner before bending double on realisation that it isn't.

As the half-time whistle blows both sides could, with some justification, claim they are deserving of the lead, but the Wise effort is the closest either have come to breaking the deadlock.

When the teams re-emerge Chelsea are playing to my right, and the second half starts as the first ended; scrappy football, neither side finding the necessary quality to hold possession, to create genuine chances.

But Chelsea have the advantage in the stands and we step up again to try to make the difference.

"Chelsea, Chelsea, Chelsea, Chelsea..." followed by *"Carefree"*, *"Celery"* and others that have been sung home and away year after year.

These are the songs that form our Greatest Hits, the tunes that survive generation after generation, the songs that still seep into our minds on a summer's day when Chelsea are at rest, not play.

And at times like this they drift from our collective mouths without thought, our bid to keep the tempo going, to give a small lift to our team playing in our name.

And it seems to be working, Chelsea are getting on top.

They're not dominating, not ripping through the Stuttgart backline, but they are turning the vice, slowly increasing the pressure.

A free-kick comes to nothing; a corner comes to nothing; Wise and Vialli shots briefly get us to our feet but come to nothing.

But the vice is getting tighter, tighter, tighter...

We lift the volume a touch more - *"CHELSEA, CHELSEA, CHELSEA, CHELSEA..."* - and down on the Stuttgart bench Joachim Löw, sensing the danger, makes the first change of the night as defender Jochen Endress replaces the struggling Thomas Schneider.

The Chelsea support returns to singing about men mowing meadows before, as the hour-mark passes, Poyet volleys well wide and Granville draws a save from Wohlfahrt.

It's largely one-way traffic now, but it remains congested so the man with the proven skills to find space is about to enter the fray.

"Zola, la, la, la, la Zola, la, la, la, la, Zola..."

As our Sardinian sorcerer walks to the touchline, his name is ringing out across all four sides of the ground.

And when the ball bounces out for a Stuttgart throw, Zola - elbows pumping - runs straight to the centre-forward position in place of the departing Flo.

As he takes up his position Stuttgart get the ball back in to play and move it down their right flank, where Granville intercepts on his chest and passes to the feet of Poyet... who moves it to Wise, who knocks in into the feet of Zola...

But the substitute's first touch is a poor one and he runs into a Stuttgart challenge which deflects the ball back to Wise.

Zola, though, ever aware, continues his run forward and Wise spots the opportunity.

His lofted pass bisects the defence and is met by Zola on the edge of the box who, majestically, first-time, on the half-volley, thunders away a crisp right-footed shot.

The on-rushing Wohlfahrt is beaten and the ball hammers into the top corner.

We're gone.

Me and Scott, two nine-year-olds first bonded by a love of Second Division Chelsea, are locked in embrace to celebrate a Zola goal in a European final in a suburb of Stockholm.

From Swindon to Sweden and plenty in between we've been on quite the journey, and it is an honour to be sharing this moment with him.

All around us the ground is a cauldron of noise. Somewhere behind one of the goals a fire-cracker goes off, and in front of us David Lee and other members of the Chelsea second string are going as loopy as the rest of us.

As Zola's name again rings out we look at the clock; there's still around 20 minutes to go and we're now more nervous than we've been for any of the previous 70.

Stuttgart make another change with midfielder Kristijan Djordjevic replacing Marco Haber and then, turning up the heat as Chelsea pack men behind the ball, they make another with number nine Sreto Ristic increasing attacking options in place of Matthias Hagner.

But within seconds Chelsea are forced to make another change of their own when Poyet, one of the stand-out performers on the night, stretches to win a defensive tackle and immediately signals that he needs to be withdrawn.

Eddie Newton is the man to come on in his place - a cool head needed in an increasingly tense, backs-to-the wall, environment.

Stuttgart have the upper hand now and Gerhard Poschner fires a speculative shot wide, but we can see the finishing line in sight.

"We shall not, we shall not be moved, we shall not, we shall not be moved, until we win the Cup Winners' Cup, we shall not be moved..." we sing, struggling to comprehend that - after 26 barren years - we are now on the brink of a third piece of silverware in just 12 months.

Stuttgart continue to push though and they swing in a

dangerous free-kick from their right corner that bounces around before eventually being cleared to Zola, who takes control before releasing the advancing Di Matteo.

It's a chance to wrap it up but, like so much that has gone before, only another half chance as our midfielder struggles to control and fails to beat the last man.

The ball is quickly played back up field as Stuttgart push one more time and Chelsea struggle to regain their shape.

In the middle of the pitch Dan Petrescu dives in for a foul on Murat Yakin.

We roar our approval at the Romanian stopping a potential dangerous break, but are then silenced as referee Braschi flashes a straight red card.

Shit.

With six minutes still to play, Chelsea are down to 10 men. It's time to dig deep, hang on, avoid the torture of extra-time a man light.

Each minute feels like 10, but Chelsea are doing everything to run the clock down as they hold the ball in the corners and win throws deep in Stuttgart territory; but it's not enough to repel all threat and with fewer than two to go Stuttgart win back-to-back corners.

From the second they lob the half-cleared ball back into the box and De Goey gathers comfortably.

We roar again, powerless to do anything more as Chelsea seek to see out the final seconds.

But Stuttgart come back again and Di Matteo concedes another corner. It's wasted again, we roar again, and more precious seconds pass before the Germans flood forward one more time.

This time, as they try to find space on the edge of the Chelsea box, keeper Wohlfahrt joins the attack.

As we desperately whistle for full-time, someone - maybe Vialli, maybe Wise, we're beyond caring - gets a crucial touch and the ball falls to Granville with an open pitch and unguarded net in front of him.

An audacious strike from his own half could place him in Chelsea folklore, but instead he shows professionalism and heads down the line before playing a ball across the box to win a corner.

The move is celebrated almost as enthusiastically as a goal because that, surely, is that... keep the ball in the corner and it must be game over.

But with the ball still out of play Braschi has got the red card out again, and this time Stuttgart's Gerhard Poschner is the recipient.

We've no idea what the dismissal is for, and we have no time to debate it because seconds later - seconds after the corner has been taken - Braschi blows his whistle three times and waves his arm in the air.

It's all over. Chelsea are European Cup Winners' Cup winners.

The team of Zola, Di Matteo and Vialli, of Wise, Petrescu and Clarke, have matched the domestic and European cup achievements of the legendary team of the early '70s - the team of Osgood, Webb and Harris, of Bonetti, Baldwin and Cooke.

They've still got their memories; but now we've got ours.

From behind both goals a small number of Chelsea fans climb the fences to celebrate with the players, but are quickly encouraged off as a stage is erected for the trophy presentation.

And when the moment comes, it's right in front of us, our VIP seats now paying dividends.

"CHELSEA ARE BACK, CHELSEA ARE BACK," we sing as the presentation begins.

And this time, more than any other time, it's true.

Chelsea, European-trophy-winning Chelsea, are back.

Last up to collect his medal, milking every second, is our captain Dennis Wise.

Our record-signing in 1990 took time to reach his full potential, but he has provided a bridge between the lows and highs of the decade; been a constant presence from mid-table mediocrity to a 12-month trophy treble.

So there he stands, directly in front of us, briefly calling for quiet from his adoring fans to maximise the trophy-lifting roar to follow.

And then he lifts the trophy and, as fireworks fill the sky, we party; for the third time in 12 months, we party.

None of us want to leave but, of course, we eventually have to, and the carnival atmosphere pours from stadium to street.

And as it does so attention is quickly drawn to the balcony of a flat above, where a bare-breasted blonde is enthusiastically congratulating the massed Chelsea support.

She gets, not surprisingly, a warm response.

So it is with that final image of a wonderful night safely filed in the memory box that Scott, Paul, Sean and I step from the crowd and straight through the door of our apartment.

When we enter it's our host who speaks first, her English impeccable.

"Well done Chelsea, congratulations...

"Now, do you know what happened to my window?"

Adrenalin means sleep doesn't come easy but we force ourselves to grab a couple of hours and are on the road by 4am, just beating the rising sun in a part of the world where the late-spring days are long.

We leave a note offering our host our further thanks, repeating an offer she'd already refused for a contribution towards the cost of her window.

And as we set off, I'm impressed that the streets around The Dick Turpin are already on the brink of having all evidence of the Chelsea invasion removed; an army of road sweepers quietly removing the carpet of cans, glass and litter to ensure the streets are spotless for the morning dog walkers.

It is incredibly efficient and, however brief our visit may have been, another reminder that Stockholm has been a wonderful host.

The long journey back to Kristianstad is done in shifts - Paul and I splitting driving, Scott and Sean sharing shot-gun duties to keep the weary driver awake and an eye out for elk.

And unlike the journey out, the lunchtime return flight is full of Chelsea as those who departed across two to three days converge for the first plane home.

As it comes in to land, *One Man and His Dog Spot* is again being happily sung by one and all.

As we get to nine - *"nine men, eight men, seven men, six men, five men, four men, three men, two men, one man and his dog Spot..."* - a quick-thinking flight attendant takes control.

"I know what comes next," she says over the speaker system in soft southern Irish tones. "Don't you DARE stand up."

It gets a laugh, and it does the job. As the wheels touch the Stansted ground an ear-splitting *"ten men went to mow"* is being sung by a very happy, but very firmly seated, plane-load of Chelsea.

With Celine at work, my first stop on arrival home is to see Mum and Dad.

Overly conscious that it's time to start putting the needs of others back before my own, I put the key in the door, walk down the hall, and - before saying anything else - ask the question I don't want to ask.

"How's Pap?"

But I don't need a reply; the face of my grieving mum tells me all I need to know.

Alf Gardner, an honourable, loving man, passed away peacefully at about the same time a football was being put through a Stockholm window.

I hug my mum.

And then I cry.

European Cup Winners' Cup Final

Chelsea 1 VfB Stuttgart 0

CHAPTER SEVENTEEN
1998/1999

Celine and I were married on August 1, 1998 - three weeks after hosts France beat Brazil in the World Cup Final and two weeks before the new season began.

And I know I'm contractually obliged to say this, but it truly was a magical day.

Pupils from Celine's primary school were there to watch her walk in to church; a church that was filled with the finest collection of family and friends one could wish for.

Reception speeches from the father of the bride, and my Dad and Scott - fulfilling joint best-man duties - brought the house down. And if I say so myself, my speech wasn't too shabby either.

At the evening reception the dancefloor was packed from beginning to end, while the bar was - literally - drunk dry.

Finally, in honour of the fact that we were only officially there because Chelsea finally won the cup, Celine and I departed to our wedding-night suite to the sound track of the 1997 FA Cup Final song, Blue Day.

"The only place to be, every other Saturday, strolling down the Fulham Road..."

Our honeymoon was spent in the beautiful Italian city of Florence, where we spent the week marvelling at the architectural wonder of the Duomo di Firenze, queueing for the Uffizi gallery, watching illegal street hawkers play cat-and-mouse with city polizia, and trying to spot pint-sized child pick-pockets that were clearing thousands of Euros per day.

Chelsea played a pre-season friendly against nearby Parma while we were there, but with the game held on neutral turf in Sicily attendance wasn't an option so I watched it on Italian TV in our hotel room with bottles of the cheapest local beers I could find and my new wife in my arms.

On our final night we dined in one of the city's many fine squares, the food washed down with such volumes of Italian red wine that - when we stood to leave - we discovered our legs no longer worked.

After stumbling back to the hotel, a minor incident involving rapidly-reappearing wine and crisp-white sheets resulted in me dumping the bed linen in a bath of water before collapsing fully-clothed ahead of an early-morning flight home.

The morning alarm call came far too soon. Stumbling around the room collecting our belongings, sitting on suitcases, and stubbing toes on every available piece of furniture, I remembered the bed sheets in the bath.

'They can't stay there, I'll hang them from the window to dry...'

Grabbing them in both arms I approached our fifth-floor window which overlooked a Florentine side street; a street so narrow you could almost touch the walls on both sides with arms outstretched.

Holding tightly on to two corners I tossed a sheet into the early Sunday morning warmth - neglecting to recall the second sheet wrapped inside and now tumbling to ground as a dead weight.

As it fell time stood still, because as it fell there was the unmistakable buzz of an approaching Vespa...

Slowly down went the sheet, 'bzzzzzz' went the Vespa; continually down went the sheet, 'bzzzzzz' went the ever-closer Vespa.

Down, 'bzzzzzz', down, 'bzzzzzz', down...

Finally, 'thud' went the sheet; hitting the ground a yard or so in front of a startled Vepsa youth who was last seen swerving into the distance, his confused head spinning to the skies with a stream of Italian obscenities filling the air... *'figlio di puttana...'*

Had it landed just a split-second later I would almost certainly have spent the first few years of married life familiarising myself with the Italian prison system.

Carefully planning my own nuptials to coincide with the football calendar I returned in time for the new season, but still missed the first game at Coventry City due to not one, but two, weddings of friends.

By the time we'd concluded proceedings at the church ceremony of the first wedding in Northamptonshire, Darren Huckerby and Dion Dublin had fired the hosts into an early 2-0 lead.

Gus Poyet reduced the margin of defeat as we headed to Essex to attend the reception of our second wedding of the day, but for a second year in succession it was to be a shock opening-day defeat at Highfield Road for a Chelsea side that had again been improved with fresh sprinkles of summer star-dust.

Making their competitive debuts on a hot August day were Catalonian full-back Albert Ferrer, signed from Barcelona for £2.2m; Italian international forward Pierluigi Casiraghi, joining from Lazio for £5.4m; and - fresh from lifting the World Cup with France - Marcel Desailly.

Of all the signings, centre-half Desailly - picked up for £4.6m from AC Milan - was the biggest statement of Chelsea intent.

In addition to the World Cup he was a double European Cup winner and was coveted by clubs across Europe before electing to join French teammate - and fellow World Cup winner - Frank Leboeuf in west London.

Alongside Casiraghi, Ferrer and Brian Laudrup - the fourth big-name signing of the summer after completing his much-teased free transfer from Rangers - Desailly's purchase completed what was widely considered to be the most exciting squad in the country and immediately put Chelsea among the pre-season title favourites... as long as, that is, the new boys could all settle and stay fit.

Joining Leicester-bound Frank Sinclair in leaving the club, meanwhile, was Stockholm medal winner Danny Granville and the man whose semi-final goal sent Chelsea to Sweden - Mark Hughes.

Arriving as a despised figure courtesy of his time at Manchester United, the Welshman left for Southampton having booked his place in the Stamford Bridge history books due to a 'never-say-die' contribution across three seasons.

"Oh Hughesy, Hughesy, the only decent thing to come from Manchester..."

Completing the list of notable departures was Mark Stein, the prolific 1994 marksman heading to Bournemouth almost three years after his last appearance, and his fellow forgotten-man David Rocastle.

Despite making a significant contribution to help guide Chelsea to the semi-finals of the European Cup Winners' Cup in his debut 1994/95 season, 'Rocky' would make just one appearance in the following campaign before struggling with injury and form and, eventually, drifting into loan moves to Norwich and Hull.

Leaving Chelsea for a final playing-hurrah in Malaysia, few Stamford Bridge fans gave him much further thought until - in February 2001 - Rocastle announced he was suffering from non-Hodgkin's lymphoma, an aggressive form of cancer which attacks the immune system.

His death, at the tragically young age of 33, was announced just weeks later on March 31, 2001.

While rightly best remembered for his time as an Arsenal title winner, his contribution to Chelsea in the mid-'90s should also never be forgotten - one of a number of signings of the time that raised standards and, ultimately, laid the foundations for the success that was now being enjoyed.

That success would see yet another trophy added to the cabinet when, following a 1-1 draw against Newcastle to get the home campaign up and running, Chelsea travelled to Monaco to face Real Madrid in the Super Cup - the showpiece UEFA clash between the previous season's European Cup and Cup Winners' Cup champions.

With Laudrup making his debut from the bench, Chelsea got the better of a side managed by their future boss Guus Hiddink when substitute Gus Poyet struck from the edge of the box for the only goal of the game.

Real Madrid 0 Chelsea 1... it was a long way from defeats to the likes of Bristol City and Tranmere Rovers just a few years previously.

It was perhaps fitting, then, that with Chelsea hitting a new pinnacle of achievement the longest-serving squad member decided it was time to bring his Stamford Bridge career to a close.

From his debut in a struggling team in January 1987 to his last appearance in the winning side in Stockholm, Steve Clarke had earned the honour of being a True Blue legend ahead of joining the new Newcastle manager Ruud Gullit as assistant boss.

Signed from St Mirren for the bargain price of £420,000, in his 11 years at Chelsea Clarke made more than 400 appearances, scored 10 goals, suffered one relegation, and won one promotion, one League Cup, one FA Cup and one European Cup Winners' Cup.

The 1994 Player of the Year, he developed from traditional right-back to wing-back, to centre half and to one of a back three to become - a brief blip under Bobby Campbell aside - a guaranteed starter for every manager under which he served.

Pound for pound he departed as one of the greatest signings in Chelsea history, but added further gloss to his legend by later returning to Stamford Bridge as youth team coach before being promoted to double title-winning assistant manager alongside José Mourinho.

Currently earning plaudits as the boss of Scotland, a further return should not be ruled out as a future manager of Chelsea on any of the multiple occasions the opportunity arises at the modern-day Stamford Bridge.

That, though, is for another day and back in 1998 a Clarke-less Chelsea picked up from their Super Cup success with a need for league points, but were left still searching for their first win of the campaign after a 0-0 draw against Arsenal.

Despite the Gunners being reduced to 10 men for the final 30 minutes after the sending off of Lee Dixon, the hosts failed to find a way through and found themselves in the bottom three of the early league table when the final whistle blew.

That, it's fair to say, wasn't in the pre-season script... but Vialli's men were simply warming to the task.

The first league win finally came three days later at home to Nottingham Forest; Zola's goal after just 24 seconds doubled by Poyet before Forest reduced the arrears in the second-half.

Another win came as the defence of the European Cup Winners' Cup got under way with an underwhelming 1-0 first-leg defeat of Swedish part-timers Helsingborg.

And another came in a seven-goal Monday-night thriller at Blackburn's Ewood Park that saw two penalties, two sending offs, the lead change hands three times and Chelsea run out eventual 4-3 winners.

Giving little indication of the drama ahead, Zola opened the scoring after 15 minutes with a free-kick before future Chelsea flop Chris Sutton levelled for the hosts seven minutes later.

Chelsea took the lead again through a Leboeuf second-half penalty, only for Blackburn to equalise again through Sebastien Perez.

But the game really heated up when Perez was involved in a double sending off with Graeme Le Saux 10 minutes after his goal; the Chelsea man the primary aggressor in retaliation for a nasty challenge.

With 10 against 10 Blackburn looked to have taken all three points when Sutton scored his second of the night after Duberry brought down Swedish striker Martin Dahlin for a penalty, only for Tore Andre Flo to steal the headlines with two late strikes.

Having made just one start since the beginning of the campaign, Flo had been introduced in place of Casiraghi moments before the Blackburn third.

With time ticking down he first met a Laudrup cross to poke

home on the volley with his first touch before, just four minutes later, he ran on to Ferrer's long pass to beat Tim Flowers.

Forward-momentum continued with a 2-0 defeat of Middlesbrough and a second-leg 0-0 draw at Helsingborg ahead of a Sunday afternoon trip to face a Liverpool side sitting a place above Chelsea in the table.

"Look la, 'issa bloke in a dress! Shows ya fanny..."

The youth giving Scott his full attention down one of the run-down terraced streets that surround Anfield was the very definition of Scouse scally - near impenetrable accent, battered shoes, scruffs for clothes and wielding a large stick that he seemed intent on using to confirm my mate's gender.

And if there hadn't been 10 of us there to protect Scott's modesty, who was facing the indignity of going to the game in a wedding dress as his stag weekend came to its exhausted conclusion, I'm sure he would quite happily have done so.

The weekend had started on the Friday night in the Welsh village of Betws-y-Coed, where we were due to participate in some climbing and caving adventure.

On the Saturday it moved on to Llandudno after - thanks to some minor Anglo-Welsh misunderstandings - we were politely asked to leave our original hotel, and on the Sunday it eventually made its way along the north Wales coast and through the Mersey Tunnel for the Chelsea game.

And Scott, in his beautiful bridal gown, was quite the attraction.

All that was now needed to complete the perfect weekend was a Chelsea win, and we so nearly got our wish.

Casiraghi was never a prolific scorer with his 58 goals in 210 Serie A appearances making him a one-in-four man, but after seven Chelsea starts he was still long overdue a first goal.

And to the delight of a noisy Chelsea following it came after just 10 minutes of play when Roberto Di Matteo's long pass released him to round Liverpool keeper David James and roll the ball into an empty net.

Liverpool's Phil Babb, chasing back, managed to add to the fun by sliding at speed into the post; one leg either side of the woodwork, family jewels as an airbag, and a pressing need for our scally with a stick to check everything was where it should have been.

Casiraghi might have got a second with an extravagant bid to catch James off his line from 35 yards, but the day was to ultimately end in mild disappointment when Jamie Redknapp equalised with a free-kick with fewer than 10 minutes to play.

Still, it was continued progress, and by the time Scott had walked Yvette down the aisle three weeks later Chelsea had added another four league points to the tally with a 2-1 defeat of Charlton and a 0-0 draw at Leeds that saw the hosts miss a penalty and referee Mike Reed issue an astonishing 13 yellow cards alongside a bonus red for Leboeuf.

Defence of the League Cup began with a 4-1 defeat of Aston Villa that featured a Vialli hat-trick, a Wise red card and a debut from the bench for a 17-year-old centre-half named John Terry, while the European campaign continued with a narrow 2-1 aggregate win against Copenhagen.

The Copenhagen game was a curious affair which saw wide midfielder Bjarne Goldbaek catch the eye to score the Danish side's goal in the 1-1 Stamford Bridge leg, and Brian Laudrup score the only goal of the game to secure Chelsea progression in the away tie.

Laudrup, though, had announced he wanted to leave Chelsea after just four months in London and played the game in his native Denmark in the knowledge that he would soon be joining the side he was scoring against.

And for 'soon', read the very next day... in a deal that saw Copenhagen's Goldbaek fill the empty seat on the flight home.

While Laudrup's brief stay at Chelsea may have been an unhappy one, he'd shown enough early creativity to confirm that his ability would be missed.

But if his loss after just five starts and two substitute appearances was a blow, worse news was around the immediate corner.

Trailing to an early Neil Ruddock goal at West Ham, after 25 minutes Casiraghi pushed into the six-yard box to meet a Zola cross.

In an accidental collision with Rio Ferdinand and Shaka Hislop, the Italian was left stricken.

The injury immediately appeared serious and, at the conclusion of a game that saw Babayaro scramble a second-half equaliser, confirmation of precisely how serious came quickly - Casiraghi had suffered season-ending, and ultimately career-ending, knee ligament damage.

The devastating news meant that in the space of just three days two of the four summer signings that were set to fire Chelsea to a title challenge had been stripped from the squad.

It was, to put it mildly, a bit of a pisser...

But in times of trouble a trip to north London is often all that is required to put a smile back on Chelsea faces, and so it proved in the fourth round of the League Cup at Arsenal.

With both sides ringing the changes for the least-desired of their season's trophy targets, Goldbaek made his Chelsea debut alongside - from the bench - Luca Percassi, a Milanese defender who would go on to make just one further substitute appearance for Chelsea.

But on a hugely enjoyable night, the goals - all five of them without reply - came from the old hands of Leboeuf from the penalty spot and Vialli and Poyet with two apiece.

It was Arsenal's worst home defeat for 73 years, and Chelsea's biggest win against the Gunners in 90 years of competitive fixtures.

"Who scored a goal at Highbury? Arthur, Arthur," the Chelsea fans sang. *"Who scored a goal at Highbury? Arthur fucking Chelsea..."*

With Chelsea now on a run of 15 games unbeaten in all competitions, further confirmation of the season's potential came in a near-perfect performance against Wimbledon.

Unbeaten in their last four league trips to Stamford Bridge we were well used to Wimbledon putting us back in our box, but they were no match for a Chelsea side determined to prove there was life without the departed Laudrup and injured Italian Casiraghi.

Zola opened the scoring just after the half-hour mark and celebrated by holding aloft the number 10 shirt in honour of his fallen countryman, before Poyet and Petrescu completed the 3-0 score-line in the second half to move Chelsea up to fourth.

The winning run was extended to 17 at Leicester with Zola, twice, and Poyet and Flo on target as Chelsea held off a fightback from the hosts to win 4-2.

The day was also notable for skirmishes in the ground as the increasingly-unpleasant relationship between the two sets of fans that had grown throughout the '90s again turned nasty.

The main difference this time though was that among those on hand to capture the build-up to the day's troubles was undercover journalist Donal MacIntyre; his resulting BBC documentary giving a couple of Chelsea faces their 15 minutes of fame when it was broadcast at a later date.

The unbeaten run finally came to an end when - sandwiched between a disappointing 1-1 draw at home to Sheffield

Wednesday and goalless trip to Everton that saw Wise again sent off - Wimbledon proved there was life in the old Dons yet by avenging their recent league defeat to dump Chelsea out of the League Cup.

The 2-1 quarter-final defeat may not have been as crushing as it would have been a couple of years and a few trophies previously, but it was a game Chelsea should have won and hinted there was still work to be done if this side was to fulfil its potential.

Central to fulfilling that potential was avoiding unnecessary suspensions and captain Dennis Wise - chief mischief maker with two reds in the campaign to add to one picked up in pre-season - was set to miss his latest run of games over the Christmas period.

Before the suspension kicked in though, he was sent a 'must do better' message by Vialli when he was dropped to the bench for a crucial midweek league visit of Aston Villa.

Villa went into the game, rearranged following the postponement of the original October fixture due to a waterlogged pitch, top of the table and with just one defeat to their name.

With a December double-header against Manchester United also on the near horizon it had all the ingredients of a must-win game but, despite hitting the woodwork twice in a dominant second half, it looked like Chelsea would fail to add to Zola's first-half free-kick that was quickly cancelled out by Lee Hendrie.

But then, with the clock showing 90, Vialli flicked on Roberto Di Matteo's corner from the right and Flo powered home with his head - 2-1.

"It's goals like that which win you the title," we probably said as we walked on to the Fulham Road.

And it's goals like the one in the 90th-minute of the next game at Derby County that cost you them...

Up to third following the Villa win, Chelsea were set to go top with a 2-1 win in the East Midlands before a late Dean Sturridge lunge stripped away two points to send them to Manchester United still one behind their fellow title contenders.

Chelsea were missing Leboeuf through suspension and Desailly through injury for the trip to Old Trafford, but United also started with David Beckham, Ryan Giggs and Teddy Sheringham on the bench as they chased honours of their own on multiple fronts.

But the hosts still had Andy Cole in their starting 11, and he lifted Old Trafford to its feet with the opener on the stroke of half-time. Chelsea, meanwhile, still had Zola in their 11... and he scored his ninth goal of the campaign when he lifted the ball over Peter Schmeichel for a share of the points with seven minutes to play.

Chelsea finally went top for the first time since 1989 a week before Christmas, and to add to the smug sense of satisfaction it was Tottenham that were the visitors.

Capitalising on a shock Manchester United defeat at home to Middlesbrough and with Aston Villa not playing for another 48 hours, Chelsea left it late but came out victorious.

Helped by Tottenham being reduced to 10 men when Chris Armstrong was sent off after an hour, Poyet grabbed his 10th of the campaign when he reacted to a Vialli flick to score off the post with 10 to play.

And before the day was over it was two; Flo heading home Dan Petrescu's cross with the final whistle ready to blow and we were top of the league, say we were top of the league...

Villa briefly knocked Chelsea off their perch when they won their game in hand at Charlton, but Chelsea again went top with a 2-0 Boxing Day win at Southampton as their title rivals slipped to defeat at Blackburn.

Flo, again, and Poyet, again, were the marksmen at The Dell, but it was not without serious cost - the Uruguayan being carried off with a knee injury that would keep him out until April after already missing much of the previous campaign.

Those of you paying attention will recall I bought a house in February 1997 as a direct result of not being present for Chelsea's 1-1 draw at home to Manchester United.

Our new abode was precisely 23 steps to the village pub and we were made immediately welcome at a gloriously happy time in our lives.

Bordering on spit and sawdust, our new local had a preference for drinkers not diners and a landlord more than happy to take a casual attitude to closing time as long as the pints kept pouring.

It was perfect. Or perfect, that is, until Anna found the camera.

Long after official closing one summer night in 1998 we were drinking with Anna and her husband Andy - good neighbours and friends of similar age and interest - when, from the toilet door, she beckoned Celine for assistance.

Sitting on the loo, Anna's four-pint curiosity had encouraged her to poke at a tiny pinhole in the wallpaper directly opposite her.

In turn, that led her to discover a hollow space behind the

paper.

And that led her to pull at the paper to discover a small hidden camera pointing at anyone using the single female cubicle.

No wonder our genial host was so generous with his lock-ins.

After a shocked Anna and Celine had returned to the table and quietly filled us in on the tawdry details, we locked eyes with the landlord, downed what would be the last beer we would ever drink in the pub, crossed the road and called the police.

When the local constabulary finally arrived in the early hours they found a hole where the camera once sat, magazines on spy surveillance and a 'collection of video tapes' at the bottom of a wardrobe.

But the court process is a lengthy one, and in the months that followed before he was finally found guilty of 'insulting behaviour' our disgraced publican was free to stay open, free to keep serving… and free to load bullets with our name on them to the limited number of undesirables that remained happy to prop up his bar.

And it was a collection of those undesirables that, between the Christmas and New Year of 1998, walked across to our house to use Celine's car as a makeshift bouncy castle.

I was out at the time, having walked to the village shop to buy a bottle of wine, but returned to find all my neighbours in the street, obvious signs of chaos, and the news that Celine had set off in search of the aggressors.

Fearing for them, Andy joined me for a tour of the neighbouring streets where first we found a furious Celine and then the group she'd set off to castrate.

"The police are on their way," I said in their direction. "Wait there, we'll send them your way."

Big mistake.

"Send the fucking police," came the immediate reply, followed by a flurry of drink-and-drug-fuelled fists and boots.

It was six on three, one of whom was my wife. They must have been Tottenham.

But, regardless, there we were… Andy and I trying to hold off all six of them from one direction and Celine from the other; all while taking multiple punches and trying to get away from the madness.

By the time we made our eventual escape the police had, indeed, arrived outside our home - immediately adding Andy's broken nose to the lengthy list of questions they already had in mind.

Ironically, the evening after the brawl - a brawl that completed a timeline of events that could be traced back to not going to that Manchester United game almost two years previously - United were again the Stamford Bridge visitors as Chelsea looked to retain top spot.

With Celine packed off to spend an evening with her parents I dragged my bruised ribs down to London, but on this occasion I wished I hadn't bothered as my mind was elsewhere and Chelsea did little to divert my attention in a 0-0 draw that sent Aston Villa back to the top.

Going in to the new year, though, Chelsea were well set... second in the table, their bid to retain the Cup Winners' Cup on track and the FA Cup campaign getting off to a winning start courtesy of a Vialli brace at Oldham Athletic.

It was the league, though, that everyone wanted and Chelsea went back to the summit at the first opportunity 1999 offered.

Ruud Gullit's troubles as Newcastle manager following a very public falling out with Toon legend Alan Shearer were yet to come, and his first season on Tyneside was ticking along in mid-table mediocrity as he prepared to welcome his former club to St James' Park.

With Steve Clarke by his side it was a chance to get one over on his old club; a chance to prove he - not his Chelsea successor Vialli - was the top dog; and a chance to become just the second manager to secure a league win against Chelsea as the season headed towards the business end.

And if it hadn't have been for Ed de Goey he may have earned his bragging rights, with the Dutch stopper keeping Chelsea in the game with a string of saves from Shearer, Dietmar Hamann, Nolberto Solano, Didier Domi and Gary Speed.

And again showing the signs of potential champions, they were saves that led to all three points as - on a rare first-half break - it was Chelsea that scored the only goal of the game when Dan Petrescu found space to fire home at the far post.

Gullit was full of praise for his former side but couldn't resist adding to the pressure for the team he'd helped build by stating the league leaders were now clear title favourites.

"Chelsea have to win the championship now because there is so much quality in their side," he said.

On a free-scoring Saturday that saw Liverpool fire seven past Southampton and Manchester United score six at Leicester,

Chelsea had to work much harder for their next three points but again came out on top with another last-minute winner against Coventry City.

Having already scored a first-half stoppage-time goal through a Leboeuf screamer to cancel out Darren Huckerby's early opener, the game was in to its 94th-minute when Di Matteo slid on to a Wise knock-back to secure the win.

"It's goals like that which win you the title," we probably said, again, as we walked on to the Fulham Road.

Another last-minute goal was required to keep Chelsea in the FA Cup, a Leboeuf equaliser from the spot sparing blushes for those of us on the terrace at Oxford United, before a second league defeat of the season that recent performances had been threatening finally came at the hands of Arsenal.

It was a bad one to lose with Dennis Bergkamp's single goal of the game, combined with a late Manchester United win at Charlton Athletic, making things even more congested at the top.

With 15 games to go United now led the table on 44 points, with Chelsea and Aston Villa a point behind and Arsenal just an additional point off the pace in fourth.

Adding to Chelsea's troubles was an injury to Flo in the early January game at Oldham that was set to keep him out for up to six weeks, so Vialli had to dig deep into his resources to maintain the push for trophies.

One of the beneficiaries was Mikael Forssell, a highly-promising 17-year-old Finnish striker picked up on a free summer transfer from HJK Helsinki who grabbed his opportunity with both hands when given his first start in the FA Cup replay against Oxford.

Vialli's men fell behind to an early Phil Gilchrist goal before Wise levelled, Zola gave Chelsea the lead and Forssell got his career off to the best of possible starts with two excellent finishes from range.

But there was still to be a sting in the tail with Oxford reducing the margin of defeat from the spot after Dennis Wise handled to, once again, receive a red card.

This time he would miss four domestic games, due to kick in after a 1-0 home win against Southampton that would keep Chelsea in second and an FA Cup Fifth Round win at Sheffield Wednesday by the same score-line.

Without him, Chelsea immediately dropped points in a 1-1 draw to relegation-threatened Blackburn and suffered another temporary loss of an attacking force when Vialli saw red alongside the visitor's Marlon Broomes.

Scott came up trumps for Chelsea's next game, a trip to Nottingham Forest's City Ground, by using his business contacts to secure two seats in an executive club running the entire length of the Trent End.

Preparing for a day watching our Ps and Qs it was something of a pleasant surprise to discover that the vast majority of those cheering on from behind the glass were Chelsea; creating a band of blues wedged between two tiers of Forest reds.

We had the perfect view as Dave Beasant was involved in a defensive mix-up to gift Forssell his first league goal after just six minutes, were sitting even more comfortably when Goldbaek doubled the advantage 20 minutes later, and were quickly toasting all three points with a pint when the Dane completed the 3-1 score-line with five minutes to play.

Meanwhile, Graeme Le Saux could never be accused of being a shrinking violet...

From a youthful elbow to the jaw for Luton's Graham Rodger back in '91, to an on-pitch fracas with Blackburn teammate David Batty in 1995, right up to his Chelsea sending off at Ewood Park for going toe-to-toe with Sebastien Perez in the current campaign... if retribution needed serving, the England international was rarely backwards in coming forwards.

But never was his anger more justified than when Robbie Fowler did the taunting as Chelsea kept up the title push with a 2-1 Stamford Bridge defeat of Liverpool at the end of February.

With Chelsea two to the good and the second half warming up, as he prepared to take a free kick Le Saux was infuriated by Fowler repeatedly bending forward and waving his backside in front of him.

The taunt - the clear taunt - related to baseless terrace tittle-tattle about Le Saux's sexuality.

The linesman, feet from the incident, did nothing despite roars of disapproval from Chelsea's West Stand. Referee Paul Durkin did act though... showing Le Saux - refusing to restart the game until action was taken - a yellow card for time-wasting.

There was only one thing for Le Saux to do then and that was to administer his own justice, which he did in style by striking a blow to the back of the Liverpool man's head once Durkin's back was turned.

Three days after the game the FA charged both Fowler and Le

Saux with misconduct - Fowler eventually receiving a two-match ban, and Le Saux a one-match ban and a £5,000 fine.

For his part Fowler later apologised for the incident while - more than 20 years later - Le Saux continues to be the go-to non-gay defender of gay rights whenever the media discusses homophobia in the game.

But back to the football...

With Flo back from injury, the first week of March saw Chelsea competing in two cup quarter finals - one in Europe, and one in Manchester.

Norwegian side Valerenga were seen off without drama in a 3-0 first-leg Cup Winners' Cup win at Stamford Bridge, before more than 8,000 Chelsea fans made the trip to Old Trafford for the FA Cup.

The most memorable moment of the day came on Sir Matt Busby Way when, inadvertently caught in a United ambush of Chelsea fans, one of our group executed a perfectly-timed volley to a Mancunian backside.

It was to prove to be the best shot we saw all afternoon, with the game rarely living up to expectation as Chelsea held on for a goalless draw after Di Matteo collected the visitors' eighth red card of the season.

United's Paul Scholes was also sent off with fewer than five minutes to play, but both he and Di Matteo were still available for the replay three days later with suspensions not kicking in for a fortnight.

Following the cagey stale-mate at Old Trafford a goal came just four minutes into the replay, but unfortunately for those in blue it was United's Dwight Yorke that set the tone for a frustrating night.

The statistical analysis would show Chelsea would have 16 efforts on goal compared to United's four, but the record books would show a 2-0 defeat with Yorke adding to his early goal with a second-half second.

To add league insult to FA Cup injury, in the very next game Chelsea would also give United a major title-chase advantage with a desperately disappointing first home league defeat of the campaign at the hands of West Ham.

Chelsea huffed and puffed but couldn't find the breakthrough, and found themselves chasing the game when Paul Kitson gave the East Londoners a 75th-minute lead.

This time there would be no last-minute goal to rescue something from the day, and with 10 games to go Chelsea had now fallen seven points off the pace - albeit with a game in hand.

A 3-2 win at Valerenga confirmed progression to the European Cup Winners' Cup last four, but as Vialli's men prepared for a league visit to Aston Villa they knew they could afford no further West Ham-type howlers if they were to stay in the title hunt.

Villa had fallen from grace following their strong start to the season, taking just one point from their previous seven games, and Chelsea made easy work of the challenge despite leaving it late to guarantee all three points.

Flo fired Chelsea in front just before the hour before, in the final five, first Goldbaek and then Flo again gave the final score a more realistic look.

With Chelsea needing everyone available for the run-in, Poyet made a long-awaited and welcome return from the bench as an early Di Matteo goal secured a 1-0 win at Charlton but the best news came elsewhere - Manchester United and Arsenal held by Wimbledon and Southampton respectively.

The two-point swing on both meant that with eight to play and a game in hand on both teams above them, Chelsea were once again just four points off top spot.

The small matter of the first leg of the Cup Winners' Cup semi-final against Real Mallorca felt like light relief compared to the increasing stress of the league campaign, but on a disappointing night Chelsea required a Flo equaliser to set up a tricky trip to the Balearics a fortnight later.

But before that came three crucial league games - Wimbledon and Middlesbrough away... and Leicester City at home.

With Vialli now being supported in his managerial duties by Ray Wilkins following the jailing of Graham Rix - the disgraced coach sentenced to 12 months for having underage sex with a 15-year-old girl - the first hurdle was cleared with relative comfort as Poyet and Flo put Chelsea in control ahead of a late Wimbledon consolation.

Middlesbrough, where a win would have put Chelsea top, proved a little more troublesome with a one-on-one Zola effort saved by Mark Schwarzer the closest the game came to a goal.

The draw was no great disaster though, and a win against a Leicester side in the bottom half of the table would keep Chelsea within a single point of Manchester United.

So, Chelsea fans of a nervous disposition may wish to look away now...

After a bright start Chelsea pressure told after 30 minutes when a Di Matteo ball released Zola to beat the advancing Kasey Keller with a sublime lob.

But with no further goals by the time the hour-mark had passed, there was a growing feeling around the ground that the safety belt of a second was needed... and it came on cue, with Di Matteo again the provider as he released Petrescu to clip a shot off the post and across the line.

Relief and much celebration all round then.

But then, in the 82nd minute, a cross from the Leicester left, a failure to clear, a poke from Matt Elliott, a deflection off a flat-footed Michael Duberry, and it's 2-1 - the Chelsea substitute putting in to his own net.

"Don't panic Chels, just run the clock down, just run the clock down..."

And the clock was running down, and it said 88 minutes when Robbie Savage played a short ball to Steve Guppy, again on the left.

Looking up, the Leicester man cut back on Petrescu.

He advanced to the corner of the box, looking dangerous, very dangerous... and in gut-wrenching slow motion curled a sublime finish beyond the diving hands of De Goey.

Stunned into silence, we knew immediately what it meant.

With that single swing of Steve Guppy's right foot, the title chase was over - Chelsea were still a point ahead of Arsenal, but a fatal three behind United having now played a game more than both.

The hangover continued for a week.

On the Thursday the defence of the Cup Winners' Cup came to an end with a 1-0 defeat in Mallorca, and on the following Sunday Chelsea were held to a third league draw in succession at Sheffield Wednesday.

Driving up to Hillsborough we were given a glimmer of fresh hope when news came through that Manchester United had been held to a 1-1 draw at Leeds, but Chelsea failed to respond in a 0-0 bore-fest.

It meant Chelsea had now taken just three points from the last nine available, hitting the proverbial wall at the precise point they required a sprint to the line.

Perhaps relieved of the pressure, free-flowing football returned for a 3-1 demolition of Everton before Chelsea confirmed a top-three finish and qualification for the following season's Champions League with a Poyet header in a 1-0 defeat of Leeds.

Going into the penultimate game at Tottenham on a Monday night Chelsea were - mathematically at least - still in the title race, but knew they would have to win both of their remaining games while hoping Manchester United and Arsenal would take no more than a single point each from their remaining two matches.

No-one thought it was possible, but we knew for certain when Tottenham's Steffen Iversen and David Ginola both scored past Kevin Hitchcock - making his last Chelsea appearance - to over-turn Poyet's fourth-minute opener.

The Spurs fans couldn't believe their fortune, finding their collective voices to celebrate the final nail in Chelsea's title chase and their first win against the Blues since February 1990 - a run they'd found increasingly difficult to stomach with each of the passing 19 games.

Watching on from the Chelsea seats in the corner of the ground, the Spurs goading was difficult to take. Losing the league was one thing, but losing to Tottenham?

Thank you, then, Bjarne Goldbaek.

On as a second-half substitute, the season's consolation Dane collected the ball on the right.

Around 30 yards from goal he took a couple of steadying touches, moved forward a yard or two and fired his place into Chelsea folklore with a laser-line net breaker.

It wasn't enough to take the title to the last day, but it maintained the unbeaten run against Tottenham - a memorable consolation prize wrapped in a Goldbaek bow.

The Spurs fans didn't take it well and formed a welcoming committee as we spilled out of the exit gates on the final whistle.

Leaving the ground with Gaz, my Stockholm-saviour Paul and one of his daughters we were immediately separated as we walked into a flurry of fights breaking out to our left, to our right, to the front, and to the back.

On the tight Park Lane street it was one of those rare moments from which there was no clear escape, all sense of who was who lost in the dark of the night, and I was forced to swerve a swing of a Chelsea fist as I was accused of being Tottenham.

"Do I look like bloody Tottenham? I'm Chelsea. You dickhead…"

I wasn't happy, but as I edged my way through the scuffles I began to ponder on a season that had promised so much but had ultimately fallen agonisingly short.

The answers to my ponderings were numerous - the injury to

Casaraghi, the early departure of Laudrup, the lengthy loss of Poyet, the brief loss of Flo, the multiple suspensions of Wise, the disruptive jailing of Rix, Dean Sturridge's late leveller at Derby, Zola's one-on-one at Middlesbrough, and Steve Guppy... Steve fucking Guppy.

The final full season of the decade concluded with a 2-1 win against Derby as Stamford Bridge saw manager Vialli score his last Chelsea goal in his last game as a player, and said farewell to a number of other favourites from across the previous years... Michael Duberry, Eddie Newton and keeper Dmitri Kharine all playing one last time.

Cup final scorer Newton had made his debut in '92, Kharine had joined in '93 and Duberry had first pulled on the shirt in '94 - long-serving players that had contributed to the Chelsea progression from annual no hopers to FA Cup winners, League Cup winners, European Cup Winners' Cup winners, Super Cup winners and Champions League qualifiers.

And on the back of that unexpected run of success, as I walked from the ground at the conclusion of the campaign I allowed myself to dream again...

Perhaps one day, I naively thought, I still might see Chelsea win the league.

CHAPTER EIGHTEEN
BOLTON AND BEYOND

Moments after Frank Lampard had fired Chelsea 2-0 ahead at Bolton Wanderers on April 30, 2005, I was standing on my seat behind the goal, the lights gone from my eyes, arm around the shoulders of my brother Andrew for emotional and physical support while declaring in song what was now beyond all doubt... for only the second time in 100 years - 50 years after the first time - we were going to win the league.

As I stood there singing, exhausted, elated, I later discovered the television cameras had briefly focused on me in full flow. Sweating and emotional, I certainly wasn't looking my best.

But more than 9,000 miles away my unkempt appearance was of no concern as it brought a smile - and I like to think a tear - from a guest member of the Chelsea Perth Supporters' Club.

Scott had first announced he and Yvette were emigrating to Australia with their young family as we travelled down to see Chelsea win 4-1 at Fulham the previous November.

I was furious and we (well, I) argued all day as Lampard, Robben, Gallas and Tiago maintained Chelsea's lead at the top of the table in what was already looking like it could be the year that we would break our lifelong title wait.

I gave the game limited attention as I couldn't understand why he would go when Chelsea were so close to our ultimate shared dream.

I couldn't understand what Perth had that Northamptonshire didn't.

I couldn't understand why he would wish to leave his wide circle of friends and family.

And, most importantly, I couldn't understand what I was going to do without him.

In short, I was heart-broken.

"Why Perth?" I pleaded. "You've never even been to Perth. I wouldn't move to fucking Norwich without going and checking it out first."

Why Norwich I've no idea, but the point stood - I felt the ultimate in life-changing decisions was being made without necessary due diligence.

He'd previously done this to me a few years earlier when he'd moved overseas to support Yvette in a new job, but that was always only temporary so I muddled through for 18 months, went to enough games with Dad, Andrew or my other mates to just about keep me happy, and waited to pick up where we left off when he came home.

This time was different though, because this time the plan was permanent.

So, as the final whistle at Bolton blew, the tears of my own that threatened to flow weren't just because Chelsea had won the league but because I knew *Phase Two* of my life as a football fan was now officially over.

But before we get there, let's go back to *Phase One*.

Phase One is how all true football addicts start.

At a young age you are taken to the game by an elder - for those of my generation, most likely your dad - and from the moment you first see that pitch, first hear that roar, you are hooked.

Phase One is a beautiful time, a life-defining time.

Every ground is a new ground, every team a new team, every new signing a poster-boy hero.

Your views on games and players are not really your views but those of your dad as you hang on to his every word, building a common bond that will last for life.

At that first stage my dad created a monster who, over the following years, would spend too much money, turn down wedding invites and throw too many sulks all in the name of a club in blue with a rampant lion on its shirt.

And I still thank him for doing so every single day.

My wonderful dad was a talented club-level sportsman in his own right so Saturdays were largely spent playing cricket or golf, passions he also involved his three children in.

As a result I wasn't a week-in-week-out regular at Stamford Bridge in my formative years, but come a forecast for heavy rain at the start or end of the cricket season, or the first sign of snow in the winter, then it was straight off to Stamford Bridge.

Night games were another favourite if they were within post-school driving distance, so that's why most of my childhood memories of 'the Chels' are either under floodlights or nearly freezing to death in The Shed. I didn't, it's fair to say, do many roasting Saturday afternoons in August or May...

But we always did enough games to keep me hooked... just two or three in the first couple of years, growing to five or six, seven or eight and ten to 12 as the years passed by and I became increasingly more insistent that 'it looked like it might snow'.

Sitting or standing alongside Dad I fell in love with a wide range of players from the likes of Clive Walker and Petar Borota, through to Pat Nevin and Kerry Dixon, and on to Steve Clarke and Tony Dorigo.

Even the likes of John McNaught and Jerry Murphy had a certain appeal in the right light.

But after one game I stopped holding Dad's hand when we walked from the ground - neither of us knowing at the time that the last time had already passed.

The next step was to leave him on the terrace while I nipped to the loo or to the refreshment hut, taking a little longer than necessary to explore the darker corners of the Shed under my own steam.

And finally - a Friday night at Birmingham City in 1988 to be precise - I announced to Dad for the first time that I was moving further down the stand to enjoy the game away from his watchful eye.

He didn't mind as, in truth, it was definitely a good year or two later than he would have expected it to happen, but he still had the last laugh.

Having had the good grace to take not just me but also Scott and Aidy to the game at St Andrews, he once again bought tickets among the home support as, by now, you'll know was his way.

But with the seated Chelsea support down the far end of the same stand, I announced we were off in a bid to cross the narrow divide of segregation.

As we approached, a steward rightly asked where we thought we were going.

"To sit there," I said, full of teenage cockiness.

"Who do you support then?" came the not unreasonable reply.

I thought this might happen, but I had a foolproof response prepared.

"The Blues," I said confidently...

"Nice try," he smirked, seeing straight through my cunning plan and sending me back in the direction of Dad with my tail between my legs and Scott and Aidy calling me for the idiot that I was.

Freedom wasn't far away though and at the start of the next season *Phase Two* was officially launched with Scott and I taking the train down to Chelsea on our own - no need for rain, no need for snow, unlimited access from August to May.

From this day forward the roles would be reversed; Dad would now primarily go to Chelsea only when *I* asked if *he* wanted to go.

The new phase started in the 1989/90 season and went into immediate overdrive with maiden trips to the likes of Anfield, White Hart Lane and Highbury - grounds which had thus far eluded me when reliant on Dad for attendance but grounds to which I would return many, many times across the following years.

For games at Stamford Bridge the first step was to move from the Bovril entrance that had become the natural home with Dad to the middle of The Shed. I was a very youthful 16-year-old, no more than 5ft 2ins and still a good four years away from needing a first shave, but I was a Shed Boy now and there was nothing anyone could do about it.

As the previous pages testify, *Stage Two* saw me and Scott follow Chelsea over land and sea and Leicester. Beautiful, wonderful years with stories and adventures to bond the best of friendships... and then he went and buggered off to Australia.

The honest truth, though, even if I didn't like to admit it at the time, is that my best mate was doing me a favour - forcing me to try to cut back on an addiction that I hadn't got the willpower to kick on my own.

After he left I continued to do as many games as I could in that 2004/05 title-winning campaign but it was always with a tinge of guilt as, by this stage, Celine and I had two amazing young boys of our own - William, four, and Euan, one - and I was spending far too much of the little money we had on Chelsea when I should have been spending it on them.

The following season I still joined my brother for an opening-day trip to Wigan Athletic to see Hernan Crespo introduce himself to his adoring new supporters with a last-minute wonder strike, and I went to Anfield, to Upton Park and to a handful of home games, but when Chelsea beat Manchester United in April to retain the title I was watching at home - the totting up of the games I'd attended falling well short of the required number to qualify for a ticket.

I didn't particularly mind though because I'd had my title-winning moment the year before, and - more importantly - I'd already had my highlight of the season... the launch of *Stage*

Three.

Twenty-six years and one month after Dad took me to my first Chelsea game at Luton Town, the generation game continued when I took William to his first match at Middlesbrough.

It was far from the most obvious of selections for a first game but was chosen because tickets were easily accessible, it was a safe away end with a good view of the pitch... and I needed a reason to justify a trip to the north-east for a game I wanted to see.

Despite starting the game an incredible 15 points clear at the top of the table, Chelsea did what Chelsea do and lost 3-0.

"This isn't very good is it Daddy?" my disappointed five-year-old accurately observed as the home side brushed us aside.

His first trip to Stamford Bridge came the following season in a League Cup game against Aston Villa, and in 2010 Euan joined us for the first time in a comfortable FA Cup win against Watford.

With my niece Vicky also now bitten by the bug, year by year the number of games started to grow again, history started to repeat itself and one day - I'm not sure when - my boys stopped holding my hand.

William and Euan have seen Chelsea at Wembley, The Emirates, Old Trafford and Anfield.

They've seen them at Wolves, Stoke, Hull, Sunderland, Everton and many more beyond.

They've seen them home and abroad, and now they are ready to move on.

These pages were penned during the Covid-19 pandemic, with the lockdown prompting me to search through the hundreds of Chelsea programmes and fanzines I've collected along the way to put memories down in print.

In the one game we managed to attend in the Covid-affected 2020/21 campaign - a campaign played almost entirely in empty stadiums that somehow ended with Chelsea winning a second European Cup - William didn't sit with me but with a mate; his first step on his own inevitable *Stage Two* journey.

I hold on to Euan for now, but soon *they* will be asking me if *I* want to go.

So, finally, what of Scott and Aidy, my two best mates of 40 years?

Aidy was one step ahead of Scott when he moved to Australia in 1999 to study, settle, fall in love, marry, and raise a beautiful daughter.

He now has the word 'Professor' before his name and is a highly-respected medical research statistician, but he still speaks to me on a regular basis to talk cobblers and Cobblers - the nickname of the Northampton Town team he still follows avidly from afar.

Scott, meanwhile, called his Australian adventure short (I did try to tell him, to be fair) and briefly returned home before heading off again for more than a decade living and working in south-east Asia, where he currently remains.

He leads a wonderful life with his wonderful wife, but I wish he would come home now… I'm ready for *Stage Four*.

POSTSCRIPT

The date is April 30, 2022, and I signed off the final proof of *For Better or Worse* eight weeks ago.

But on the very same day I signed off that final proof, the existence of Chelsea Football Club was dramatically thrown into doubt.

It was thrown into doubt because shortly after 9.15am on March 10, our Russian owner Roman Abramovich's plans to sell Chelsea following his country's invasion of Ukraine were halted when the oligarch was sanctioned by the UK government.

The move meant Abramovich's considerable assets, including Chelsea, were frozen and the club was told it couldn't generate any revenue through the sale of match tickets, merchandising or the sale of players.

In addition, some club sponsors ran for the hills as everything we have known and enjoyed since Abramovich walked into the club in 2003 threatened to collapse before our eyes.

It was an irrelevance, of course, in comparison to the atrocities witnessed in Ukraine, where - at the time of writing - innocent people continue to lose their lives, flee their homes and stand to fight aggression.

But it still mattered.

It mattered deeply to me, to my Chelsea family and friends, and to the millions of other Chelsea fans that can now be found across the globe.

It mattered because for a period everything looked grim, very grim indeed, with genuine fears that - with limited access to funds - Chelsea could fall into administration or, even worse, liquidation.

But then, with word coming from the government that it would still be open to the club being sold on condition that proceeds would not go to the sanctioned Abramovich, potential new owners and consortiums stepped forward to take part in a billionaires' beauty parade.

From America to Saudi Arabia, London, Switzerland and beyond they came to wave their wallets in front of American investment firm Raine Group, which had been tasked with selling the reigning European Cup, European Super Cup and Club World Cup champions.

A postscript I wrote on March 10 to acknowledge the potential impact of the sanctioning of Abramovich was quickly out of date; as was another one I wrote on March 18 as potential new owners started to step forward.

I held on in a bid to seek confirmation of the new owners of Chelsea Football Club before sending this book to print.

I then held on some more… and then held on some more… but deadlines have now been stretched to breaking point and I can hold on no more.

Until yesterday, April 29, the battle for ownership was between three groups - a consortium headed by LA Dodgers co-owner Todd Boehly, one led by former Liverpool chairman Sir Martin Broughton, and one fronted by Boston Celtics co-owner Stephen Pagliuca.

But then, out of the blue, came a sensational new bid of more than £4.25bn from Sir Jim Ratcliffe - one of Britain's richest men and chairman of petrochemical giant INEOS.

It was a shock 11th-hour move that lit up social media and the news websites… but within minutes of Fleet Street's finest filing their copy things changed again, with word coming that it was the Boehly consortium - linked to the takeover from the very start – that was to be put forward as the preferred bidder.

And that, with an extended publishing deadline to desperately meet, is as far as I can take this story.

The Boehly bid - which includes, among others, backing from US investment firm Clearlake Capital and Swiss businessman Hansjorg Wyss – appears to be in the driving seat to take Chelsea into a new era.

The truth is, though, that I still can't say - certainly with any certainty - how things are going to unfold in the coming days and weeks.

The sale should go through ahead of a May 31 Government deadline, but it may not.

Boehly looks likely to win the race, but he still may not.

And he… or still potentially Pagliuca, or Broughton, or Ratcliffe, or someone entirely new… may prove to be a worthy owner, but he may not.

If all goes to plan under new ownership we can be optimistic that Chelsea will continue to prosper, and continue to compete for league titles, European Cups and Club World Cups.

But if it doesn't, well, let's be honest... we're long overdue a relegation.

That wouldn't be the *Stage Four* I had in mind when I signed off that final proof of *For Better or Worse* eight tortuous weeks ago but, quite frankly, who cares?

Wherever the future takes us, whatever the future holds, we'll still be there, still smiling and still cheering.... cheering on through the sun and rain, 'cause Chelsea, Chelsea is our name.

In the meantime, I'll sign off by leaving you with one final thought... if you don't already own a Chelsea Pitch Owner share, now might still be a good time to consider buying one: www.chelseafc.com/en/cpo

Up the Chels!

DEDICATION

To Celine; my beautiful wife who still (mostly) humours my Chelsea obsession. It was clearly meant to be gorgeous... we've won it another six times since!

To our wonderful boys William and Euan, who make us laugh, smile and burst with pride every single day.

To Sue and Simon for their support and guidance.

To Scott, to Aidy, to Stewie and to the many other good friends that have joined me on the Chelsea journey... you know who you are.

To Gaz and Laura; great friends that were tragically taken far too young and whom we think of often.

And finally...

To my sister Amanda, brother Andrew and their respective others for all bringing so much love and joy to our family.

To my amazing, dearly-loved Mum; one half of an incredible double act who has always put children and grand-children first.

And, of course, to Dad; forever loved, forever missed, forever by my side at Stamford Bridge xx.

GATE 17
THE COMPLETE COLLECTION
(SUMMER 2022)

CHELSEA

Over Land and Sea – Mark Worrall
Chelsea here, Chelsea There – Kelvin Barker, David Johnstone, Mark Worrall
Chelsea Football Fanzine – the best of cfcuk
One Man Went to Mow – Mark Worrall
Making History Not Reliving It –
Kelvin Barker, David Johnstone, Mark Worrall
Celery! Representing Chelsea in the 1980s – Kelvin Barker
Stuck On You, a year in the life of a Chelsea supporter – Walter Otton
Palpable Discord, a year of drama and dissent at Chelsea – Clayton Beerman
Rhyme and Treason – Carol Ann Wood
Eddie Mac Eddie Mac – Eddie McCreadie's Blue & White Army
The Italian Job, A Chelsea thriller starring Antonio Conte – Mark Worrall
Carefree! Chelsea Chants & Terrace Culture – Mark Worrall, Walter Otton
Diamonds, Dynamos and Devils – Tim Rolls
Arrivederci Antonio, The Italian Job (part two) – Mark Worrall
Where Were You When We Were Shocking? – Neil L. Smith
Chelsea, 100 Memorable Matches – Chelsea Chadder
Bewitched, Bothered & Bewildered – Carol Ann Wood
Stamford Bridge Is Falling Down – Tim Rolls
Cult Fiction – Dean Mears
Chelsea, If Twitter Was Around When... – Chelsea Chadder
Blue Army – Vince Cooper
Liquidator 1969-70 A Chelsea Memoir – Mark Worrall
When Skies Are Grey, Super Frank, Chelsea And The Coronavirus Crisis – Mark Worrall
Tales Of The (Chelsea) Unexpected – David Johnstone & Neil L Smith
The Ultimate Unofficial Chelsea Quiz Book – Chelsea Chadder
Blue Days – Chris Wright
Let The Celery Decide – Walter Otton
Blue Hitmen – Paul Radcliffe
Sexton For God – Tim Rolls
Tales From The Shed – Edited by Mark Worrall
For Better Or Worse – Jason Gibbins
Come Along And Sing This Song – Johnny Neal's Blue And White Army
Days I'll Remember All My Life – Kelvin Barker

FICTION

Blue Murder, Chelsea Till I Die – Mark Worrall
The Wrong Outfit – Al Gregg
The Red Hand Gang – Walter Otton
Coming Clean – Christopher Morgan
This Damnation – Mark Worrall
Poppy – Walter Otton

NON FICTION

Roe2Ro – Walter Otton
Shorts – Walter Otton
England International Football Team Quiz & Trivia Book – George Cross

www.gate17books.co.uk

Printed in Great Britain
by Amazon

17340127R00135